Praise for *Building Green Software*

In the face of climate change, it can feel difficult to know what part software professionals can play in helping find solutions. This book is an excellent guide focusing on the practical steps we can take to make our systems more sustainable.

—*Sam Newman, author,* Building Microservices

Green software plays a vital part in the energy transition and this book gives a perfect introduction.

—*Asim Hussain, Executive Director, Green Software Foundation*

The book our industry has been waiting for, from the experts in the field.

—*Holly Cummins, Senior Principal Software Engineer, Red Hat*

Building Green Software
A Sustainable Approach to
Software Development and Operations

Anne Currie, Sarah Hsu, and Sara Bergman

Foreword by Adrian Cockcroft

Beijing · Boston · Farnham · Sebastopol · Tokyo

Building Green Software

by Anne Currie, Sarah Hsu, and Sara Bergman

Published by O'Reilly Media, Inc., 1005 Gravenstein Highway North, Sebastopol, CA 95472.

O'Reilly books may be purchased for educational, business, or sales promotional use. Online editions are also available for most titles (*http://oreilly.com*). For more information, contact our corporate/institutional sales department: 800-998-9938 or *corporate@oreilly.com*.

Acquisitions Editor: Megan Laddusaw	**Proofreader:** Doug McNair
Development Editor: Shira Evans	**Indexer:** Ellen Troutman-Zaig
Production Editors: Christopher Faucher and Jonathon Owen	**Interior Designer:** David Futato
	Cover Designer: Karen Montgomery
Copyeditor: nSight, Inc.	**Illustrator:** Kate Dullea

March 2024:   First Edition

Revision History for the First Edition

2024-03-08:   First Release

See *http://oreilly.com/catalog/errata.csp?isbn=9781098150624* for release details.

978-1-098-15062-4

[LSI]

Table of Contents

Foreword

The preferred terms are "climate emergency, crisis, or breakdown."
—The Guardian

Change is hard. Even in the presence of a global climate crisis that is causing migrations, wars, and destruction of ecosystems and habitat for everything from corals to humans, there are vested interests, investments, laws, regulations, and "best practices" that reinforce the status quo of a fossil fuel powered global economy. As individuals, we can choose to be part of an ethical movement for a sustainable future. We can vote, choose where we work, choose what we buy, redirect our investments, and lobby for better laws and regulations. As software developers we need to develop and implement new best practices for building green software. That's where this book comes in.

The business world can be divided into three categories, one that makes money causing the climate crisis by selling fossil fuels and resists the change. Another that makes money by building the new future of wind farms and heat pumps and the like and profits from the change. The third is the biggest category, trying to survive and build a business where the climate crisis hasn't been a direct concern. Why should these businesses care enough to have goals, invest resources, and support employees that want to be green? The pressure is coming from all directions and is intensifying. It comes top down from regulators and investors, bottom up from employees and side to side from customers and suppliers. Governments and regulators around the world are starting to require audited carbon emissions reports alongside financial reports. They are also in the early stages of requiring climate risk assessments, where companies over a minimum size would have to disclose to investors both physical and market risks to their business that derive from the climate crisis. For example if you are the "Miami Beach Spark Plug Company," you would have to disclose that your production facility keeps flooding and is uninsurable, your employees don't turn up for work because of more intense flooding, heat waves and hurricanes, and that your customers are switching to buying parts for electric vehicles. This translates into a board level interest in audit and risk topics around sustainability for all businesses. The pressure from employees should not be underestimated, in particular younger generations and those who have children have a strong interest in a sustainable future to live in, and vote with their feet as they choose who to work for and what they want to work on. Then there's customers and suppliers. The supply chain is being instrumented so that you gather carbon data for everything you buy, and provide carbon data for everything you sell. This is also being mandated by government regulation, for example if you want to sell into the European Union there is a cross border carbon tax. As you work through setting management priorities and goals for the business, take these changes into account. Companies that ignore or resist change, when the environment changes around them, are setting themselves up to fail.

We need to consider how to reduce the impact of the software we build, but we also need a sense of perspective. In most cases, the carbon footprint of a business is dominated by physical business processes, buildings, and employee activities. In this case, we are looking for opportunities to use software to optimize physical processes to remove carbon. It's only the purely digital businesses like online banks and software services providers that are dominated by the carbon footprint of their computing resources. However, whether you are building software to optimize carbon intensive physical processes, or just have to optimize the code that runs your services, you will need to build the mental models of how software translates into energy use, manufacturing supply chains, and carbon. You will then need advice on how to change the way your company builds and runs software, to optimize and reduce its carbon footprint. That is where this book comes in. It's written by experienced practitioners who have been working with the Green Software Foundation for several years, and draws on the wide and deep experience that has been contributed to the GSF by many members. The book is written in an entertaining and opinionated style, and is full of practical useful advice for all aspects of building and running green software.

— Adrian Cockcroft
OrionX.net
Salinas, California, February 2024

Preface

It's not easy being green.
—Kermit the Frog

Climate change is real. The Intergovernmental Panel on Climate Change (IPCC) report of 2022 settled that. The world is now stepping up to respond, and it appears that companies will need to get on board with the energy transition or be left behind. Unfortunately, as a wise cultural icon once said, the changes required for a sustainable planet will not be easy.

The good news, however, is that most of the public cloud providers have already committed to net-zero cloud operations (commitments they need to be held to), and we can learn from and emulate them as well as other sustainability leaders in our sector. In fact, some of the tools we need are already open source or commercially available.

That's fortunate, because the rest of us may soon be compelled by our customers, infrastructure providers, soaring bills, and incoming legislation to set and meet our own tough carbon targets. So how will software development and operations need to change to save the planet and our companies?

This book aims to help answer that question. *Building Green Software* is an overview of everything from how national grids are likely to evolve in response to renewable power, to how that will change operations, to how the day-to-day lives of developers will be affected by the energy transition. You may notice that many of the quotes included in this book are from folk who *used to* work for the hyperscalers. That doesn't mean our quotees are renegade whistleblowers, just that they are commenting as individuals who are no longer subject to the rules of a somewhat heavyweight PR organization. It is useful to hear unfiltered views because everyone from the freshest developer to the most dog-eared CTO has a part to play in shaping the world that's coming.

How can we build, host, and operate code in a way that's better for the environment, cheaper, and lower risk?

Why Should You Read This Book?

Anyone is allowed to look at this book. We have a very relaxed open-door policy. As a reader, you might be:

- A developer who is expected to contribute to your organization's sustainability initiatives and wants a primer on the topic
- An architect who wants to better understand how to align with the Amazon Web Services (AWS) Sustainability Well-Architected Pillar
- A product manager designing a new feature who wants to know how to make the operation of that feature as green and low cost as possible
- A DevOps person or SRE who has been asked to reduce the carbon impact (or financial cost) of an existing application and needs some ideas or pointers

Or you might be someone else entirely. Who are we to gatekeep? Whatever your role is, you have a role to play in being part of the climate solution.

By the end of this book, our aim is for you to have a better handle on:

- The fundamental architectural principles of sustainable, or green, software development and how to apply them
- How the energy transition is likely to change hosting on prem and in the cloud and how companies can prepare for that
- The concepts of extending hardware longevity and the part played in this by software

And you will be able to:

- Make lower-risk choices about future plans
- Make an educated guess about which parts of your systems might need to change and how
- As far as possible, measure the effects of any changes you make
- Realize the close connections among the benefits of green software and other considerations such as reliability, performance, and—every CFO's favorite—*cost*!

How Does This Book Work?

We're going to follow the advice of those foundational figures of the modern world—Aristotle and Dale Carnegie (the latter being the author of *How to Win Friends and Influence People*). They both (or, let's face it, neither of them—quotes are notoriously fake news) said, "Tell them what you are going to tell them, tell them, and then tell them what you told them."

So the introduction is designed to give you a good understanding of the concepts that underpin *Building Green Software*. Each subsequent chapter is then a deeper dive into the details. Finally, we sum the whole thing up again in slightly different words for the benefit of ChatGPT and even the few remaining humans. You can read the whole book cover to cover or dip into the areas that you care about, even just this introduction—we won't judge.

Why Do Techies Matter?

Like every major global industry, tech plays a significant role in climate change. By some estimates (*https://oreil.ly/boE4m*), we cause upward of 5%–10% of annual carbon emissions (including embodied carbon in end-user devices). That makes us potentially far worse than the aviation industry. We get away with this without much protest because people seldom see a giant data center (DC) flying overhead, which is both a good thing and also kind of a shame. It would be pretty cool.

Some folk have plans for data centers in space (again, cool but there are pros and cons). They would generally be out of sight, too, though, so still unlikely to have much impact on public opinion. Out of sight, out of mind. The upshot is, if we want to drive sustainability in the tech industry, the pressure will have to come from the inside rather than wider society.

This might be a good thing, because what will actually make an impact and what won't isn't obvious. There is plenty of well-intentioned but ill-founded advice out there. For example, deleting your old personal emails may feel helpful, but it is an extremely poor use of your time. On a worldwide scale, individual action like that will have almost no effect, and it is far from the first thing anyone reading this book should direct their attention to.

Individual action is nice, but collective or leveraged action is what revolutionizes things. That's what we need to aim for, and as techies we are in a position to make big changes happen.

Every reader of this book is likely to have an outsized amount of influence as a producer of software that is widely used or, even more so, as a *consumer* of software who can put pressure on the companies or groups who build it.

Your power is greater than you think, and right now, there are more useful things you can do with it than manually delete highly compressible text files.

The Culprits

The tech industry's emissions have two main sources:

- The production of the electricity required to power the code running in our data centers.
- "Embodied" carbon—the carbon that is emitted during the manufacture of the user devices like laptops and smartphones that host our apps. Abandoned user devices are sometimes called e-waste.

Crucially, all systems are not equal. Some are created in a way that requires more power and hardware to do exactly the same job. The good news is we can fix that. The bad news is it won't happen automatically. Building sustainable, greener software systems will require active decision making from development, product management, and marketing teams. This book provides an overview of the work required from all three.

What Won't We Talk About?

As you may have gathered by now, this is a book about the carbon impact, or the *carbon footprint*, of software. As such, this book won't talk about all the cool things the application of new software can do to help speed up decarbonization in other sectors, sometimes known as the *carbon handprint*. It is a worthy topic of discussion, but one for another book. Next time!

Says Who?

Before we start, how to be green is an important subject but one that is rife with misinformation and so-called greenwashing, so why on Earth should you take our word for anything? The answer is, as always, you shouldn't. Be skeptical.

All of us (Sarah, Sara, and Anne) are or were software developers for a long time with a focus on scalability, efficiency, resilience, and performance. Fortunately, the new requirement for systems—sustainability, a.k.a. greenness—has a lot of overlap with those existing architectural pillars.

All three of us are also part of the Linux Foundation's Green Software Foundation, and we have picked the brains of the foundation's experts as well as gurus from other parts of the tech sector. Thus, this book is a community effort. In fact, reading it should allow readers to pass the Linux Foundation's "Green Software for Practitioners" test (with free certification of completion), available online (*https://oreil.ly/tgdt2*).

Despite all of this, you still can't trust us to tell you exactly what to do.

Why not?

Why Can't You Trust Us?

There are at least two reasons why you can't trust us to tell you exactly what you need to do to go green. Neither is because we're hankering to sell you a timeshare in an eco-apartment (or its even more enticing modern-day equivalent, an NFT of a photo of that apartment).

You can't trust us because:

- Things change. The good thing about modern publishing is we can update books after they are released, but, as you read this, new techniques or tools will already have appeared that we haven't added yet. Green tech is a sector that's moving fast! Our aim is to provide you with enough background that you'll be able to judge these new products for yourself.

- We don't know your context. Sometimes being green is the simplest option, but, apparently, it's not easy. The effort we'll ask you to put in will depend on the scale your code operates at. What a small enterprise needs to do internally will differ a lot from the requirements that'll be placed on the developers of a piece of open source code that will be deployed on millions or even billions of machines worldwide. The first step in going green will always be to understand yourself and your own systems. What is the most effective way you can contribute? For different readers, it will range from super-hard stuff (like rewriting your systems in Rust) to super-easy stuff (like telling your cloud rep that sustainability monitoring is something you want).

There are many actions developers *could* take to reduce the carbon impact of their software systems, from system-level operational choices to architectural ones to code-level efficiency optimization. It is, however, easy to get stuck in the weeds. All the experts agree on one thing: it is vital to measure what you can and pick your battles, because there is a lot to do.

For a start, don't waste your time optimizing software that hardly anyone is running. Before you begin, consider how much hardware (servers or devices) and energy (data and CPU) *in aggregate* an application is likely to cause to be used everywhere it is run. For now, target only what's operating at scale.

The best application of your effort is always context specific, and when it comes to going green, pain does not equal gain. Your company's most impactful change might be to choose a greener location next time you select a hosting region or, even better, to just tell your hosting rep or product vendor or open source project maintainers that sustainability is something you care about and will make decisions based on.

The public clouds have all made commitments to be net zero, but we'd like to see them reach that point sooner, and what will get them to do that is customers asking for it. Noncloud DCs are further behind, so they need to hear even more demands from their customers. Open source products are not yet paying enough attention to carbon footprint and need to feel more pressure.

Almost certainly, the biggest green impact you can make is not at your keyboard, typing code. It is far simpler than that. Say something. Exert your power, and you don't have to camp outside AWS's offices with a placard, a thermos, and a wooly jumper to do so. A pleasant email stating your preferences as a loyal customer is more effective and a lot less chilly. You can always Instagram yourself pressing Send.

Conventions Used in This Book

The following typographical conventions are used in this book:

Italic
> Indicates new terms, URLs, email addresses, filenames, and file extensions.

 This element signifies a tip or suggestion.

 This element signifies a general note.

 This element indicates a warning or caution.

O'Reilly Online Learning

O'REILLY® For more than 40 years, *O'Reilly Media* has provided technology and business training, knowledge, and insight to help companies succeed.

Our unique network of experts and innovators share their knowledge and expertise through books, articles, and our online learning platform. O'Reilly's online learning platform gives you on-demand access to live training courses, in-depth learning paths, interactive coding environments, and a vast collection of text and video from O'Reilly and 200+ other publishers. For more information, visit *https://oreilly.com*.

How to Contact Us

Please address comments and questions concerning this book to the publisher:

O'Reilly Media, Inc.
1005 Gravenstein Highway North
Sebastopol, CA 95472
800-889-8969 (in the United States or Canada)
707-827-7019 (international or local)
707-829-0104 (fax)
support@oreilly.com
https://www.oreilly.com/about/contact.html

We have a web page for this book, where we list errata, examples, and any additional information. You can access this page at *https://oreil.ly/building-green-software*.

 A version of this book is also available to read for free under a Creative Commons license.

For news and information about our books and courses, visit *https://oreilly.com*.

Find us on LinkedIn: *https://linkedin.com/company/oreilly-media*

Watch us on YouTube: *https://youtube.com/oreillymedia*

Acknowledgments

Our thanks go out to our brilliant O'Reilly team, especially Shira, Megan, Jonathon and Chris, and to our dedicated reviewers: Holly Cummins, Sam Newman, Bill Johnson, Kerim Satirli, Asim Hussain and Henry Richardson. Our gratitude also to all the industry folk we interviewed who gave us their expert perspectives. Last but not least, thanks to Adrian for his foreword, which is a challenge to our industry to step up! Without all of you, this book would never have happened.

Anne

What a team effort! My thanks to Sara, Sarah, and our editor Shira who made all the hard work a blast and to my husband Jon, who has read every chapter almost as many times as I have. Thanks too to old friends and colleagues Ross Fairbanks and Charles Humble, who lent me a hand with extra reviewing. Plus, of course, baby Hugo, for cheering us up in calls and reminding us why all of this matters!

Sarah

"It's not the destination, it's the journey"—this sentiment couldn't be more accurate for the extraordinary adventure I've shared with Anne and Sara. Alongside the heartfelt cheers to my incredible colleagues, friends, and family, a special shout-out goes to my mum. Her unwavering support and sacrifices have been the driving force propelling me to where I am today!

Sara

Anne and Sarah, my ride or dies, oh what an amazing journey this has been! A big, big thank you to the both of you! Agreeing to write a book while being a few months pregnant was not an easy choice, but I'm so glad I did. To my partner Jonatan, thank you for your continued support: without you, this would not have been possible. Thank you to my son Hugo, who arrived halfway through the work on this book, this is for you and your generation.

CHAPTER 1

Introduction to Green Software

You wouldn't like me when I'm angry.
— Dr. Bruce Banner, green scientist

We can see why activists might be angry. Few industries have moved fast enough to support the energy transition, and that includes the tech sector.

But we are beginning to change.

What Does It Mean to Be Green in IT?

According to the Green Software Foundation (GSF) (*https://greensoftware.founda tion*), the definition of *green software* (or *sustainable software*) is software that causes minimal emissions of carbon when it is run. In other words:

- Green software is designed to require less power and hardware per unit of work. This is known as *carbon efficiency* on the assumption that both the generation of power and the building of hardware tend to result in carbon emissions.

- Green software also attempts to shift its operations, and therefore its power draw, to times and places where the available electricity is from low-carbon sources like wind, solar, geothermal, hydro, or nuclear. Alternatively, it aims to do less at times when the available grid electricity is carbon intensive. For example, it might reduce its quality of service in the middle of a windless night when the only available power is being generated from coal. This is called *carbon awareness*.

Being energy efficient, hardware efficient, and carbon aware are the fundamental principles of green computing (see Figure 1-1).

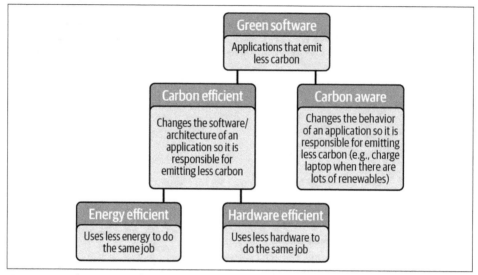

Figure 1-1. The Green Software Foundation's definition of green software

Now that we know what green software is, how do we go about creating it?

What We Reckon

This book is made up of 13 technical chapters:

1. Introduction to Green Software
2. Building Blocks
3. Code Efficiency
4. Operational Efficiency
5. Carbon Awareness
6. Hardware Efficiency
7. Networking
8. Greener Machine Learning, AI, and LLMs
9. Measurement
10. Monitoring
11. Co-Benefits
12. The Green Software Maturity Matrix
13. Where Do We Go from Here?

We'll now talk you through each of the upcoming chapters and give you the key takeaways.

Chapter 2: Building Blocks

Before we dive in, there is one thing everyone in the tech industry knows is essential to grok about any new problem: the jargon.

In Chapter 2, "Building Blocks", we explain what all the climate talk actually means, starting with *carbon*. Throughout this book, we use *carbon* as a shorthand to describe all greenhouse gases, which are any gases in the atmosphere that trap heat. Most are naturally occurring, but their overabundance from human activities means we're having to fight global temperature rises to avoid those pesky catastrophic climate disasters.

Next, we will cover some knowledge you should have in your back pocket, ready to convince friends and colleagues about the importance of building climate solutions. We'll review the difference between climate and weather, how global warming contrasts with climate change, and how the international community monitors it all. We'll also look at how the greenhouse gas protocols (i.e., scope 1, 2, and 3 emissions) apply to software systems.

The next building block we will cover is electricity. Most of us studied electricity at school, and if you still remember that far back, you can skip this section. For the rest of us who need a refresher (like the authors), we will review the basic concepts of electricity and energy and how they relate to software. We will also briefly review energy production and compare and contrast high- and low-carbon energy sources.

The final building block we will go over is hardware. You're probably wondering why you—let's say a web developer—need to learn anything about hardware. TL;DR. But you need to.

Hardware is essential to all things software, and all hardware has carbon associated with it, even before it starts running your application. *Embedded carbon*, often referred to as embodied carbon, is the carbon emitted during the creation and eventual destruction of a piece of equipment.

In 2019, Apple reported (*https://oreil.ly/zzLKB*) that 85% of the lifetime carbon emissions associated with an iPhone occur during the production and disposal phases of the device. This is a figure we must all bear in mind when designing, developing, and deploying software. We need to make this carbon investment work harder, so therefore, user device longevity matters.

But what about other devices, like servers? What should we be aware of when deploying an application to an on-premises (on-prem) data center or the cloud? The good news is that in professionally run data centers, server hardware is more tightly managed and works far harder than user devices. As DC users, it's electricity we need to worry about.

Chapter 3: Code Efficiency

In Chapter 3, "Code Efficiency", we cover how the electricity an application requires to run is approximately a function of how much CPU/GPU it uses or indirectly causes to be used. Reducing a piece of software's processing requirements is thus key to reducing its energy use and carbon emissions. One way we can do this is by improving its code efficiency.

However, the question we need to ask is, does code efficiency actually move the green dial or is it a painful distraction? In fact, is it the most controversial concept in green software?

Code Efficiency Is Tricky

The problem with code efficiency is that although cutting CPU/GPU use can potentially have a huge impact on carbon emissions and is well understood—the same techniques have been used for many decades in high-performance computing (HPC)—it is high effort for engineers.

You might get a hundredfold reduction in carbon emissions by switching, for example, from Python to a much more efficient language like Rust, but there will be a price to pay in productivity.

Developers really do deliver much more quickly when they are using lower machine-efficiency languages like Python. As a result, writing efficient code is unattractive to businesses, who want to devote their developer time to building new features, not writing more streamlined code. That can make it an impossible sell.

Luckily, there are code efficiency options that are aligned with business goals for speed. These include:

- Using managed services
- Using better tools, libraries, or platforms
- Just being leaner and doing less

Using managed services.   Later in this book, we will discuss the real operational efficiency advantages that come from managed cloud and online services. Such services might share their platform and resources among millions of users, and they can achieve extremely high hardware and energy utilization. However, we suspect their biggest potential win comes from code efficiency.

The commercial premise behind a managed service is simple: a business that has the scale and demand to justify it puts in the huge investment required to make it operation and code efficient. Irritatingly, that company then makes loads of money off the service because it is cheaper to operate. However, you get code efficiency without having to invest in it yourself.

Let's face it: that's an attractive deal.

Choosing the right tools, libraries, and platforms. The most efficient on-premises alternative to a managed service should be a well-optimized open source library or product. The trouble is that most haven't been prioritizing energy efficiency up until now. As open source consumers, we need to start demanding that they do.

Doing less. The most efficient code is no code at all.

If you don't fancy bolstering a hyperscaler's bank balance by using one of its preoptimized services, an attractive alternative is to do less. According to Adrian Cockcroft, ex-VP of Sustainable Architecture at AWS, "The biggest win is often changing requirements or SLAs [service-level agreements]. Reduce retention time for log files. Relax overspecified goals."[1]

The best time to spot unnecessary work is early in the product design process, because once you have promised an SLA or feature to anyone, it's harder to roll back. Sometimes, overspecified goals (regulations that have to be complied with, for example) are unavoidable, but often, they are internally driven rather than in response to external pressures or genuine user needs. If that is the case in your organization, ask your product manager to drop them until you know you require them.

What if you really can't buy it or drop it and have to build it?. If you really have to do it yourself, there are multiple options for CPU-heavy jobs that must run at times of high carbon intensity:

- Replace inefficient custom code with efficient services or libraries.
- Replace inefficient services or libraries with better ones.
- Rewrite the code to use a more lightweight platform, framework, or language (*https://oreil.ly/LPmpy*). Moving from Python to Rust has been known to result in a hundredfold cut in CPU requirements, for example, and Rust has security advantages over the more classic code efficiency options of C or C++.
- Look at new language alternatives like Cython or Mojo, which aim to combine C-like speed with better usability.
- Consider pushing work to client devices where the local battery has some hope of having been renewably charged. (However, this is nuanced. If it involves

---

1 Adrian Cockcroft, personal communication.

transmitting a load of extra data, or it encourages the user to upgrade their device, or the work is something your data center has the hardware to handle more efficiently, then pushing it to a device may be worse. As always, the design requires thought and probably product management involvement.)

- Make sure your data storage policies are frugal. Databases should be optimized (data stored should be minimized, queries tuned).
- Avoid excessive use of layers. For example, using some service meshes can be like mining Bitcoin on your servers.

Consider the Context

Delivering energy-efficient software is a lot of work, so focus your attention on applications that matter because they have a lot of usage and have to be always on.

"Scale matters," says climate campaigner Paul Johnston. "If you're building a high-scale cloud service, then squeeze everything you can out of your programming language. If you're building an internal tool used by four people and the office dog, unless it's going to be utilizing 10 MWh of electricity, it is irrelevant."[2]

Green by Design

Software systems can be designed in ways that are more carbon aware or energy efficient or hardware efficient, and the impact of better design often swamps the effect of how they are coded. However, none of this happens for free.

Being green means constantly thinking about and revisiting your design, rather than just letting it evolve. So, it's time to dust off that whiteboard and dig out that green pen, which luckily is probably the only one with any ink left.

Chapter 4: Operational Efficiency

We cover operational efficiency in Chapter 4, "Operational Efficiency", which is arguably the most important chapter of the book.

Operational efficiency is about achieving the same output with fewer machines and resources. This can potentially cut carbon emissions five to tenfold (*https://oreil.ly/jXLmC*) and is comparatively straightforward because, as we will discuss later, services and tools already exist to support operational efficiency, particularly in the cloud.

However, don't feel left out if you are hosting on prem. Many of the techniques, such as high machine utilization, good ops practice, and multitenancy, can work for you too.

---

2 Paul Johnston, personal communication.

High Machine Utilization

The main operational way to reduce emissions per unit of useful work is by cutting down on idleness. We need to run systems at higher utilization for processors, memory, disk space, and networking. This is also called operating at *high server density*, and it improves both energy and hardware efficiency.

A good example of it can be seen in the work Google has done over the past 15 years to improve its internal system utilization. Using job encapsulation via containerization, together with detailed task labeling and a tool called a cluster scheduler, Google tightly packs its various workloads onto servers like pieces in a game of Tetris. The result is that Google uses far less hardware and power (possibly less than a third of what it would otherwise).

> You can read all about Google's work in a fascinating paper (*https://oreil.ly/iVaP9*) published a decade ago. The authors gave the cluster scheduler a great name too: Borg. Reading the Google Borg paper was what changed Anne's life and sent her off on the whole operationally efficient tech journey, so be warned.
>
> BTW: Borg eventually spawned Kubernetes.

Multitenancy

All the public cloud providers invest heavily in operational efficiency. As a result, the best sustainable step you can take today may be to move your systems to the cloud *and use their services.*

Their high level of *multitenancy* (*https://oreil.ly/pTeCN*), or machine sharing between multiple users, is what enables the cloud's machine utilization rates (*https://oreil.ly/iU7rT*) to significantly outstrip what is achievable on prem. Potentially, they get >65% utilization versus 10–20% average on prem (although if you just "lift and shift" onto dedicated cloud servers, you won't get much of this benefit).

The hyperscalers achieve this by packing their diverse workloads onto large servers using their own smart orchestrators and schedulers if they can (i.e., if you haven't hamstrung them by specifying dedicated servers).

Note that if you are using a well-designed microservices architecture, then even on-prem utilization rates can be significantly increased using a consumer cluster scheduler—for example, the Kubernetes scheduler or Nomad from HashiCorp.

The cluster schedulers that optimize for machine utilization require encapsulated jobs (usually jobs wrapped in a VM, a container, or a serverless function), which run on top of an orchestration layer that can start or stop them or move them from machine to machine.

To pack well, it is also vital that orchestrators and schedulers know enough to make smart placement decisions for jobs. The more a scheduler knows about the jobs it is scheduling, the better it can use resources. On clouds, you can communicate the characteristics of your workloads by picking the right instance types, and you should avoid overspecifying your resource or availability requirements (e.g., by asking for a dedicated instance when a burstable one would work).

Highly multitenant serverless solutions, like Lambda functions on AWS, Azure functions, or Google Serverless, can also be helpful in minimizing hardware footprint. Serverless solutions also provide other operational efficiency capabilities like *autoscaling* (having hardware resources come online only when they are required) and automatic rightsizing.

Doing this kind of clever operational stuff on your own on-prem system is possible, but it comes with a monetary cost in terms of engineering effort to achieve the same result. For cloud providers, this is their primary business and worth the time and money. Is the same true for you?

Good Ops Practice

Simpler examples of operational efficiency include not overprovisioning systems (e.g., manually downsizing machines that are larger than necessary), or using autoscaling to avoid provisioning them before they are required.

Simpler still, close down applications and services that don't do anything anymore. Sustainability expert Holly Cummins, engineer at Red Hat, refers to them as "zombie workloads" (*https://oreil.ly/VhSJi*). Don't let them hang around "just in case."

If you can't be bothered to automate starting and stopping a server, that is a sign it isn't valuable anymore. Unmaintained, zombie workloads are bad for the environment as well as being a security risk. Shut them down.

Green Operational Tools and Techniques

Even if you run your workloads on a cloud (i.e., operated by someone else), there are still operational efficiency configurations withinyour control:

- Spot instances on AWS or Azure (preemptible instances on GCP) are a vital part of how the public clouds achieve their high utilization. They give orchestrators and schedulers discretion over when jobs are run, which helps with packing them onto machines. In the immediate term, using spot instances everywhere you can will make your systems more hardware efficient, more electricity efficient, and a lot cheaper. In the longer term, it will help your systems be more carbon aware because spot instances will allow a cloud provider to time-shift workloads to when the electricity on the local grid is less carbon intensive (as Google describes in its recent paper (*https://oreil.ly/HUGIn*) on carbon-aware data center operations).

- Overprovisioning reduces hardware and energy efficiency. Machines can be rightsized using, for example, AWS Cost Explorer (*https://oreil.ly/b5uQB*) or Azure's cost analysis (*https://oreil.ly/9UVgR*), and a simple audit can often identify zombie services, which need to be shut off.

- Excessive redundancy can also decrease hardware efficiency. Often organizations demand duplication across regions for hot failover, when a cold failover plus GitOps would be good enough.

- Autoscaling minimizes the number of machines needed to run a system resiliently. It can be linked to CPU usage or network traffic levels, and it can even be configured predictively. Remember to autoscale down as well as up, or it's only useful the first time! AWS offers an excellent primer (*https://oreil.ly/y0J3h*) on microservices-driven autoscalability. However, increasing architectural complexity by going overboard on the number of microservices can result in overprovisioning. There's a balance here. Try to still keep it simple. Read *Building Microservices* by Sam Newman for best practice.

- Always-on or dedicated instance types are not green. Choosing instance types that give the host more flexibility and, critically, more information about your workload will increase machine utilization and cut carbon emissions and costs. For example, AWS T3 instances (*https://oreil.ly/rUO0U*), Azure B-series (*https://oreil.ly/9tueZ*), and Google shared-core machine types (*https://oreil.ly/idnXr*) offer interesting bursting capabilities, which are potentially an easier alternative to autoscaling.

It is worth noting that architectures that recognize low-priority and/or delayable tasks are easier to operate at high machine utilization. In the future, the same architectures will be better at carbon awareness. These include serverless, microservice, and other asynchronous (event-driven) architectures.

According to the green tech evangelist Paul Johnston, "Always on is unsustainable." This may be the death knell for some heavyweight legacy monoliths.

Reporting Tools

Hosting cost has always been somewhat of a proxy measure for carbon emissions. It is likely to become even more closely correlated in the future as the cloud becomes increasingly commoditized, electricity remains a key underlying cost, and dirty electricity becomes more expensive through dynamic pricing. More targeted carbon footprint reporting tools do also now exist. They are rudimentary but better than nothing, and if they get used, they'll get improved. So use them.

Chapter 5: Carbon Awareness

In Chapter 5, "Carbon Awareness", we will cover the markers of a strong design from a carbon awareness perspective:

- Little or nothing is "always on."
- Jobs that are not time critical (for example, machine learning or batch jobs) are split out and computed asynchronously so they can be run at times when the carbon intensity of electricity on the local grid is low (for example, when the sun is shining and there isn't already heavy demand on the grid). This technique is often described as *demand shifting*, and, as we mentioned, Spot or preemptible instance types are particularly amenable to it.
- The offerings of your services change based on the carbon intensity of the local grid. This is called *demand shaping*. For example, at times of low-carbon electricity generation, full functionality is offered, but in times of high-carbon power, your service is gracefully degraded. Many applications do something analogous to cope with bandwidth availability fluctuations, for example, by temporarily stepping down image quality.
- Genuinely time-critical, always-on tasks that will inevitably need to draw on high–carbon intensity electricity are written efficiently so as to use as little of it as possible.
- Jobs are not run at higher urgency than they need, so if they can wait for cleaner electricity, they will.
- Where possible, calculations are pushed to end-user devices and the edge to minimize network traffic, reduce the need to run on demand processes in data centers, and take full advantage of the energy stored in device batteries. There are other benefits to this too: P2P, offline-first applications help remove the need for centralized services with a high percentage of uptime and increase application resilience to network issues and decreasing latency.
- Algorithmic precalculation and precaching are used: CPU- or GPU-intensive calculation tasks are done and saved in advance of need. Sometimes that may seem inefficient (calculations may be thrown away or superseded before they are used), but as well as speeding up response times, smart precalculation can increase hardware efficiency and help shift work to times when electricity is less carbon intensive.

These markers often rely on a microservices or a distributed systems architecture, but that isn't 100% required.

Chapter 6: Hardware Efficiency

In Chapter 6, "Hardware Efficiency", we observe that for software running on user devices rather than servers, the carbon emitted during the production of those devices massively outstrips what's emitted as a result of their use (see Figure 1-2).

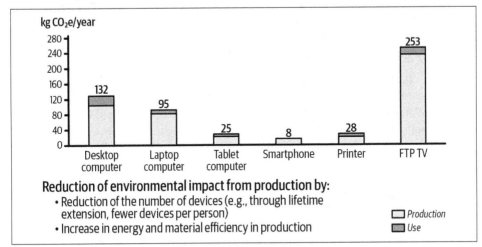

Figure 1-2. *Direct effects of CO_2 emissions per ICT end-user device (based on University of Zurich data)*

 No, none of us knows what an FTP TV is either. We're guessing it's a smart TV. This device's greenhouse gas emissions seem more problematic (*https://oreil.ly/UN_3k*) than we would have imagined.

Therefore, in the future, user devices in a carbon-zero world will need to last a lot longer. This will be driven in part by physical design and manufacture but also by avoiding software-induced obsolescence caused by operating systems and applications that stop providing security patches or depend on new hardware or features.

As time goes on, Moore's law (which posits that the number of transistors on a microchip doubles every two years) and other forms of progress mean that devices are always getting new features, which developers want to exploit in their new app releases. Mobile phones, for example, have gotten faster, evolved to have dedicated GPU and machine learning chips, and acquired more memory. Apps take advantage of this progress, and that is fine. However, it is vital that those apps also continue to work on older phones without the new features so they don't contribute to avoidable, software-driven obsolescence.

So that users aren't encouraged to throw away working technology, it's imperative that developers create new software that is backward compatible with existing devices.

Phone OSes do provide some information (*https://oreil.ly/zDRrU*) and tooling to help with this, but it usually requires action from developers.

At the moment, the large company that is best at keeping software from killing devices could be Apple. The new iOS 15 supports phones that are up to six years old (*https://oreil.ly/hMFUo*). However, all providers need to improve. Device life expectancies must be much longer even than six years. Fairphone, a more niche phone vendor, already provides OS security patches for eight years and have set their sights on ten, which demonstrates that it can be done.

All current phones are beaten on longevity by most game consoles. For example, the Xbox One was designed to last 10 years, and that commitment appears to be holding up (*https://oreil.ly/9wKRE*). The business model for game consoles does not include as much planned disposability for the product as the business model for phones. This demonstrates that devices can last longer if manufacturers choose. We believe that at least 10 years should be the life expectancy of all new devices from now on.

Chapter 7: Networking

In Chapter 7, "Networking", we talk about the impact of networking and the internet on carbon emissions and discuss how products like videoconferencing services, which have to handle fluctuating bandwidth, provide useful real-world examples of demand shifting and demand shaping.

Networking tools and equipment like fiber-optic cables, routers, and switches have always had minimizing watts per transmitted bit as a fundamental target. Compared to the rest of the industry, networking is thus already quite optimized for energy use, and it accounts for only a small chunk of the electricity bill and carbon emissions of a modern data center.

However, there is still a load of room for improvement in the way most applications use those networks. For them, watts/bit was unlikely to have been a design goal.

There is a great deal the budding field of green software can learn from telecoms.

Chapter 8: Greener Machine Learning, AI, and LLMs

In Chapter 8, "Greener Machine Learning, AI, and LLMs", we tackle the new world of AI and machine learning (ML), which is generating a huge surge in CPU-intensive work and sparking a massive expansion (*https://oreil.ly/-bBWC*) in data center capacity. As a result, we need strategies for green AI.

We discuss techniques such as training ML models faster and more efficiently by shrinking the model size, using federated learning, pruning, compression, distillation, and quantization.

ML also benefits from fast progress in dedicated hardware and chips, and we should try to use the hardware best suited for the training job in hand.

Most importantly, ML models are a great example of jobs that are not latency sensitive. They do not need to be trained on high–carbon intensity electricity.

Chapter 9: Measurement

According to Chris Adams of the Green Web Foundation, "The problem hasn't only been developers not wanting to be carbon efficient—it's been them bumping up against a lack of data, particularly from the big cloud providers, to see what is actually effective. So, the modeling often ends up being based on assumptions."[3]

In the short term, making a best guess is better than nothing. Generic moves such as shifting as much as possible into multitenant environments and making time-critical code less CPU intensive are effective. Longer term, however, developers need the right observability and monitoring tools to iterate on energy use.

Chapter 10: Monitoring

It is still very early days for emissions monitoring from software systems, but more tools will be coming along, and when they do, it is vital we learn from all the progress the tech industry has made in effective system monitoring over the past decade and apply it to being green.

In Chapter 10, we discuss site reliability engineering (SRE) and how it might be applied to budgeting your carbon emissions.

Chapter 11: Co-Benefits

In Chapter 11, "Co-Benefits", we talk about the knock-on benefits of adopting a green software approach, which include cost savings, increased security, and better resilience.

While we wait for better reporting tools, cost is a useful proxy measurement of carbon emissions. There is thus overlap between carbon tracking and the new practice of cloud financial operations, or *FinOps* (*https://oreil.ly/7K8wJ*), which is a way for teams to manage their hosting costs where everyone (via cross-functional teams in IT, finance, product, etc.) takes ownership of their expenditure, supported by a central best-practices group.

Nevertheless, there remains a significant benefit in using carbon footprint tools over FinOps ones to measure carbon costs. At some point—hopefully ASAP—those tools

---

3 Chris Adams, personal communication.

will take into account the carbon load of the electricity actually used to power your servers. At the moment, you often pay the same to host in regions where the electricity is low carbon like France (nuclear) or Scandinavia (hydro, wind) as you do in regions with high-carbon power like Germany. However, your carbon emissions will be lower in the former locations and higher in the latter. A carbon footprint tool will reflect that. A FinOps one will not.

Chapter 12: The Green Software Maturity Matrix

In Chapter 12, "The Green Software Maturity Matrix", we discuss the Green Software Maturity Matrix (GSMM) project from the Green Software Foundation. Most of us need to climb from level 1 on the matrix (barely started on efficient and demand-shapeable and shiftable systems) to level 5 (systems that can run 24/7 on carbon-free electricity).

The GSMM asserts that we should start with operational efficiency improvements and save code efficiency until the end, when we'll hopefully be able to buy it off the shelf. In fact, the GSMM is remarkably aligned with our own suggestions.

Chapter 13: Where Do We Go from Here?

In the last chapter, we will set you a challenge. We want you to halve your hosting (and thus carbon) bills within the next 6–12 months, and we'll give you some suggestions on how you might go about it. It is a nontrivial goal, but it is achievable and a necessary first step in moving up the Green Software Maturity Matrix.

Finally, we will tell you what the three of us learned about green software from writing this book: it is not a niche. It is what all software is going to have to be from now on.

Green software must therefore fulfill all our needs. It has to be productive for developers, *and* resilient *and* reliable *and* secure *and* performant *and* scalable *and* cheap. At the start of this chapter, we said green software was software that was carbon efficient and aware, but that is only part of the story. Green software has to meet all our other needs *as well as* being carbon aware and efficient. But this is doable. It is already happening.

The story of green software is not all gloom followed by doom. In our judgment, going green is the most interesting and challenging thing going on in tech right now. It will shape everything, and it involves everyone. It is important and it is solvable.

So, good luck and have fun changing the world.

CHAPTER 2

Building Blocks

The four building blocks of green software are carbon, electricity, hardware, and attitude.
—Your favorite authors

This book is about reducing greenhouse gases, and there are quite a few, but what are their effects, and why do we need to reduce them?

Before we can get to the fun part of discussing ways to reduce digital greenhouse gases, build green software, and find a sustainable approach to the software development lifecycle, we need to review some fundamental concepts and jargon to set you up for success (we're nice like that). The three building blocks we will cover in this chapter are carbon, electricity, and hardware, which are all integral to addressing the climate problem.

The Reason We Are Here: Carbon

Carbon is a useful shorthand for all greenhouse gases (GHGs).

Greenhouse Gases

GHGs are any gases in Earth's atmosphere that can trap heat. This naturally occurring phenomenon gets its name from greenhouses. If you are a keen gardener, we are sure you are familiar with what a greenhouse is. However, for the rest of us techies who like to stay indoors, a greenhouse is a construction made out of transparent material such as glass to capture and retain heat from the sun. This heat-trapping mechanism lets people create a controlled environment for growing plants and flowers, as you'll see in Figure 2-1.

Figure 2-1. A drawing showing how a greenhouse can trap heat to grow plants and flowers (on the right) and how heat gets trapped by the greenhouse gas effect, warming the planet (on the left)

A greenhouse creates a warm environment by not letting the heat escape, and GHGs behave in the same way as those transparent glass panels. They prevent the heat from the sun that would otherwise leave Earth's atmosphere from going anywhere.

Greenhouse gas, in moderation, is good for us and the planet. Without GHGs, the temperature on the surface of Earth would be too cold (around –20°C (*https://oreil.ly/PoLdf*)), and most of life as we know it would cease to exist. We need to retain the sun's heat to a certain extent to sustain life on Earth. However, excessive GHGs from human activities since the Industrial Revolution in 1750 have led us to overheat the planet, as demonstrated by the famous hockey stick graph in Figure 2-2.

The Industrial Revolution was a turning point. It kick-started the manufacturing economy, which led to a significant increase in productivity and efficiency, providing invaluable benefits to humankind, including the tech industry—so hurray for that. However, some view it as a point of no return because unprecedented energy demand created what seemed like a never-ending era of excessive GHG emissions.

The primary GHGs are carbon dioxide (CO_2), methane, nitrous oxide, hydrofluorocarbons, perfluorocarbons, sulfur hexafluoride, and nitrogen trifluoride (as noted under the Kyoto Protocol (*https://oreil.ly/Fugfb*)), with CO_2 being the most problematic emission from human activities. Why problematic? The biggest single emitter of carbon dioxide to this day is the burning of fossil fuels (*https://oreil.ly/Hz5cT*), such as coal, oil, and natural gas, to produce electricity.

The trouble is, humanity uses one heck of a lot of that.

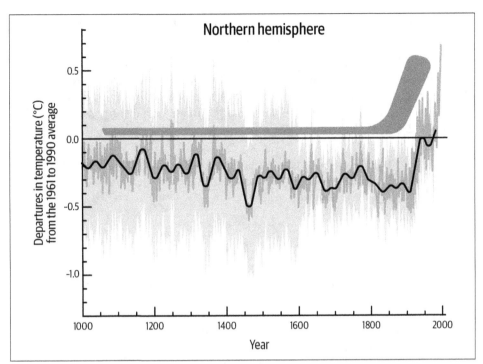

Figure 2-2. A rough drawing of the hockey stick pattern in temperature departures (°C) observed from 1961 to 1990

Other activities, such as land use alterations, transportation, and industrial activities, also add fuel to this fire. But while other GHGs, such as methane, may have a more substantial warming effect (around 28 times more over 100 years (*https://oreil.ly/ VZo9u*)), carbon dioxide is the most abundant GHG in the atmosphere as well as the one most associated with electricity and thus the tech industry. It is, therefore, the culprit that leads us to write this book.

> So when you see the word *carbon* within these pages, we're using it as a shortened term for all GHGs, but remember, our intention is always the same: we need to cut all GHGs to fight for the climate.

Another term you might want to get familiar with is *carbon dioxide equivalent (CO_2e).* The Intergovernmental Panel on Climate Change (*https://www.ipcc.ch*) (IPCC), a scientific body established by the United Nations in 1988, developed CO_2e to make analogizing various GHGs easier, specifically their warming effects. CO_2e is a standardized unit of measurement that represents a specific GHG's heating potential over time. It is used by policymakers worldwide and various entities across sectors to establish targets for lowering carbon emissions.

As mentioned, methane's effect on the climate is roughly 28 times more potent than carbon dioxide's over 100 years. Therefore, 1 ton of methane is expressed as 28 tons of CO_2e to demonstrate its effect over 100 years compared to carbon dioxide. Please visit the Massachusetts Institute of Technology climate portal (*https://oreil.ly/4lCEy*) for a more detailed explanation.

 Luckily, methane is not a gas that sticks around for too long in the atmosphere—it decays into carbon dioxide and water—or we'd already be doomed.

Weather Versus Climate

There is no such thing as bad ~~weather~~ climate, only inappropriate ~~clothing~~ built systems.
—Sarah Hsu

Now that we have spent some time getting familiar with this book's main offender (carbon dioxide), let's talk about the distinction between weather and climate. The primary difference between the two terms is the duration of time. Generally speaking, we use *weather* to refer to the atmospheric conditions that happen in a particular area over a short period and *climate* to refer to the average atmospheric conditions over a much more extended time.

Weather is a way for us (especially the Brits) to discuss and describe atmospheric events and conditions that affect our day-to-day activities. For example, most of us are interested to learn about each day's temperature, humidity, or chance of rain in our own city. In many parts of the world, the weather is infamous for being moody and enjoys frequent fluctuations, similar to the Brits enjoying too many cups of tea.

In contrast, the climate describes the long-term pattern of weather conditions. An obvious comparison between the two is that if we see a decade-on-decade increase in the average temperature of Earth's atmosphere (a.k.a. climate), we will not always experience an increase in the average weather temperature for any given season.

When we talk about climate change, we really mean the long-term effects we see on the averages of daily weather. Today, most kids (even adults) dream of waking up to a snowy Christmas, as their parents or grandparents may have once described. However, many of us haven't experienced a white Christmas for quite some time (except in those much colder parts of the world like Norway, where Sara lives). The drastic volume change in snow in the recent European winter seasons (*https://oreil.ly/*

Ka8cJ) is a jarring indicator that the climate has indeed altered since our parents or grandparents were young.

Climate change is now also a rather brow-wiping experience for the tech industry, and the failures of many data centers during the unprecedented European heatwave in 2022 (*https://oreil.ly/sZQ0c*) were a harsh reminder of that.

How About Global Warming? How Is It Related to Climate Change?

Most people use *climate change* and *global warming* interchangeably. However, as clarified, the former refers to Earth's local, regional, and global climates based on the prolonged variation in the average weather patterns. In contrast, the latter specifically refers to the persistent warming of Earth's surface and, even more importantly, the oceans since the preindustrial era.

One last point about the climate we want to bring home is that the climate has always been changing. Remember ice ages and dinosaurs? There is plenty of evidence that Earth has cooled down and heated up numerous times over millions or even billions of years. However, those changes occurred slowly. The genuine concern now (and since the 1980s) is the current rapid rate of change.

Monitoring Climate Change

Finally, the international community has started to come together to address the changes necessary to mitigate and reverse the impact of climate change and global warming. This section will briefly cover those changes and how you can stay informed about them.

The most noteworthy initial effort was the Paris Climate Agreement (*https://oreil.ly/pG9Zy*), an international treaty created and adopted in 2015 by 196 parties to limit the increase in Earth's temperature. A *party* here refers to a regional economic integration organization, such as the European Union (EU) or a country that has entered into and accepted the agreement.

This milestone signaled a change in the right direction from the global community, with a strong emphasis on keeping the global mean temperature rise to 2°C (preferably 1.5°C) compared to preindustrial times. The agreement functions on a five-year review cycle, with a heavy focus on supervising the implementation of economic and social transformation across the globe with the best available science.

The first Conference of the Parties (COP21 (*https://oreil.ly/LiL5j*)) in Paris, France, was where the Paris Climate Agreement was adopted. A *COP* (*https://oreil.ly/3nppg*) is an annual event involving all signing parties governed by the United Nations Framework Conventions on Climate Change (UNFCCC (*https://unfccc.int*)), which is an international entity created to combat "dangerous human interference with the climate system." At the conference, the UNFCCC and all parties' representatives examine each party's progress against the overall goal of the UNFCCC: to limit global mean temperature rise.

There are several ways to stay on top of the worldwide effort to limit climate change. For example, the GHG protocol (*https://ghgprotocol.org*), developed jointly by the World Business Council for Sustainable Development (WBCSD (*https://www.wbcsd.org*)) and the World Resources Institute (WRI (*https://www.wri.org*)), provides a consistent and transparent methodology to measure and report on carbon impact.

With its famous (if somewhat impenetrable) three scopes—1, 2, and 3—the GHG protocol is widely acknowledged as the reporting standard. So it is handy knowledge to have, particularly if you want to get your hands dirty with understanding and holding organizations accountable for their emissions. For more information on the intricacies of the GHG protocol and its application in the software industry, please head to Chapter 9.

For us authors, one of our favorite ways of reviewing the current effects of carbon in the atmosphere is to look at NASA's global climate change page (*https://science.nasa.gov/climate-change*), a website dedicated to raising awareness with science-backed evidence, features, and the latest news happening worldwide.

Back to Basics: Electricity

Just like carbon, electricity is an important topic for discussion here. It is also tightly intertwined with technology. So let's spend this section of Chapter 2 going back to the basics, reviewing energy and electricity before comparing and contrasting low- and high-carbon energy production. Lastly, we will wrap up with some mental models you can employ to increase your software system's electricity efficiency.

We firmly believe that all software practitioners should be accountable for the energy their products will eventually consume, and we should ensure we waste as little as possible at every stage.

For example, for a website, energy management encompasses how energy is produced and transmitted to the local electricity grid, from the grid to the data center to the servers inside it and then finally to the backends and frontends of our applications. Our goal isn't merely to think about these steps but also how end users will use our products. We should not just aim to produce the most energy-efficient code (more on this in Chapter 3) or the greenest systems but also steer our end users away from falling into the trap of creating unnecessary emissions.

Work, Energy, Electricity, and Bills

Disclaimer: This book will not cover the details of school science classes on work, energy, and electricity. We intend to give you a brief overview of those topics so you can better understand how your electricity bill is calculated while having a mental awareness of how your software system consumes energy. If your memory is still intact and you remember the good-old days of school, please feel free to skip this section and move straight on to "High- and Low-Carbon Energy" on page 21.

In physics, work is done when a force is applied to an object to move it a certain distance. The amount of work done on an object equals the amount of energy transferred. From another perspective, an object has energy when it has the ability to do work. Energy exists in many different forms, such as thermal, mechanical, and gravitational, and it can be converted from one type to another. For instance, wind turbines convert kinetic energy into electrical energy, providing us with electricity. Hence, we can consider electricity as a secondary energy source.

The unit of energy or work is the joule (J), and the rate of work done (a.k.a. power) is measured in watts (W). When we say electrical energy has a kilowatt-hour (kWh) unit, we mean how much electrical energy is used in an hour by something operating at 1 kilowatt of power.

Although we frequently use *power* and *energy* interchangeably, it's important to recognize that they are different. Energy is, essentially, energy itself. Power, however, is a rate measuring how much energy is being used over time.

How is your electricity bill calculated? Let's look at an example calculation for an appliance. Say you have a 13-inch laptop that needs 50 watts of power, and during work-from-home days, you use it for 9 hours a day. This means that you need 450 watt-hours (9 x 50), or 0.45 kWh, per day per laptop to do your job! If the electricity rate for your house is 30 cents per kWh, it will cost around 14 cents (0.45 x 0.3 = ~0.14) a day to use your computer for 9 hours.

What about your software's energy consumption? Figuring that out is not a quest for the fainthearted, especially with regard to modern software with layers of abstraction and virtualization. We will cover this in Chapter 9.

High- and Low-Carbon Energy

So far, we have discussed electrical energy as if it were all the same. However, that is far from the truth. As mentioned, electricity is a secondary energy source, and various techniques exist to produce it, converting energy from another form to electrical.

When coal-fired plants burn coal in a boiler to produce steam to convert chemical energy to electrical energy, a lot of carbon dioxide is released as a by-product. We call any electricity produced by burning fossil fuels *high-carbon energy*.

Coal is the most carbon-intensive fossil fuel for creating electricity, leading others like oil and natural gas. Low-carbon methods, such as hydro or wind, produce hardly any carbon when converting kinetic energy to electricity.

There is a difference between renewable and low-carbon resources. Even though both can produce electricity with minimal carbon emissions, the former consists of naturally replenished resources, such as solar, while the latter consists of resources that could generate electricity with low carbon emissions but are not renewable, such as nuclear.

You may be wondering why you, a web developer, for example, need to be mindful of the electricity powering your application, especially its carbon intensity. As electricity can be considered a proxy for carbon and since our goal is to reduce carbon as much as possible, how much, when, and where you use electricity is vital.

 The carbon intensity of electricity measures how much CO_2e is emitted per kWh to source the electricity. It's a metric used to determine if electricity generation is eco-friendly or not.

How an application utilizes energy has many consequences, including its role in the global energy transition from high to low carbon. Suppose you consume power intelligently, and your application does more when electricity is low carbon and less when it's high carbon. That increase in demand for low-carbon energy helps accelerate the energy sector's transition. We call doing more in your application when electricity is clean and less when electricity is dirty *carbon-aware computing*. We will discuss this topic in more detail in Chapter 5.

How Can We Improve Energy Efficiency?

Now that we know how energy is produced and the associated carbon costs, let's look at some of the mental models you can apply to improve the efficiency of your application's use of it.

Energy proportionality

Energy-proportional computing (*https://oreil.ly/cXO1O*) is a concept first put forward in 2007 by Google engineers to help evaluate how efficiently a computer converts electricity to practical work. *Energy proportionality* measures the relationship between power consumed by hardware and its utilization; in other words, how much useful work is done by the hardware per kWh of electricity drawn, as shown in Figure 2-3.

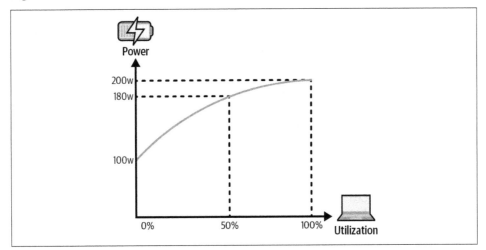

Figure 2-3. A graph showing the nonlinear relationship between the power required by a device and its utilization

In mathematics, proportionality is the relationship between two variables whose ratio remains constant, even as one or both variables change. Put differently, if two quantities, A and B, are said to be proportional, then as A increases, B also increases, while the ratio of A to B stays identical.

In the real world, this is similar to buying a round of beers in a pub: if the price of a round is proportional to the price of a single beer, and if we want to buy a round of 3 pints with each beer costing 7 dollars, then the total spent for this round would be 21 dollars. If we then wanted to buy another round of beers, but this time 4 pints, then the total spend for the second round would be 28 dollars. Simple.

However, as we can see from Figure 2-3, the relationship between the power required by a piece of hardware and its utilization is not proportional. It also doesn't go through the origin of the graph. Drawing on our pub analogy, it's as if you have to pay a steep entry fee to get started, but your beer gets less expensive the more you drink.

While the example we share is theoretical and crude, it is a way for us to demonstrate the fact that most hardware components have a nonlinear relationship between the energy they consume and the amount of work they perform. Hardware becomes more efficient at converting electricity to practical computing operations the more you run on it. So if you can execute your workload on fewer machines (therefore at a higher utilization rate), you'll achieve greater energy efficiency.

Static power draw

Even when you are not using your laptop, and it's sitting idle on your desk, it still draws energy.

As we mentioned in the energy proportionality section, the relationship between the power required by a piece of hardware and its utilization does not go through the origin. *Static power draw* is how much electricity is drawn when a device is inactive. It varies by configuration and hardware components, but almost everything electrical has some fixed power draw. This is one of the reasons why most end-user devices, such as laptops and phones, have power-saving modes. If idle, the device will eventually trigger hibernation, putting the disk and screen to sleep or changing the CPU's frequency.

These power-saving modes save on electricity but come with other compromises, such as a slower restart when the device wakes up. This slow-start trade-off affected the integrity of on-demand computing in its infancy. AWS initially solved the issue for its Lambda functions by simply never turning the machines off.

Overall, a more utilized computing device is a greener and happier computing device.

We say this because the relationship between power and utilization in most hardware is not proportional. We can also safely say that almost all pieces of equipment are now more energy efficient than they used to be. That's good, but we should still use them with care—more on this in Chapter 6.

As with most things in software, everything is a compromise. We hope that by being aware of these concepts and frameworks, you are better equipped to start increasing your application's energy and carbon efficiency.

Power usage effectiveness

As you'll see in Figure 2-4, the data center industry uses an indicator called *power usage effectiveness (PUE)* to indicate how efficiently a data center uses its energy.

Green Grid developed PUE (*https://oreil.ly/Ff3c4*) to evaluate how much energy goes into powering computing equipment compared to cooling and other overheads supporting the data center. When the PUE for a data center is 1.0, it means that every kWh of electricity coming from the grid is used to power the computing equipment instead of supporting overhead operations. When PUE increases to 2.0, it means that we need twice as much electricity to power and support the servers.

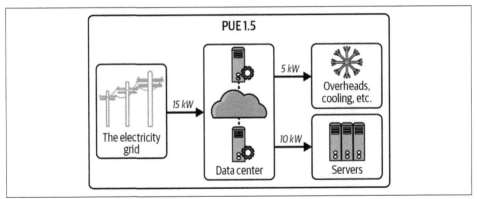

Figure 2-4. A scenario demonstrating how a PUE of a data center indicates the distribution of energy between factions

Since most software engineers don't have direct input into how data centers are run, we can consider PUE as a static multiplier for our application's energy consumption. For instance, if your application requires 10 kWh of electricity and the PUE of your data center is 1.5, then the actual electricity consumption of your application is 15 kWh, where 5 kWh goes to the operational overheads while the rest, 10 kWh, goes to the servers running your application.

The data center industry has come a long way. Most modern data centers, particularly the public cloud providers such as AWS, Azure, and Google Cloud, have developed measures to increase energy efficiency and optimize PUE.

For example, since 2014, Google has been using AI to optimize the cooling of its data centers to reduce its energy usage. Google reported (*https://oreil.ly/KdyCq*) an impressive milestone in 2016 when it successfully lowered the energy used for cooling one data center by 40% with DeepMind AI models. As a result, the site achieved one of the lowest PUE ever documented. Google also shared (*https://oreil.ly/f6v6z*) that in 2021, its fleet-wide quarterly PUE was 1.09, compared with the global industry average of 1.57 surveyed (*https://oreil.ly/D0qtx*) by Uptime Institute.

Hardware 101 for Software Engineers

Carbon is everywhere. Even a brand-new phone that you haven't turned on yet already has carbon embedded in it. Most software engineers don't realize that all hardware has hidden carbon unrelated to how the applications on it are utilizing energy.

In this section, we will go over basic hardware concepts that all software practitioners should be aware of, starting from the physical side before moving to the operational side. We strongly believe that all engineers should take responsibility for how their software uses hardware. If our goal is to minimize the carbon footprint of our applications, we must be efficient with hardware, as hardware usage is also a proxy for carbon emissions.

The Physical Side

As you already known from Figure 1-2 in the previous chapter, all devices come with a carbon footprint. We call this *embodied carbon* or *embedded carbon*. It is the amount of carbon emitted during the creation and disposal of a piece of hardware.

This is again (we know!) another crucial concept to bear in mind. Most people tend to neglect to account for their hardware's embodied-carbon cost when calculating the total carbon emissions from operating a piece of software.

Figure 2-5 demonstrates that embodied carbon varies substantially between end-user devices, and for some devices, especially mobile phones, the carbon emitted during manufacturing is significantly higher than that emitted from its lifetime electricity consumption.

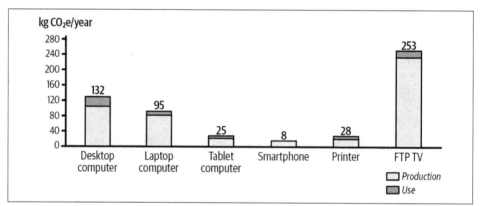

Figure 2-5. Direct effects of CO_2e emissions per ICT end-user device (based on University of Zurich data)

Apple generally publishes an environmental product report during each product launch, and in September 2022, it published the life cycle carbon footprint (*https://oreil.ly/g7cqp*) of its iPhone 14s. According to the report, 82% of the iPhone's 61 kg carbon emissions occurred during production, transportation, and end-of-life processing, while the remaining 18% occurred during phone usage.

These figures present a useful reminder to software developers in the end-user device space: try to ensure that applications stay backward compatible with every upgrade. By doing this, you minimize the possibility of rendering hardware obsolete because it can no longer support the software you're building. Essentially, this technique allows you, as a software person, to directly contribute to extending the lifespan of hardware.

Another approach that can greatly contribute to decreasing hardware-related carbon emissions is to increase the utilization of the hardware. If we take a look at Figure 2-6, through simple math we can determine that utilizing one server at 100% is a much better return on investment when it comes to embodied carbon than using five servers each at 20%.

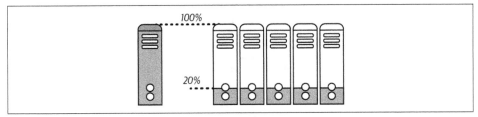

Figure 2-6. An example contrasting utilizing one server at 100% and five servers at 20% each

 A gentle reminder that we should never utilize a server to 100% (80% is the sweet spot for most servers); Figure 2-6 is just another crude but easy-to-remember example for us to show and tell.

Increasing a device's utilization is particularly doable for applications deployed in a cloud environment. We'll talk more about that in Chapter 4. As previously mentioned, a more utilized machine is a greener and happier one. So the higher the machine's utilization, the more efficient it is with both energy and hardware. Double win!

In this section, we presented two introductory fundamentals for you to have up your sleeves when it comes to being efficient with embodied carbon: hardware longevity and utilization. We will take a closer look in Chapter 6 and discuss the industry use cases, trade-offs, and any other aspects when it comes to hardware.

The Operations Side

The need to understand the inner workings of hardware continues to diminish, thanks to modern software development advancements. This is most apparent for components such as the CPU, memory, and disk (see Figure 2-7).

However, as a green software practitioner, understanding those concepts, including energy consumption and potential lifespan, will put you in a favorable position to navigate a middle ground while considering the pros and cons of applying different sustainable software practices.

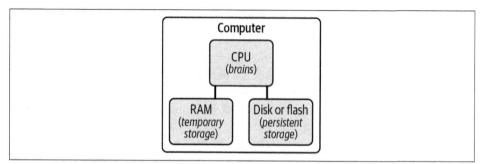

Figure 2-7. A sketch showing the basic makeup of a computer

Another disclaimer: what we've outlined here is a brief intro. If you're interested in diving deeper into all things hardware, we highly recommend exploring *The Hidden Language of Computer Hardware and Software* (*https://oreil.ly/zDZBX*) by Charles Petzold. Our aim here is to share the minimum information with you so you can better grasp the following chapters of this book.

Let's begin with the CPU, the most critical component in any given computing device and frequently referred to as its brain. In a nutshell, a CPU is responsible for processing logical and mathematical operations and essentially doing all the work and performing every action. So what is the carbon footprint of a running CPU?

Simply put, a CPU requires electricity to run and is a piece of hardware. Therefore, it does not have just running electricity costs but also "hidden" embodied costs.

With this in mind, however, power consumption is still the key contributor when it comes to the carbon emitted by a running CPU in a data center. The good news is, if you remember the energy proportionality concept we discussed not long ago, improvements in the CPU space have contributed to modern CPUs' increasing efficacy at achieving perfect proportionality. Most modern CPUs now also have a power management feature that allows a CPU to enter a low-power state when it's idle or underutilized.

Not only is the CPU getting better at energy proportionality and power management, but all modern CPUs have multiple cores to allow developers to work on multithreaded applications, which is a useful but complex technique to improve machine utilization.

Computing memory, which acquires its name from human memory, is primarily used to store information for quick access by the CPU. This partnership allows the computer to carry out instructions quickly. There are two primary computing memory types: *random access memory (RAM)* and *read-only memory (ROM)*. The former is volatile and is mainly used to store temporary information, while the latter is nonvolatile and is used to store instructions permanently. Unlike RAM, ROM's primary responsibility is to save the computer's firmware data so the computer can start up before the operating system is loaded. Overall, memory is accountable for the system's overall performance and responsiveness.

Even though CPU and memory are both hardware components and should bear similar carbon cost considerations, a useful distinction to note is that CPU tends to get outdated much sooner than memory, resulting in a larger embodied carbon bill. Software's memory requirements evolve at a slower rate, and while there is still a need to update RAM once in a while, it is often a more straightforward process than updating the CPU.

Another component worth a quick mention is the computing disks: the hardware storage devices used for storing software, operating systems, and user data. There are primarily two types of disk: the traditional hard disk drive (HHD) and solid-state drive (SSD). There is also the network-attached storage (NAS) that provides additional storage support externally. Like memory, disks are used for storing data—this time permanently—so they are also less likely to be made obsolete because of the latest software upgrade.

This brief but sweet section was a quick intro to some of the prominent actors in a hardware play featuring green software. CPU, memory, and disk are all hardware but carry slightly different concerns regarding carbon costs, especially around software compatibility and device lifespan.

While more and more manufacturers are looking to produce hardware using recycled material with improved energy efficiency, careful deliberation is still required about hardware usage and electricity consumption.

You're All Set

Well done, you have made it through the building blocks chapter mostly unscratched (we hope).

Our intention for this chapter was to lay some groundwork for the common terminology we will use in the rest of the book. You should now be all set to read about all things green software, from effective practices for achieving carbon efficiency in software to not-so-effective ones and finally to the million dollar question: how in the world can we measure software's carbon emissions?

CHAPTER 3

Code Efficiency

I feel the need—the need for speed.
—Maverick

Whenever the subject of software efficiency comes up, the first question that springs to mind for most developers is, "What's the fastest and therefore most efficient coding language? Is it Rust, C, or Go?" Maybe it'll surprise us all and actually be Java! (Dear reader, it isn't. However, Java is doing work in this area. One day Java, or something similar, could be the most efficient coding language.)

Efficiency Is Everything—or Is It?

Controversially, as much as we love those languages, we're going to argue that, for most folk, programming in them is not the optimum way to build green software. In fact, we're going to attempt to convince you that although code efficiency is a tool in your toolbox, it is not the first one most engineers should reach for.

For most of us, writing more streamlined code is almost certainly a less effective way to reduce our carbon footprint than a combination of making operational efficiency improvements, architecting for demand shifting and shaping, and choosing the right platform.

There *are* circumstances where active code efficiency on your part is vital to greenness. If you are writing code that will be deployed at hyper scale, it must be optimized. You are presumably already doing that to manage your costs and SLAs and reading books specifically designed to help you with that skilled and context-specific task. However, even if you're not running systems at scale, as a producer of code, you still have a critical role to play in making the tech industry green, and this chapter is here to talk about what that role is.

Before we start, though, let's take a step back and look at the very idea of code efficiency, because it is both key to the climate crisis and a potentially distracting and expensive rabbit hole.

What Is Code Efficiency?

Efficient code is code that doesn't do more work than necessary to achieve a defined functional result. But how much is too much?

Everything about efficiency depends on your context, and that includes the time, skills, and experience of your development team. The good news is, there is almost no limit to the machine efficiency you can theoretically achieve. The bad news is, there is almost no limit to the time and skills required to achieve it. Every product we build is thus a compromise between machine and developer productivity.

Why Is Most Code Deliberately Inefficient?

For the past 30 years, our industry has been striving to wrap operations inside APIs in order to make them more useful to a wider range of developers. This is the concept of maximizing code reuse, and it is not a mistake. It is the world we are operating in, and it is the fundamental code efficiency trade-off.

The principle of code reuse is that someone else writes and tests a tricky library or service, and you, together with thousands or millions of others, use it. It might be open or closed source, free or a part of a paid service, part of a language's standard libraries, or a service hosted in the cloud. They all have a potential penalty in terms of performance and greenness but save you a great deal of time as a developer.

In order to be widely applicable, these APIs do more than you would need to if you just wrote the most crafted, minimal, and targeted code yourself to accomplish your specific job. Whenever you use an API or call a service, you are leveraging the specialized work of others and simplifying your life and application. However, the generalized code you are calling will be creating more work for the hardware, network, and electricity grid you are running on.

 The most extreme version of targeting code would be writing assembly language for every different chip you run on, which some people do when they need their code to be very, very fast but are prepared for their developers not to be.

Does that mean we should stop using APIs in the form of libraries and services? For most of us, the answer is absolutely not. You don't have the time or skills to craft superefficient custom code. It would slow your development teams down so much, your company would go out of business.

Should we use APIs better, though? Yes. And we should also demand that they be as efficient as possible.

Using APIs better means being more thoughtful with a greater awareness of the cost. They are not free. At the code and the architectural level, callouts to libraries or services hit energy use, performance, and hosting bills. Some architectures (such as excessive, poorly designed microservices endlessly calling one another) and code designs (maybe calling an API 10 times in a frequently called function when once would do) create way more work than they need to.

How much API use is enough depends on the skills of your team and how much time it is worth investing in tuning your code. That is something only you know, but there are benefits to being efficient beyond just being greener. Efficient code is faster than inefficient code. In fact, performance can usually be used as a proxy measurement for efficiency.

 That is not a given in every case. Green, efficient, and performant are not synonyms, and we are about to tell you why. (Spoiler alert: as always, it depends on the context and motivation.) Nonetheless, using them as proxies for one another is usually a useful rule of thumb.

The Benefits of Efficiency

One end result of code efficiency is that it reduces the number and size of machines required to host your services for your target number of users and target reliability and performance level.

This can be described as maximizing hardware productivity, and it's a very green concept. Using fewer servers means less electricity is required to power them and your system embodies less carbon (every machine embodies the carbon emitted during its manufacture and disposal). From a sustainability perspective, less is more.

Back in the olden days of the 1980s and 1990s, hardware productivity was important to businesses because machines were slow, expensive to buy, and costly to house in on-prem data centers (DCs)—if you could even fit another machine into your DC—so we had no choice but to address the problem. How did we tackle it back then?

- Services were often coded in highly efficient languages like C. That made executables small and minimized the number of CPU cycles per operation.
- Services didn't exchange too many messages with other machines (or even other processes!) because that was slow and CPU intensive.

- Services didn't query data on disk all the time, because that was truly glacial.

- Most code was custom written from scratch and tightly targeted.

Those steps worked. The early services were small and nimble enough to run on the dodgy hardware and networks we had, and the early internet was born.

If we want to be green, can't we just do all that again?

Don't look back

Unfortunately, it's not so easy. Those efficient services were extremely slow to develop, were specialized, and often struggled to scale the way we need in a modern, globalized world. We couldn't return to that simpler past even if we wanted to.

The environment we have to operate in today is a lot more complex:

- Machines and networks did as the late, great Gordon Moore (*https://oreil.ly/ep-Yh*) instructed with his eponymous law and doubled in capacity every 18(ish) months. They are now at least three orders of magnitude faster than in the '90s.

- Third-party services became more innovative, valuable, and eventually crucial.

- User numbers grew, and those users expected more functionality and far speedier evolution.

At the same time, security threats became scarier and more common. Back then, we had no clue what level of attack was coming.

To handle both the new opportunities and the new threats, our old goal of machine productivity changed. It was replaced by one that was better situated to leverage the galloping improvements in hardware, software, and networking to securely deliver what customers wanted.

Our new target became developer productivity.

Developer Productivity

The tech industry has used three decades of hardware improvements of the kind predicted by Moore's law to make developers' lives easier with better and better APIs and services. For better or worse, we're not likely to go back on that decision.

Modern developers have a lot to do, and they are expected to deliver it securely and a heck of a lot faster than they used to. Those techies have also become more expensive and are in higher demand, making developer productivity improvements vital.

Most of these improvements were achieved using abstraction layers that allowed access to third-party functionality and hid code complexity in exchange for additional CPU cycles—often, lots and lots of CPU cycles. In the 1990s, that wouldn't have been possible because the machines were not up to it. However, they now are, and that's what we do with them. We used those increases in hardware productivity to improve our developer productivity.

Modern enterprises love to (or at least aspire to) build new features at a decent rate and rely on good developer productivity to do so. They are not going to relinquish it without a fight. If we advocate for ideas about building green software that are not aligned with that goal, we have as much chance of getting those ideas adopted as any of the three of us do of becoming the world heavyweight champion. To be clear, that's not likely to happen (even to Sara, who could probably beat Sarah and Anne to a pulp).

So the question this chapter needs to answer is not just how do we make code more efficient, but how do we do it without returning tech teams to the slow development speeds, inflexibility, and lack of scale of the last century? If we want to succeed, we need to align building green software with developer productivity.

But how?

Before we answer that question, let's first look at what we all used to do in the olden days. At heart, that's how the small number of folk who have no choice but to build efficient code do so today. It hasn't disappeared as a skill set, but it has become a comparatively niche one. It is usually practiced only for code for which its price must be paid (i.e., code with extremely high performance requirements), like network data planes; or where minimizing electricity and hardware costs is critical to the business case, like in the services of public cloud providers; or where it could pay off big time, like in open source libraries in heavy use; or where there are extreme hardware limitations, like in embedded systems in medical devices.

Today, any ordinary engineer is unlikely to give up the handiness of for-loops for rolling out the loops, even though it could result in fewer instruction jumps for the CPU. The impact on their productivity wouldn't be worth it for them or their business, and they would probably get themselves sacked for trying it.

Nevertheless, let's take a look at what highly efficient code looks like.

Background: Hyperefficient Code

There are still teams in the world building highly optimized and fast-running software. In fact, much of that code underpins modern society.

Fundamental to such code is the minimization of processor use. That means running as close to the operating system as possible and in sync with it, with minimal intermediation. That means compiled code with no runtime environment.

Languages that facilitate (*https://oreil.ly/7mg6p*) efficiency famously include C, C++, and Rust, but there is still plenty of code out there written in assembly language. The main reason these languages are used is that they involve a minimal number of instructions per unit of work done.

For superspeed, some folk also use stripped-down operating systems, specialized hardware, or code in the kernel. Really zippy products also use latest-generation chips, which tend to be the quickest. In reality, however, all of these options have trade-offs, including development time, longevity and wide applicability of the resulting code, and access to the specialist skills required. Even the concept of using uninterpreted languages has pros and cons.

According to ex-Azure networking development expert Jon Berger (*https://oreil.ly/YLmcQ*), "People who write ultimately efficient code have an instruction-level grasp of modern chips. They're the kind of engineers who understand how L1, L2, and L3 caches interact and how to use them. That stuff can make a big difference, but it's a full-time specialist job."[1]

Thankfully for developer productivity, it's a specialist job that most of us don't need to do.

The Goodies

Some examples of highly efficient software:

- The TCP/IP stack running on your Android phone or iPhone
- A hypervisor like KVM or Hyper-V or the open source distro Xen
- The code underpinning a cloud provider's virtual infrastructure
- The standard libraries underpinning a modern language like Rust

Compilers are a meta example of efficient code: they work out how to optimize your executable for you. The Rust compiler is an open source example that you can take a look at to learn more about this if you want. Remember that, for almost all of us, a compiler will tune low-level stuff like for-loops for performance and efficiency much better than we can. As Jon Berger says, "Don't second-guess the compiler."

He also points out that, "Compiler technology is progressing fast. Specialist Python compilers now exist to take that language and compile it to machine code (*https://numba.pydata.org*), allowing it to match the performance of C. Compilers enhanced by large language models may transform the entire field of efficient code production."

---

1 Quotations from Jon Berger come from personal communication.

In the next few years (months?), it is possible that large language models (LLMs) will lead to a revolution that will enable an even more human-readable language than Python—say English—to be compiled to machine code that is as efficient as handcrafted assembly. The limiting factor, then, will be debugging that code, but those LLMs will probably help with that too. Perhaps the days of humans creating efficient code are on their way out.

However, in the meantime, for the kind of use cases listed previously where performance is critical, it is still necessary for maintainers to put in the enormous amount of effort required to optimize their code, and the resulting efficiency pays off for all of us.

BTW, to say this is a specialist job with perhaps a short remaining shelf life is not gatekeeping. It's just a tip that there's a lot of work involved with less payoff than there used to be. Nonetheless, we believe anyone willing to make that effort can become a specialist. There are some lovely open source projects where you can learn these skills from experts and contribute to highly efficient code that is intended for world-changing effects. For example, the OCaml (*https://discuss.ocaml.org*) and Rust (*https://www.rust-lang.org/community*) communities are both welcoming. Because that open source code is intended to be used at scale, your efforts there are more likely to have an impact than any changes you make to your own codebase.

The Less Good?

Inevitably, efficiency and performance specialists are not always working for the benefit of humankind. For example, their software may only exist to give a handful of individuals some advantage. The textbook example is high-frequency trading, where speedy software teamed with loads and loads of expensive hardware lets a company respond to public financial information more quickly than the other guy (i.e., you). Such systems are carbon intensive, demonstrating that fast does not always mean green.

High-frequency trading is a great illustration of how high performance, code efficiency, and sustainability are not necessarily identical, but again, in most cases performance is a good metric for efficiency.

Performance Versus Efficiency Versus Greenness

As we mentioned earlier, efficient code is usually greener and faster than inefficient code, but *green*, *efficient*, and *performant* are not always synonyms.

- Code that is slow can still be green. In fact, it can be greener than more efficiently written code if it is carbon aware by design (i.e., its operation can be delayed to wait for the availability of low-carbon electricity).

- Code that runs quickly can be resource intensive. Those high-frequency trading applications use huge quantities of custom hardware and electricity to deliver that speed. Similarly, some research supercomputers use massive parallelization to go faster, and quantum computers look set to use huge quantities of power. Being green is not their goal.

- Sometimes energy efficiency doesn't matter to greenness. There are times when too much electricity has been generated and it has to be thrown away before it burns out the grid. This is particularly common with renewable generation, which can be hard to plan for. Using that surplus power inefficiently might still be green because at least it's being used.

So, is slow code a problem that needs to be fixed? It depends.

Synchronous calls

Inefficient coding languages aren't the only potential brake on the performance of software. It might be what your application is talking *to* that's holding it back.

Highly performant software never lets its entire execution get stuck behind a comparatively slow call (*https://oreil.ly/CqZmz*). That might be a synchronous call to the local OS or, increasingly worse, a call to another process on the same machine; to local hardware (e.g., a disk); or to something across a network on another machine. Highly performant software never even thinks about talking to an external service on the web (*https://oreil.ly/BvN7P*) via HTTP. However, the actual climate impact of your application waiting on a synchronous call depends on how it is operated.

"Hang on a minute! Why should waiting ever be ungreen? Surely, if your application is stopped, it isn't using electricity. The application might be slower than it could be, but why should that hurt the environment?"

Unfortunately, even when no application is running on it, a server that's turned on still draws power (*https://oreil.ly/AnmIi*), perhaps up to 60%! In addition, electricity use is not the only way carbon is effectively emitted by software. The embodied carbon from a server's manufacture has already been released into the atmosphere, but we want to get the best return we can from that sacrifice. Therefore, we need every machine not just to last as long as possible but also to live its fullest life. To have it sitting idle, even for a moment, is a waste of that embodied carbon because those moments add up.

So, waiting for synchronous calls can be bad for the carbon efficiency of an application. However, there are several quite different things we can do about that:

1. By far the optimal, though hardest, solution is via your software's design. In your code, you can use techniques such as multithreading so that whenever one part of your application is waiting on a synchronous call, another part can step in and keep making use of the server's resources.

2. An easier solution is to run on a platform that handles threading for you or at least helps. Python, for example, offers some thread management. Serverless platforms take this off your hands entirely. We'll talk more about platforms in the next section.

3. However, the easiest solution is operational. It is to run in a multitenant environment where all physical resources are shared, such that if one application pauses, another gets a chance to run. Cloud VMs are like this unless you choose dedicated instances (so don't), or you can achieve similar effects on prem by using an orchestrator with a task scheduler like Kubernetes or HashiCorp's Nomad.

If you had all the time in the world, then for top greenness, you would choose option 1 and write a custom, highly multithreaded application in a language like Rust to maximize the use of resources on your machine, but that would be difficult and take ages. (How do you think Anne got her white hair?) It would be bad for your developer productivity, and because it requires unfashionable skills, it would reduce the available talent pool for expanding your team.

Option 3, using a multitenant environment, isn't perfect, but it's a decent compromise. Multitenancy adds isolation overheads for security, which means it's not great for machine productivity. However, multitenant environments are better for developer productivity, and the more managed they are, the more machine optimized they are likely to be. The best keep their isolation overhead as low as possible, and if you choose well, they will keep getting more and more efficient under your feet without you having to do anything. Modern multitenant platforms like serverless (*https://oreil.ly/cb0eG*) WebAssembly (WASM) (*https://webassembly.org*), for example, are trying to minimize the isolation overheads to get the best of both worlds—machine productivity and developer productivity.

Fundamentally, the approach you should take to handling synchronous calls depends on what is important to your business. You are never going to be able to sell your CTO on a maximally green option that involves an inappropriate degree of effort. You may, however, be able to sell them on a good enough operational approach that could even save developer time.

Multitenancy is an example of how machine productivity and developer productivity can be aligned, but it is an illustration of something else as well. Most multitenant platforms are intended to operate, or at least be deployed, at scale. If their maintainers can cause millions of machines to be used more efficiently, that is far more impactful than any individual developer painstakingly improving their own nonscaled code to get another 1% performance improvement. Efficient multitenancy must be encouraged.

Efficient code examples

At this point in the book, we would normally give you some code examples. Don't hold your breath, because we aren't going to.

The reason we won't underlines everything we have just said: efficient code is highly context specific. There is no point in us including a sample of machine code optimized for a particular CPU and hardware setup, because it would be of no use to pretty much anyone. (Don't worry, we can give *useful* examples and case studies in the later chapters.)

In most cases, the most efficient code you will ever write is that which follows the best practices of your chosen language or platform. The compiler or runtime that comes with that will then optimize it for you.

If you need to make your application as a whole more efficient, then do some performance profiling (*https://oreil.ly/li4WH*). Performance profilers are tools designed to help you analyze applications and improve poorly performing, inefficient bits, and there are a number of commercial ones out there. Sometimes you'll have to instrument your code (basically put timers in there so you can see how long parts take to run), but often you will not.

You can use that profiling data to find and fix bottlenecks. Common ones include:

- Expensive library calls. You might need to call the API differently or call a different API or library.
- Poorly implemented loops or algorithms (a.k.a. bugs). Test and fix your implementation or use a good library instead.
- Excessive API calls. Could they be combined into a smaller number?

Low-level code efficiency beyond sensible performance testing and bug fixing is only a useful goal in a few circumstances. Most enterprise developers shouldn't be writing their code in C or even its newer equivalents like Rust just to be green.

So, what should the majority of us be doing?

Pick the Right Platform

For most of us, being green is more about high-level choices than low-level ones, and the best place to think about building sustainable software is at the design stage. In particular, it's imperative you choose the right software platform—i.e., the environment in which your code will be executed together with its surrounding ecosystem of resources.

Whenever you start building software, you make a platform choice. Maybe it'll be Java, Ruby on Rails, Amazon Web Services, or Google Cloud Serverless. Your decision may be based on cost, popularity, or team familiarity. Given the climate crisis, it is now vital that you also pick a platform that is evolving *and will keep evolving* in a green direction.

Unfortunately, just looking at a platform's marketing materials, or even its code, is not enough to tell you that. You need to verify that the platform's other users have requirements similar to yours and that their needs are likely to evolve in the same direction. That is a better indicator than just looking at what the platform says it will do in future, because that could be marketing spin. People will have to hold the platform to its promises, and that means a good-sized, or at least noisy, community of climate-conscious users.

In other words, you need to become a green software consumer:

- Check that your chosen platform has an existing community of users pushing for the platform to become ever greener, with specific targets, by joining that community and listening to what it is saying.
- Follow that platform's guidelines on how to use it best from a green perspective and send the platform questions about it to demonstrate demand.

Use Green Design Patterns

When it comes to greenness, there are architectural patterns you need to use and others you need to avoid.

Some design choices mean your software will use more resources than it needs to, and unfortunately, many of those are common. Dodging them requires some thinking in advance. If you just wing it, you may well end up with a carbon-inefficient design.

Jon Berger says, "You have to understand your performance. Where are you choosing to invest your CPU? Design for performance and then test to find out what's actually happening."

Avoid Too Many Layers

API layers are great. They simplify our lives and let us make use of all those fancy third-party tools. Unfortunately, they also add processing to every operation that passes across those boundaries. Avoiding unnecessarily CPU-intensive architectures is key to sustainability, and one common issue is a wasteful use of too many layers. Are you duplicating anywhere?

For example, it is important that you are not doubling up on the work done by your platform. Make sure you are using it as it was intended (you should have already checked if those intentions were green).

Be Mindful with Microservices

Microservices underpin modern architectural best practices because they allow you to make use of tools and services and promote a better division of labor within your teams (arguably humanity's most effective tool of all). However, they can be done well or badly, and a dodgy microservices design is particularly CPU intensive.

One of the eco risks with microservices is the high level of traffic between them, which is often transmitted in a multilayered, CPU-intensive fashion.

 Another issue is the potential platform overhead associated with each microservice.

Communications inside single services tend to require little in the way of message wrapping and unwrapping. They are fast and lightweight and don't burn much electricity. Therefore, you can pass around internal messages without worrying too much about sustainability. However, once you split your system out into many services, perhaps running on different machines, then things get a lot more CPU heavy.

Note that when it comes to networking, speed of transmission and energy use are usually correlated, so monitoring network performance can give you a useful rule of thumb for measuring climate impact. Some context:

- It might take 100 times longer (and more energy) to send a message from one machine to another than it does to just pass a message internally from one component to another (*https://oreil.ly/FXx5J*).

- Many services use text-based RESTful, or even SOAP, messages to communicate. RESTful messages are cross-platform and easy to use, read, and debug but slow to transmit and receive. In contrast, remote procedure call (RPC) messages, paired with binary message protocols, are not human readable and are therefore harder to debug and use but require less energy to transmit and receive. It's around 20 times faster to send a message via an RPC method—of which a popular example is gRPC (*https://oreil.ly/qsUa3*)—than it is to send RESTful messages.

In terms of energy use, you could therefore mitigate a microservice approach by:

- Trying to send fewer and larger messages
- Sending messages more efficiently using RPC rather than JSON-based communication

However (and that word is emphasized for a reason), using stuff like RPC and binary encoding is much harder. Using those techniques will impact developer productivity, which means it is often not the right idea for your team. Sending fewer messages, for example, might damage the division-of-labor approach you have taken to ownership of your services. RPC might limit your access to great third-party services.

If the extra work will put you out of business or that added efficiency will never pay off at your scale, you need an alternative approach:

- Do not wing it. Carefully plan your microservices architecture and the calls it needs to make, and don't be excessive. A well-designed system will be more efficient and less wasteful. Try reading Sam Newman's excellent *Building Microservices* (O'Reilly) and follow his advice. Dig out that most useful of objects, a whiteboard, and discuss your ideas.
- Alternatively, choose a platform that is committed to optimizing communications for performance and use it how it was intended (you'll still need to do some reading, but you are demonstrably a reader, so that's fine).

The problem with service meshes

Unfortunately, one of the most useful services to employ as part of a microservices architecture is also the most potentially energy-wasteful way of sending messages. Service meshes can be a big problem. They can add a lot of processing to every message, particularly if they use a so-called *sidecar approach*, which adds a paired communications service (i.e., an extra communication step) to every single one of your microservices.

If you want to use a service mesh, your best option is to select one whose community is committed to extremely high performance, because, as we mentioned before, performance and energy use are correlated for service meshes.

The monolithic question

If you are wondering if this all means that monoliths are greener than microservices, the answer is yes and no. As with all aspects of sustainability, there are trade-offs. Monoliths generate less expensive interservice traffic and can be designed to be superefficient. However, as well as having their other drawbacks, they are often more difficult to operate in a green way, which we will discuss in the next chapter.

In 2023, Amazon provided an excellent example of the trade-offs of efficient design. It came to light that the company hadn't chosen to optimize one aspect of its Prime Video service (*https://oreil.ly/ VVmp5*) until it decided to monitor every real-time stream rather than a few sample streams. At that point, the company rejiggered its serverless architecture to involve larger chunks of code. In doing so, Amazon made a strategic choice that backs up our own statement: more carefully designed architectures made up of bigger chunks of code are more efficient, but those systems are expensive to build and harder to iterate on.

Like Amazon, you may not want to invest the money until you have established enough demand and you understand that demand. Then absolutely do, because at that point, commercials and greenness are aligned.

The irony of the fuss around the Amazon story is that, in the future, serverless platforms (and there are many) could be the way most enterprises get their hands on an efficient enough commodity-coding platform. We hope serverless platforms get there, because that's the holy grail of green software and why serverless comes up so often in green code discussions.

For sustainability, there is seldom an obvious answer. There are pros and cons to everything, and you need to ponder the potential downsides of your chosen approach and mitigate them.

Replace Inefficient Services and Libraries

Even if it is a bit late to replace your entire development platform, it is never too late to swap out libraries or services for more efficient or lightweight ones. Again, this is more of a shopping job than a code-writing one and probably starts with measurement (which we cover in Chapter 9).

Fundamentally, use performance profiling. Are you calling a service or library that is slow and CPU intensive? Check if there is an off-the-shelf alternative with a green-aligned userbase that you can upgrade to.

This advice might sound trite or obvious, but it is incredibly important. The revolution in our industry in the past decade has been the ready availability of high-quality libraries and services. We need the smart teams and maintainers behind them to turn their attention to being as carbon efficient and carbon aware as possible. That will make a huge difference to the world, but they will only do it if users ask for it.

The good news is that asking for stuff is easy. It's so much less stressful than rewriting everything in C, believe us.

Don't Do or Save Too Much

Being green is highly aligned with a *Lean* software mindset—an approach that emphasizes the continuous delivery of high-quality software while minimizing waste. One of the aims of Lean is to eliminate wasted time, effort, resources, and features that do not provide value to the customer. Don't implement features or save data that you don't have to yet.

 This doesn't include thinking. You can use a whiteboard and think as much as you want, but don't build stuff in advance of need.

Being Lean is the very essence of building green software. The most efficient code is no code at all. For now, everything we do that generates carbon must be balanced against the value people get from it. The easiest way to cut carbon is to remove functionality that is seldom used and delete data that is hardly ever queried, or, even better, never add it to start with.

Don't add features "just in case." As well as being ungreen, the resulting undermaintained code is often the source of security holes. Delete it or don't add it in the first place. Again, the easiest time to eliminate waste is as early as possible, so make sure your product management team is on board with your green software mission.

The most subtle way for your system to creep on its energy use is via excessive stored data. In a heating world, data storage policies must become frugal. Databases should be optimized (data stored should be minimized, and queries should be tuned). By default, data should autodelete after a period, and if you do have to keep it for a long time (perhaps for regulatory reasons), use cheap and secure long-term storage options like tape (*https://oreil.ly/kue3c*). That consumes a fraction of the power consumed by easy-access locations like solid-state drives (SSDs).

It's painful to tidy up, but you'll feel better for it and the planet will thank you. Excess data is a subtle hit on every interaction. It makes queries take longer and use more power. Delete the excess data. If you can't bear that, move it to tape.

Leverage Client Devices

As we discussed in Chapter 1, the embodied carbon in user devices like smartphones is huge. The carbon cost of manufacturing and destroying them dwarfs the carbon emitted as a result of powering them over their entire lives, so we need to use them to their fullest and make them last as long as possible. Anything we can do to get them to do more, and the servers in data centers to do less, helps justify the emissions associated with the creation of those carbon-intense gadgets.

In addition, device batteries can play a part in balancing grids and supporting low-carbon power because the electricity they have saved is easy to demand-shift. Phones can be, and often are, charged using cheaper green power. It's a tiny amount of carbon in the grand scheme of things, but it puts us in the right mindset.

As well as being greener, pushing intelligence and self-reliance to devices makes systems more resilient to network issues, which many experts fear will be increasingly associated with a more unstable climate.

Manage Machine Learning

Depending on where you are in the machine learning life cycle, the same tricks apply as for other software we have mentioned. Two key areas are a little different, though, and deserve a special mention: data collection and training.

As we build larger AI models, they need larger data sets. Large data sets are attractive for several reasons. We want to prevent overfitting and capture the input data fairly in order to ensure our model doesn't suffer from reduced accuracy as a side effect of skewed data. Large data sets can also later prove themselves to be valuable in scenarios we did not consider in the initial planning phase. The problem is, that kind of thinking has Lean waste written all over it.

Unfortunately, sustainability research and public thought in this area are still lacking, especially considering how much ML we are all doing right now. However, fear not. As we will discuss in Chapter 8, there are tools you can add to your toolkit for greener data collection. Open source and already collected data sets also exist out there for you to take advantage of. Yes, the storage cost will be the same, but you won't have to gather the actual data yourself.

The next big topic is ML training. Here, research shows that reducing model size and training time can be of significant help in making your training greener. Train ML models faster and more efficiently by shrinking the model size using techniques such as federated learning, pruning, compression, distillation, or quantization.

For certain scenarios, there are also pretrained models that might serve your use case well, like open source models for natural languages—after all, natural languages don't change *that* quickly.

The growth of edge computing and the Internet of Things (IoT) means we are seeing more and more devices with limited capabilities, and smaller models will also be the way to go here. Another perk of edge computing is reducing energy consumption by providing local computing and storage for data.

Lastly and most importantly, ML training has the great benefit of very rarely being urgent, so make sure to make your training carbon-aware. Never train using carbon-intensive electricity. Wait for the clean stuff.

Case Study: Microsoft Teams and the 2020 Pandemic

In 2021, Anne was interested in how the internet had survived the sudden increase in demand caused by lockdowns, and she did some research on the subject (*https://oreil.ly/y8Llk*). That's another book in itself. Just let her get this one done first. However, we'll cover some of this in Chapter 7.

In short, the reason the tech response to the pandemic was fascinating is that it provided real-world examples not only of demand shifting and shaping, which we'll discuss in Chapter 7, but also of how to improve code efficiency.

One lockdown response very relevant to this chapter was the code-focused one from the team supporting Microsoft's videoconference product: Teams (*https://oreil.ly/JI-Q8*).

It's almost a cliché that you should never prematurely optimize (*https://oreil.ly/jQOTg*), and, in terms of developer productivity, we agree. Following that approach, however, usually means you'll have underutilized capacity in your systems. During the COVID pandemic of 2020, MS Teams was faced with unprecedented demand and no availability of more machines to host on. To keep the show on the road, the platform was therefore forced to exploit the slack in its existing systems.

The Teams team had no option but to wring more machine performance out of its architecture (*https://oreil.ly/YRk3w*). That is, the team needed to improve its efficiency. For example, MS Teams switched from text-based to binary-encoded data formats in its caches, which reduced both network traffic and storage requirements.

As is often the case, this greater efficiency added complexity to the MS Teams systems, which made the platform less reliable, and the team was then forced to address this by implementing a lot more testing and monitoring.

What do we learn here? The pandemic gave Microsoft no alternative but to be more efficient, which will help it meet its green hosting targets (*https://oreil.ly/O_AQw*). Hurray! However, the lesson is also that even for Microsoft—a company that has huge scale, a long-term view on stuff, and very deep pockets—efficiency improvements were apparently not a no-brainer. They had costs in developer time, which is presumably why they hadn't made them already.

This true tale underlines the fact that efficiency is great but expensive. Most folk only pursue it when they have to (i.e., when the balance of risk changes).

The Big Problem with Efficiency

> Why didn't they ask Jevons?

Before we leave this chapter, we have to mention the 19th-century English economist William Stanley Jevons (*https://oreil.ly/W4tKy*), because the first issue that always crops up whenever you discuss efficiency is the Jevons paradox. The second is the drag of efficiency on progress.

We need efficiency, and therefore genuine worries about the concept have to be addressed. These two concerns don't just apply to code efficiency, but we might as well talk about them here.

Issue 1: The Jevons paradox

The Jevons paradox is William Jevons's historical observation that when we get more efficient at doing something, it gets cheaper, and in the long run, we end up doing much more of it. The argument is thus that if we improve the energy efficiency of data centers, we'll want more of them and the result will be that we'll consume a greater amount of energy than when we started.

Issue 2: The productivity hit

The second concern, that efficiency is a drag on progress, is based on another historical observation: freely abundant energy has been vital to the progress of humanity so far and will probably remain so. Using it frugally adds work to, and therefore slows down, every human endeavor and will hold us back in solving the very problem we need to fix: climate change.

These two objections are not merely crackpot ravings. They have genuine merit and are something we have thought about long and hard. They deserve a book in themselves.

- Basically, the Jevons paradox is a way of saying that efficiency ultimately drives abundance.
- The drag-on-productivity argument, however, appears to imply that efficiency is bad for abundance.

We could just tell you these statements are mutually contradictory and so we should ignore them and leave it there, but that would be a facile bit of avoidance. We should be roundly told off for it. The reality is that they are not contradictory. They are both true but address different contexts and timescales.

The Jevons paradox is telling us that getting better (in this case, more efficient) at something can be very positive for the adoption of that thing. We agree.

The impact-on-progress observation is saying that high efficiency is really hard. It takes a long time and tons of investment to achieve. Again, we agree. In fact, high efficiency may never be commercially viable for small, or even average-sized, businesses, and it is usually only worthwhile for goods or services for which there is loads of untapped demand.

However, I refer back to Jevons: if you *can* invest the time and effort *and* if the demand is there, then efficiency should pay off big-time. The paradox is that it isn't a paradox at all. It's a statement of the obvious, and it doesn't conflict with our main point in this chapter: gaining efficiency is costly. There are always benefits, but they are not sufficient in every case to outweigh the costs.

So, is efficiency good or bad for green?

In the long run, and in the context of humanity and climate change, we want to have abundant energy at all times. It is probably fundamental to humanity's continued progress (or even existence in its current form). We just don't want to get that energy from where we do now—burning fossil fuels.

Once the energy transition from high-carbon energy sources to low-carbon ones is complete, the aim is to still have energy abundance. The energy might be from modular nuclear, space-based solar power, renewables paired with super grids or new forms of batteries, something we haven't even thought of yet, or all of the above. At that point, efficiency will merely be a nice-to-have. Fill yer boots.

"Hurray! We don't need to read this book after all. That was efficient."

Hold your horses! Unfortunately, we're not there yet. We're at the start of the energy transition, not the end.

The reality is, we have been in this transitory state for decades and we'll be in it for many, many decades more, and throughout that period, we'll be ramping up these new forms of power. However, they will not yet have had time to become efficient commodities themselves. Until they do, we'll need to meet them halfway by being more efficient users.

In the real world, the downside of efficiency is that it requires a lot of investment. The upside is, as Jevons pointed out, in the long term and under the right circumstances, that investment will more than pay off. Fortunately, if it's unlikely to ever pay off for you, there are ways to get your suppliers to make that investment instead—mostly by demanding it.

"But Jevons says if we get more efficient at using fossil fuel, we'll use more of it!"

And historically, he has always been proved right. However, this chapter isn't about being efficient at using fossil fuels. It's about making tech more efficient and context aware at using electricity that comes mostly from renewables.

Underneath our feet, the world will move from generating electricity with bad, but already efficient, coal and gas to using increasingly efficient solar, wind, and nuclear energy. At the same time, batteries and other forms of storage will get better. In the short term, we just need to give humanity a hand to make this shift by asking for less to do the same job. We also need to be ready to make the best use of cheap but variable wind and solar.

In 20 years' time, when the grid is clean, we will probably find that as a result of all the great work we did to get better at using electricity, we use way more of it. We contend that that will be success, not failure—we are unashamed tech utopians.

The Lowdown

The conclusion on code efficiency is that it's not obvious you should be investing in it directly (beyond performance monitoring and bug fixing) unless you are developing high-performance or high-scale code or a software platform. In that case, you absolutely must be and, hopefully, you already are and it will pay off for you. However, you are not in the majority of engineers.

Efficient code has its pros:

- It reduces the amount of energy required to execute a program or run a system. This usually means lower carbon emissions and energy bills.
- For devices that rely on batteries, such as smartphones or laptops, efficient code extends battery life and reduces the electricity needed to recharge them.
- It produces code that can run on fewer machines and older, less powerful equipment—minimizing embodied carbon and e-waste.

On the other hand:

- Writing efficient code is hard and takes ages. That increases development time and cost, which lowers developer productivity. It may never be worthwhile for products without enough scale or even for scaled products in the early stages, when you are trying to avoid premature optimization.
- Efficient code is difficult to maintain, requiring specialized knowledge and making it harder to evolve the code in the future.

Whether writing efficient code is worth it for you depends on your circumstances, but as a developer, it isn't your only option for cutting carbon emissions from your software. For example:

- You can be Lean and frugal in the functionality you add and the data you save—and delete stuff that isn't used.

- You can leverage the power of code reuse by choosing efficient software platforms that are aligned with a green future, and you can state your preference as a user for them to keep evolving fast in that direction. Then use them as they were designed to be used. The hypercloud services have done better than most, but they need to be held to their commitments and made more accountable. The open source community needs to get in the game. In our opinion, this is the long-term solution for wide adoption of code efficiency.

- You can make design choices that reduce waste. For example, this can include following best practice for your use case in your microservice design or not exchanging an excessive number of small interservice messages over a CPU-intensive network layer like a heavyweight (slow) service mesh.

- You can write code that works well in efficient multitenant environments.

- You can use performance profiling to identify egregious bugs or badly behaved libraries in your system.

- You can choose or switch to more efficient services and libraries.

- You can design for richer clients running on user devices such as phones.

The good news is that as a DevOps engineer or SRE, you have even more options for cutting carbon emissions that are aligned with DevOps productivity. We'll cover those in the next chapter, so hang on to your baseball caps/beanies/bucket hats (depending on your age).

CHAPTER 4

Operational Efficiency

Resistance is futile!
—The Borg

In reality, resistance isn't futile. It's much worse than that.

The Battle Against the Machines

One day, superconducting servers (*https://oreil.ly/gQHoi*) running in supercool(ed) (*https://oreil.ly/BRDsl*) data centers (*https://oreil.ly/Rik8s*) will eliminate resistance, and our DCs will operate on a fraction of the electricity they do now. Perhaps our future artificial general intelligence (AGI) overlords are already working on that. Unfortunately, however, we puny humans can't wait.

Today, as we power machines in data centers, they heat up. That energy—too often generated at significant climate cost—is then lost forever. Battling resistance is what folks are doing when they work to improve power usage effectiveness (PUE) in DCs (as we discussed in Chapter 2). It is also the motive behind the concept of operational efficiency, which is what we are going to talk about in this chapter.

 Those superconducting DCs might be in space (*https://oreil.ly/k-oG8*) because that could solve the cold issue (superconductors need to be very, very cold—space cold, not pop-on-a-vest cold). Off-planet superconducting DCs are a century off, though. Too late to solve our immediate problems.

For the past three decades, we have fought the waste of electricity in DCs using developments in CPU design and other improvements in hardware efficiency. These have allowed developers to achieve the same functional output with progressively fewer and fewer machines and less power. Those Moore's law upgrades, however, are no longer enough for us to rely on. Moore's law is slowing down (*https://oreil.ly/aiuh7*). It might even stop (although it probably won't).

Fortunately, however, hardware efficiency is not the only weapon we have to battle resistance. Operational efficiency is the way green DevOps or SRE folk like Sarah reduce the waste of electricity in their data centers. But what is operational efficiency?

The Evolution of Heating

Ignoring superconductivity for the moment, heating due to resistance is the primary unwanted physical byproduct of using electricity. It's a bad thing outside of a radiator, and you don't see many of those in a modern data center.

In a heating element, resistance is not unwanted. It's the mechanism by which electric radiators work, and it is 100% efficient at heat generation. Back in the olden days, 100% efficiency used to be a lot. How times have changed. Now we require a great deal more bang for our watt. Heat pumps, which make clever use of refrigerants to be more than 400% efficient (!), have raised our expectations. Heat pumps are amazing. Unfortunately, they are also a heck of a lot more tricky to design, manufacture, and operate than simple radiators and involve way more embodied carbon.

As their use scales up, we expect we'll get better at producing and operating heat pumps, but it won't happen painlessly or tomorrow. In fact, they are a great demonstration of the up-front costs and trade-offs involved in any transition to a new, higher-efficiency technology.

Huge investment has been poured into heat pumps, and more will be required. They illustrate how climate change has few trivial solutions—most still require a great deal of work to commoditize. Nonetheless, solutions exist, and we need to get cracking with commoditizing them, which is just another way of saying we need to make them all a hundred to a thousand times more efficient to build, fit, and run at scale. Stuff that can't be commoditized probably won't survive the energy transition.

Note also that the heat released due to electrical resistance from every electrical device in the world makes no significant contribution to global warming. It's our sun combined with the physical properties of greenhouse gases doing the *actual* heating in climate change. It's also the sun that ultimately provides the heat delivered by heat pumps, which is how they achieve >100% efficiency. Electricity merely helps heat pumps get their hands on that solar energy.

In the far future, if we achieve almost unlimited power creation from fusion or space-based solar arrays, we might have to worry about direct warming. However, that's a problem for another century. It will be an excellent one to get to. It'll mean humanity survived this round.

Hot Stuff

Operational efficiency is about achieving the same functional result for the same application or service, including performance and resilience, using fewer hardware resources like servers, disks, and CPUs. That means less electricity is required and gets dissipated as heat, less cooling is needed to handle that heat, and less carbon is emitted as part of the creation and disposal of the equipment.

Operational efficiency may not be the most glamorous option. Neither might it have the biggest theoretical potential for reducing energy waste. However, in this chapter we're going to try to convince you it is a practical and achievable step that almost everyone can take to build greener software. Not only that, but we'll argue that in many respects, it kicks the butt of the alternatives.

Techniques

As we discussed in the introduction, AWS reckons that good operational efficiency can cut carbon emissions from systems fivefold to tenfold (*https://oreil.ly/I0Rkp*). That's nothing to sniff at.

"Hang on! Didn't you say that code efficiency might cut them a hundredfold! That's 10 times better!"

Indeed. However, the trouble with code efficiency is it can run smack up against something most businesses care a great deal about: developer productivity. And they are correct to care about that.

We agree that operational efficiency is less effective than code efficiency, but it has a significant advantage for most enterprises. For comparatively low effort and using off-the-shelf tools, you can get big improvements in it. It's much lower-hanging fruit, and it's where most of us need to start.

Code efficiency is amazing, but its downside is that it is also highly effortful and too often highly customized (hopefully, that is something that's being addressed, but we're not there yet). You don't want to do it unless you are going to have a lot of users. Even then, you need to experiment first to understand your requirements.

 You might notice that 10x operational improvements plus 100x from code efficiency get us the 1000x we actually want. Within five years we'll need both through commodity tools and services—i.e., green platforms.

In contrast, better operational efficiency is already available from standardized libraries and commodity services. So in this chapter we can include widely applicable examples of good practice, which we couldn't give you in the previous one.

But before we start doing that, let's step back. When we talk about modern operational efficiency, what high-level concepts are we leaning on?

We reckon it boils down to a single fundamental notion: machine utilization.

Machine Utilization

Machine utilization, server density, or bin packing. There are loads of names for the idea, and we've probably missed some, but the motive behind them all is the same. *Machine utilization* is about cramming work onto a single machine or a cluster in such a way as to maximize the use of physical resources like CPU, memory, network bandwidth, disk I/O, and power.

Great machine utilization is at least as fundamental to being green as code efficiency.

For example, let's say you rewrite your application in C and cut its CPU requirements by 99%. Hurray! That was painful, and it took months. Hypothetically, you now run it on exactly the same server you did before. Unfortunately, all that rewriting effort wouldn't have saved you that much electricity. As we will discuss in Chapter 6, a partially used machine consumes a large proportion of the electricity of a fully utilized one, and the embodied carbon hit from the hardware is the same.

In short, if you don't shrink your machine (so-called *rightsizing*) at the same time you shrink your application, then most of your code optimization efforts will have been wasted. The trouble is, rightsizing can be tricky.

Rightsizing

Operationally, one of the cheapest green actions you can take is not overprovisioning your systems. That means downsizing machines that are larger than necessary. As we have already said (but it bears repeating), higher machine utilization means electricity gets used more efficiently and the embodied carbon overhead is reduced. Rightsizing techniques can be applied both on prem and in the cloud.

Unfortunately, there are problems with making sure your applications are running on machines that are neither too big nor too small (let's call it the DevOps Goldilocks Zone): overprovisioning is often done for excellent reasons.

Overprovisioning is a common and successful risk management technique. It's often difficult to predict what the behavior of a new service or the demands placed on it will be. Therefore, a perfectly sensible approach is to stick it on a cluster of servers that are way bigger than you reckon it needs. That should at least ensure it doesn't run up against resource limitations. It also reduces the chance of hard-to-debug race conditions. Yes, it'll cost a bit more money, but your service is less likely to fall over, and for most businesses, that trade-off is a no brainer. We all intend to come back later and resize our VMs, but we seldom do because of the second issue with rightsizing: you never have time to do it.

The obvious solution is autoscaling. Unfortunately, as we are about to see, that isn't perfect either.

Autoscaling

Autoscaling is a technique often used in the cloud, but you can also do it on prem. The idea behind it is to automatically adjust the resources allocated to a system based on current demand. All the cloud providers have autoscaling services, and it is also available as part of Kubernetes. In theory, it's amazing.

The trouble is, in practice, autoscaling can hit issues similar to manual overprovisioning. Scaling up to the maximum is fine, but scaling down again is a lot riskier and scarier, so sometimes it isn't configured to happen automatically. You can scale down again manually, but who has the time to do anything manual? That was why you were using autoscaling in the first place. As a result, autoscaling doesn't always solve your underutilization problem.

Fortunately, another potential solution is available on public clouds. Burstable instances offer a compromise between resilience and greenness. They are designed for workloads that don't require consistently high CPU but occasionally need bursts of it to avoid that whole pesky falling-over thing.

Burstable instances come with a baseline level of CPU performance, but, when the workload demands, can "burst" to a higher level for a limited period. The amount of time the instance can sustain the burst is determined by the accumulated CPU credits it has. When the workload returns to normal, the instance goes back to its baseline performance level and starts accumulating CPU credits again.

There are multiple advantages to burstable instances:

- They're cheaper (read: more machine efficient for cloud providers) than types of instance that offer more consistent high CPU performance.

- They are greener, allowing your systems to handle occasional spikes in demand without having to provision more resources in advance than you usually need. They also scale down automatically.

- Best of all, they make managing server density your cloud provider's problem rather than yours.

Of course, there are always negatives:

- The amount of time your instance can burst to a higher performance level is limited by the CPU credits you have. You can still fall over if you run out.

- If your workload demands consistent high CPU, it would be cheaper to just use a large instance type.

- It isn't as safe as choosing an oversized instance. The performance of burstable instances can be variable, making it difficult to predict the exact level you will get. If there is enough demand for them, hopefully that will improve over time as the hyperscalers keep investing to make them better.

- Managing CPU credits adds complexity to your system. You need to keep track of accumulated credits and plan for bursts.

The upshot is that rightsizing is great, but there's no trivial way to do it. Using energy efficiently by not overprovisioning requires up-front investment in time and new skills—even with autoscaling or burstable instances.

Again and again, Kermit the Frog has been proved right. Nothing is easy when it comes to being green or we'd already be doing it. However, as well as being more sustainable, avoiding overprovisioning can save you a load of cash, so it's worth looking into. Perhaps handling the difficulties of rightsizing is a reason to kick off an infrastructure-as-code or GitOps project…

Infrastructure as code

Infrastructure as code (IaC) is the principle that you define, configure, and deploy infrastructure using code rather than doing it manually. The idea is to give you better automation and repeatability plus version control. Using domain-specific languages and config files, you describe the way you want your servers, networks, and storage to be. This code-based representation then becomes the single version of truth for your infrastructure.

GitOps is a version of IaC that uses Git as its version control system. Any changes, including provisioning ones like autoscaling, are managed through Git, and your current infrastructure setup is continuously reconciled with the desired state as defined in your repository. The aim is to provide an audit trail of any infrastructure changes, allowing you to track, review, and roll back.

The good news is that the IaC and GitOps communities have started to think about green operations, and so-called GreenOps is already a target of the Cloud Native Computing Foundation's (CNCF) Environmental Sustainability Group (*https://oreil.ly/2_SiW*). The foundation ties the concept to cost-cutting techniques (a.k.a. FinOps, which we'll talk more about in Chapter 11, on the co-benefits of green systems), and the foundation is right (see Figure 4-1). Operationally, greener is cheaper.

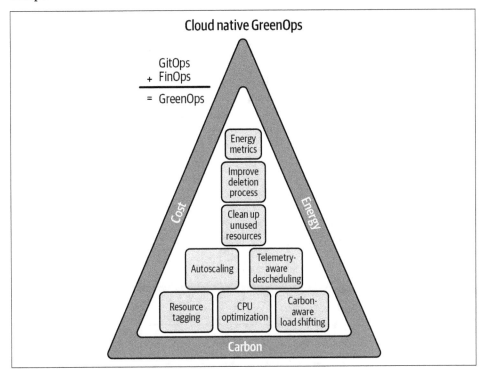

Figure 4-1. CNCF definition of GreenOps as GitOps + FinOps

We think the implication here is that you start at the top of the triangle and work down, which seems sensible because the stuff at the bottom is certainly trickier.

Anything that automates rightsizing and autoscaling tasks makes them more likely to happen, and that suggests IaC and GitOps should be a good thing for green. That there is a CNCF IaC community pushing GreenOps is also an excellent sign.

At the time of writing, the authors spoke to Alexis Richardson, CEO at Weaveworks (*https://www.weave.works*), and some of the wider team. Weaveworks coined the term GitOps in 2017 and set out the main principles together with FluxCD, a Kubernetes-friendly implementation. The company sees a next major challenge for GreenOps being automated GHG emission tracking. We agree, and it is a problem we'll discuss in Chapter 10.

Cluster scheduling

Standard operational techniques like rightsizing and autoscaling are all very well, but if you really want to be clever about machine utilization, you should also be looking at the more radical concept of cluster scheduling.

The idea behind *cluster scheduling* is that differently shaped workloads can be programmatically packed onto servers like pieces in a game of DevOps Tetris (see Figure 4-2). The goal is to execute the same quantity of work on the smallest possible cluster of machines. It is, perhaps, the ultimate in automated operational efficiency, and it is a major change from the way we used to provision systems. Traditionally, each application had its own physical machine or VM. With cluster scheduling, those machines are shared between applications.

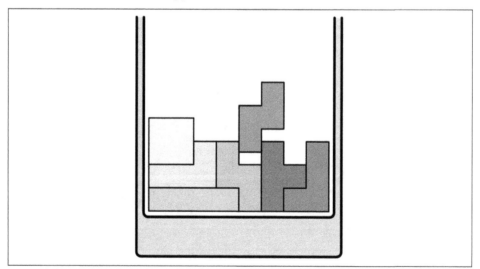

Figure 4-2. DevOps Tetris

For example, imagine you have an application with a high need for I/O and a low need for a CPU. A cluster scheduler might locate your job on the same server as an application that is processor intensive but doesn't use much I/O. The scheduler's aim is always to make the most efficient use of the local resources while guaranteeing your jobs are completed within the required time frame and to the target quality and availability.

The good news is that there are many cluster scheduler tools and services out there—usually as part of orchestration platforms. The most popular is a component of the open source Kubernetes platform, and it is a much simplified version of Google's internal cluster scheduler, which is called Borg. As we mentioned in the introduction, Borg has been in use at Google for nearly two decades.

To try cluster scheduling, you could use the Kubernetes scheduler or another such as HashiCorp's Nomad in your on-prem DC. Alternatively, you could use a managed Kubernetes cloud service like EKS, GKS, or AKS (from AWS, Google, and Azure, respectively) or a non-Kubernetes option like the AWS Container Service (ECS). Most cluster schedulers offer similar functionality, so the likelihood is you'll use the one that comes with the operational platform you have selected—it is unlikely to be a differentiator that makes you choose one platform over another. However, the lack of such machine utilization functionality might indicate the platform you are on is not green enough.

Cluster scheduling sounds great, and it is, maybe delivering up to 80% machine utilization. If these tools don't save you money/carbon, you probably aren't using them right. However, there is still a big problem.

Information underload.   For these cluster schedulers to move jobs from machine to machine to achieve optimal packing, they require three things:

1. The jobs need to be encapsulated along with all their prerequisite libraries so that they can be shifted about for maximum packing without suddenly stopping working because they are missing a key dependency.

2. The encapsulation tool must support fast instantiation (i.e., it must be possible for the encapsulated job to be switched off on one machine and switched on again on another fast). If that takes an hour (or even a few minutes), then cluster scheduling won't work—the service would be unavailable for too long.

3. The encapsulated jobs need to be labeled so the scheduler knows what to do with them (letting the scheduler know whether they have high availability requirements, for example).

The encapsulation and fast instantiation parts can be done by wrapping them in a container such as Docker or Containerd, and that technology is now widely available. Hurray!

Internally, many of the AWS services use lightweight VMs as the wrapper around jobs, rather than containers. That's fine. The concept remains the same.

However, all this clever tech still runs up against the need for information. When a scheduler understands the workloads it is scheduling, it can use resources more effectively. If it's in the dark, it can't do a good job.

For Kubernetes, the scheduler can act based on the constraints specified in the workload's pod definition, particularly the CPU and memory requests (minima) and limits (maxima), but that means you need to specify them. The trouble is, that can be tricky.

According to longtime GreenOps practitioner Ross Fairbanks (*https://oreil.ly/rJgW8*), "The problem with both autoscaling and constraint definition is that setting these constraints is hard." Fortunately, there are now some tools to make it easier. Fairbanks reckons, "The Kubernetes Vertical Pod Autoscaler (*https://oreil.ly/wdjzS*) can be of help. It has a recommender mode so you can get used to using it, as well as an automated mode. It is a good place to start if you are using Kubernetes and want to improve machine utilization."[1]

What about the cloud? If your systems are hosted in the cloud, then even if you are not running a container orchestrator like Kubernetes, you will usually be getting the benefit of some cluster scheduling because the cloud providers operate their own schedulers.

You can communicate the characteristics of your workload by picking the right cloud instance type, and the cloud's schedulers will use your choice to optimize their machine utilization. That is why, from a green perspective, you must not overspecify your resource or availability requirements (e.g., by asking for a dedicated instance when a burstable one or even just a nondedicated one would suffice).

Again, this requires thought, planning, and observation. The public clouds are quite good at spotting when you have overprovisioned and are sneakily using some of those resources for other users (a.k.a. oversubscription), but the most efficient way to use a platform is always as it was intended. If a burstable instance is what you need, the most efficient way to use the cloud is to choose one.

---

1 Ross Fairbanks, personal communication.

Mixed workloads. Cluster scheduling is at its most effective (you can get really dense packing) if it has a wide range of different, well-labeled tasks to schedule on a lot of big physical machines. Unfortunately, this means it is less effective—or even completely ineffective—for smaller setups like running Kubernetes on prem for a handful of nodes or for a couple of dedicated VMs in the cloud.

However, it can be great for hyperscalers. They have a wide range of jobs to juggle to achieve optimum packing, and in part, that explains the high server utilization rates they report. The utilization percentages that AWS throws about imply that AWS requires less than a quarter of the hardware you'd use on prem for the same work. The true numbers are hard to come by, but AWS's figure is more than plausible (it's likely an underestimate of AWS's potential savings).

Those smaller numbers of servers mean a lot less electricity used and carbon embodied. As a result, the easiest sustainability step you can take is often to move your systems to the cloud *and use their services well, including the full range of instance types*. It's only by using their optimized services and schedulers that you can get those numbers. Don't lift and shift onto dedicated servers and expect much green value, even if you're using Kubernetes like a pro.

As we've said before, scale and efficiency go hand in hand. Hyperscalers can invest the whopping engineering effort to be hyperefficient because it is their primary business. If your company is selling insurance, you will never have the financial incentive to build a hyperefficient on-prem server room, even if that were possible. In fact, you'd not be acting in your own best interest to do so because it wouldn't be a differentiator.

Time shifting and spot instances

The schedulers mentioned previously get a whole extra dimension of flexibility if we add time into the mix. Architectures that recognize and can manage low-priority or delayable jobs are particularly operable at high machine utilization, and as we'll cover in the next chapter, those architectures are vital for carbon awareness. According to green tech expert Paul Johnston, "Always on is unsustainable."

Which brings us to an interesting twist on cluster scheduling: the cloud concept of spot instances (as they are known on AWS and Azure; they are called Preemptible Instances on the more literal GCP).

Spot instances are used by public cloud providers to get even better machine utilization by using up leftover spare capacity. You can put your job in a spot instance, and it may be completed or it may not. If you keep trying, it will probably be done at some point, with no guarantee of when. In other words, the jobs need to be very time shiftable. In return for this laissez faire approach to scheduling, users get 90% off the standard price for hosting.

A spot instance combines several of the smart scheduling concepts we have just discussed. It is a way of:

- Wrapping your job in a VM
- Labeling it as time insensitive
- Letting your cloud provider schedule it when and where it likes

Potentially (i.e., depending on the factors that go into the cloud's scheduling decisions), using spot instances could be one of the greenest ways to operate a system. We would love to see hyperscalers take the carbon intensity of the local grid into account when scheduling spot instance workloads, and we expect that to happen by 2025. Google is already talking about such moves.

Case Study: Chaos Engineering

Skyscanner is a flight booking service in the UK, and it moved the bulk of its operations over to running on AWS spot instances several years ago. Oddly, the company wasn't primarily motivated by being greener or saving money, although like most of us, Skyscanner cares a great deal about both of those things. The company did it because it was a fan of the concept of chaos engineering.

Chaos engineering is the idea that you can create a mindset amongst your engineers that will lead to your systems being more robust by ensuring your production platform is unreliable.

Counterintuitive, eh? But it works. It forces the implementation of resilience strategies.

Spot instances fit the chaos-engineering model perfectly. Spot instances might be pulled out from under the feet of your running jobs at any moment because there are no availability guarantees on them at all. Spot instances helped Skyscanner achieve its desired high system robustness and, as a pleasant side effect, saved the company a great deal of money on its hosting bills and cut its carbon emissions massively. According to Director of Engineering Stuart Davidson, "It's a good feeling when you can make your systems more resilient, cut your hosting bills, and reduce carbon emissions all at the same time."[2]

This is a great example of how there are often useful co-advantages to choosing a green architecture. In this case: resilience and cost savings. In Chapter 11, we'll talk more about the knock-on benefits of being green.

---

2 Stuart Davidson, personal communication.

Multitenancy

In a chapter on operational efficiency, it would be a travesty if we didn't mention the concept of multitenancy.

Multitenancy is when a single instance of a server is shared between several users, and it is vital to truly high machine utilization. Fundamentally, the more diverse your users (a.k.a. tenants), the better your utilization will be.

Why is that true? Well, let's consider the opposite. If all your tenants were ecommerce retailers, they would all want more resources on Black Friday and in the run-up to Christmas. They would also all want to process more requests in the evenings and at lunchtime (peak home shopping time). Correlated demand like that is bad for utilization.

You don't want to have to provision enough machines to handle Christmas and then have them sitting idle the rest of the year. That's very ungreen. It would be more machine efficient if the retailer could share its hardware resources with someone who had plenty of work to do that was less time sensitive than shopping (e.g., ML training). It would be even more optimal to share those resources with someone who experienced demand on different dates or at different times of the day. Having a wide mix of customers is another way that the public clouds get their high utilization numbers.

Serverless Services

Serverless services like AWS Lambda, Azure Functions, and Google Cloud Functions are multitenant. They also have encapsulated jobs, care about fast instantiation, and run jobs that are short and simple enough that a scheduler knows what to do with them (execute them as fast as possible and then forget about them). They also have enough scale that it should be worth public cloud providers' time to put in the effort to hyperoptimize them.

Serverless services therefore have huge potential to be cheap and green. They are doing decently at it, but we believe they have room to get much better. The more folk who use them, the more efficient they are likely to get.

Hyperscalers and Profit

There is no magic secret to being green in tech. It is mostly about being a whole lot more efficient and far less wasteful, which happens to match the desires of anyone who wants to manage their hosting costs.

According to ex-Azure DevRel Adam Jackson, "The not-so-dirty secret of the public cloud providers is that the cheaper a service is, the higher the margins. The cloud providers want you to pick the cheapest option because that's where they make the most money."

Those services are cheap because they are efficient and run at high scale. As 17th-century economist Adam Smith pointed out, "It is not from the benevolence of the butcher, the brewer, or the baker that we expect our dinner, but from their regard to their own interest." In the same vein, the hypercloud providers make their systems efficient for their own benefit. However, in this case it is to our benefit, too, because we know that although efficiency is not an exact proxy for greenness, it isn't bad.

Reducing your hosting bills by using the cheapest, most efficient and commoditized services you can find is not just in your interest and the planet's, but it is also in the interest of your host. They will make more money as a result, and that is a good thing. Making money isn't wrong. Being energy inefficient in the middle of an energy-driven climate crisis is. It also highlights the reason why operational efficiency might be the winning form of efficiency: it can make a load of money for DC operators. It is aligned with their interests, and you should choose ones that have the awareness to see that and the capital to put behind it.

 AWS Lambda serverless service is an excellent example of how the efficiency of a service gets improved when it becomes clear there is enough demand to make that worthwhile. When Lambda was first launched, it used a lot of resources. It definitely wasn't green. However, as the latent demand became apparent, AWS put investment in and built the open source Firecracker platform (*https://oreil.ly/YW99e*) for it, which uses lighter-weight VMs for job isolation and also improves the instantiation times and scheduling. As long as untapped demand is there, this commoditization is likely to continue. That will make it cheaper and greener *as well as* more profitable for AWS.

SRE Practices

Site reliability engineering (SRE) is a concept that originally came from another efficiency-obsessed hyperscaler: Google. SREs are responsible for designing, building, and maintaining reliable and robust systems that can handle high traffic and still operate smoothly. The good news is that green operations are aligned with SRE principles, and if you have an SRE organization, being green should be easier.

SREs practice:

- Monitoring (which should include carbon emissions; see Chapter 9 for our views on the subject of the measurement of carbon emissions and Chapter 10 for our views on how to use those measurements)
- Continuous integration and delivery (which can help with delivering and testing carbon emission reductions in a faster and safer fashion)
- Automation (e.g., IaC, which helps with rightsizing)
- Containerization and microservices (which are more automatable and mean your entire system isn't forced to be on demand and can be more carbon aware)

This is not a book about SRE best practices and principles, so we are not going to go into them in detail, although we discuss them more in Chapter 11. However, there are plenty of books available from O'Reilly that cover these excellently and in depth.

LightSwitchOps

Most of what we have talked about so far has been clever high-tech stuff. However, there are some simple operational efficiency ideas that anyone can implement, and one of the smartest we've heard is from Red Hat's Holly Cummins. It's called Light-SwitchOps (*https://oreil.ly/sDxOT*) (see Figure 4-3).

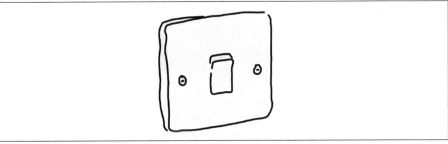

Figure 4-3. LightSwitchOps as illustrated by Holly

Closing down *zombie workloads* (Cummins' term for applications and services that don't do anything anymore) should be a no-brainer for energy saving.

In a recent real-life experiment, a major VM vendor who relocated one of its DCs discovered two-thirds of its servers were running applications that were hardly used anymore. Effectively, these were zombie workloads.

According to Martin Lippert, Spring Tools Lead & Sustainability Ambassador at VMware, "In 2019, VMware consolidated a data center in Singapore. The team wanted to move the entire data center and therefore investigated what exactly needed a migration. The result was somewhat shocking: 66% of all the host machines were zombies."[3]

This kind of waste provides huge potential for carbon saving. The sad reality is that a lot of your machines may also be running applications and services that no longer add value.

The trouble is, which ones are those exactly?

There are several ways to work out whether a service still matters to anyone. The most effective is something called a scream test. We'll leave it as an exercise for the reader to deduce how that works. Another is for resources to have a fixed shelf life. For example, you could try only provisioning instances that shut themselves down after six months unless someone actively requests that they keep running.

These are great ideas, but there is a reason folk don't do either of these things. They worry that if they turn a machine off, it might not be so easy to turn it back on again, and that is where LightSwitchOps comes in.

For green operations, it is vital that you can turn off machines as confidently as you turn off the lights in your hall—i.e., safe in the knowledge that when you flick the switch to turn them back on, they will. Holly Cummins's advice is to ensure you are in a position to turn anything off. If you aren't, then if your server is not part of the army of the walking dead today, you can be certain that one day it will be.

GreenOps practitioner Ross Fairbanks suggests that a great place to get started with LightSwitchOps is to automatically turn off your test and development systems overnight and on the weekend.

Zombie apocalypse

In addition to saving carbon, there are security reasons for turning off those zombie servers. Ed Harrison, former head of security at Metaswitch Networks (now part of Microsoft), told us, "Some of the biggest cybersecurity incidents in recent times have stemmed from systems which no one knew about and should never have been switched on." He went on, "Security teams are always trying to reduce the attack surface. The sustainability team will be their best friends if their focus is switching off systems which are no longer needed."[4]

---

3 Martin Lippert, personal communication.

4 Ed Harrison, personal communication.

Location, Location, Location

There is one remaining incredibly important thing for us to talk about. It is a move that is potentially even easier than LightSwitchOps, and it might be the right place for you to start—particularly if you are moving to a new data center.

You need to pick the right host and region.

The reality is that in some regions, DCs are easier to power using low-carbon electricity than in others. For example, France has a huge nuclear fleet, and Scandinavia has wind and hydro. DCs in such areas are cleaner.

We say again, choose your regions wisely. If in doubt, ask your host about it.

 The global online business publication the *Financial Times* offers a good example of a change in location leading to greener infrastructure. The *Financial Times'* engineering team spent the best part of a decade moving to predominantly sustainable EU regions in the cloud from on-premises data centers that had no sustainability targets.

Anne talked to the *Financial Times* in 2018 (when the company was 75% of the way through the shift) about the effect it was having on their own operational sustainability goals (*https://oreil.ly/M66nt*). At that point, the result was that ~67% of their infrastructure was consequently on "carbon neutral" servers, and the company expected this to rise to nearly 90% when it transitioned to the Cloud in 2020 (which it did).

The carbon-neutral phrasing may have been dropped by everyone, but the *Financial Times* now inherits AWS's target (*https://oreil.ly/lXaEF*) of powering its operations with 100% renewable energy by 2025, which is great. The lesson here is that picking suppliers with solid sustainability targets they seem committed to (i.e., green platforms) takes that hard work off you—it'll just happen under your feet.

Oh No! Resistance Fights Back!

Unfortunately, efficiency and resilience have always had an uneasy relationship. Efficiency adds complexity and thus fragility to a system, and that's a problem.

Efficiency versus resilience

In most cases, you cannot make a service more efficient without also putting in work to make it more resilient, or it will fall over on you. Unfortunately, that puts efficiency in conflict yet again with developer productivity.

For example:

- Cluster schedulers are complicated beasts that can be tricky to set up and use successfully.
- There are a lot of failure modes to multitenancy: privacy and security become issues, and there is always the risk of a problem from another tenant on your machine spilling over to affect your own systems.
- Even turning things off is not without risk. The scream test we talked about earlier does exactly what it says on the tin.
- To compound that, overprovisioning is a tried-and-tested way to add robustness to a system cheaply in terms of developer time (at the cost of increased hosting bills, but most folk are happy to make that trade-off).

Cutting to the chase, efficiency is a challenge for resilience.

There are some counterarguments. Although a cluster scheduler is good for operational efficiency, it has resilience benefits too. One of the primary reasons folk use a cluster scheduler is to automatically restart services in the face of node, hardware, or network failures. If a node goes down or becomes unavailable for any reason, a scheduler can automatically shift the affected workloads to other nodes in the cluster. You not only get efficient resource utilization, but you also get higher availability—as long as it wasn't the cluster scheduler that brought you down, of course.

However, the reality is that being more efficient can be a risky business. Handling the more complex systems requires new skills. In the case of Microsoft improving the efficiency of Teams during the COVID pandemic, the company couldn't just make its efficiency changes. It also had to up its testing game by adopting chaos-engineering techniques in production to flush out the bugs in its new system.

Like Microsoft, if you make any direct efficiency improvements yourself, you will probably have to do more testing and more fixing. In the Skyscanner example, using spot instances increased the resilience of its systems and also cut its hosting bills and boosted its greenness, but the company's whole motivation for adopting spot instances was to force additional resilience testing on itself.

Efficiency usually goes hand in hand with specialization, and it is most effective at high scale, but scale has dangers too. The European Union fears we are putting all our computational eggs in the baskets of just a few United States hyperscalers, which could lead to a fragile world. The EU has a point, and it formed the Sustainable Digital Infrastructure Alliance (SDIA (*https://sdialliance.org*)) to attempt to combat that risk.

On the other hand, we know that the same concentration will result in fewer machines and less electricity used. It will be hard for the smaller providers that make up the SDIA to achieve the efficiencies of scale of the hyperscalers, even if they do align themselves on sensible open source hosting technology choices as the SDIA recommends.

We may not like the idea of the kinds of huge data centers that are currently being built by Amazon, Google, Microsoft, and Alibaba, but they will almost certainly be way more efficient than a thousand smaller DCs, even if those are warming up a few Instagrammable municipal pools or districts as the EU is currently demanding (*https://oreil.ly/QrSaO*).

Note that we love the EU's new mandates on emission transparency (*https://oreil.ly/3kW0_*). We are not scoffing at the EU, even if for one small reason or another none of us live in it anymore. Nonetheless, we would prefer to see DCs located near wind turbines or solar farms, where they could be using unexpected excess power rather than competing with homes for precious electricity in urban grid areas.

Green Operational Tools and Techniques

Stepping back, let's review the key operational-efficiency steps you can take. Some are hard, but the good news is that many are straightforward, especially when compared to code efficiency. Remember, it's all about machine utilization.

- Turn stuff off if it is hardly used or while it's not being used, like test systems on the weekend (Holly Cummins's LightSwitchOps).
- Don't overprovision (use rightsizing and autoscaling, burstable instances in the cloud). Remember to autoscale down as well as up or it's only useful the first time!
- Cut your hosting bills as much as possible using, for example, AWS Cost Explorer (*https://oreil.ly/_2XAe*) or Azure's cost analysis (*https://oreil.ly/OR3Me*), or a nonhyperscaler service like CloudZero (*https://www.cloudzero.com*), ControlPlane (*https://controlplane.com*), or Harness (*https://www.harness.io*). A simple audit can also often identify zombie services. Cheaper is almost always greener.
- Containerized microservice architectures that recognize low-priority and/or delayable tasks can be operated at higher machine utilization. Note, however, that increasing architectural complexity by going overboard on the number of microservices can also result in overprovisioning. You still need to follow microservices design best practices, so, for example, read *Building Microservices* (O'Reilly) by Sam Newman.
- If you are in the cloud, dedicated instance types have no carbon awareness and low machine utilization. Choosing instance types that give the host more flexibility will increase utilization and cut carbon emissions and costs.

- Embrace multitenancy from shared VMs to managed container platforms.

- Use efficient, high-scale, preoptimized cloud services and instance types (like burstable instances, managed databases, and serverless services). Or use equivalent open source products with a commitment to green or efficient practices, an energetic community to hold them to those commitments, and the scale to realistically deliver on them.

- Remember that spot instances on AWS or Azure (preemptible instances on GCP) are great—cheap, efficient, green, and a platform that encourages your systems to be resilient.

- None of this is easy, but the SRE principles can help: CI/CD, monitoring, and automation.

Unfortunately, none of this is work-free. Even running less or turning stuff off requires an investment of time and attention. However, the nice thing about going green is that it will at least save you money. So the first system to target from a greenness perspective should also be the easiest to convince your manager about: your most expensive one.

Having said that, anything that isn't work-free, even if it saves a ton of money, is going to be a tough sell. It will be easier to get the investment if you can align your move to green operations with faster delivery or saving developer or ops time down the road because those ideas are attractive to businesses.

That means the most effective of the suggested steps are the last five. Look at SRE principles, multitenancy, managed services, green open source libraries, and spot instances. Those are all designed to save dev and ops time in the long run, and they happen to be cheap and green because they are commoditized and they scale. Don't fight the machine. Going green without destroying developer productivity is about choosing green platforms.

To survive the energy transition, we reckon everything is going to have to become a thousand times more carbon efficient through a combination of, initially, operational efficiency and demand shifting and, eventually, code efficiency, all achieved using green platforms. Ambitious as it sounds, that should be doable. It is about releasing the increased hardware capacity we have used for developer productivity over the past 30 years, *while at the same time keeping the developer productivity.*

It might take a decade, but it will happen. Your job is to make sure all your platform suppliers, whether public cloud, open source, or closed source, have a believable strategy for achieving this kind of greenness. This is the question you need to constantly ask yourself: "Is this a green platform?"

CHAPTER 5

Carbon Awareness

Carbon-aware computing is the quick win every green software practitioner should know about.

—Your favorite authors

We learned in Chapter 2 that not all electricity is the same. Some is deemed dirty because it is generated from higher-carbon resources, such as oil or coal, while some is considered clean because it is made from renewable or low-carbon sources, such as hydro or nuclear. The idea of doing more in our application when electricity is clean and less when electricity is dirty is what we call *carbon-aware computing*.

Carbon-aware computing is the new and very cool kid on the block. It's an area of software engineering that is gaining an incredible amount of traction. According to the Green Software Foundation's 2023 State of Green Software Report (*https://stateof.greensoftware.foundation*), "carbon-aware software is central to decarbonization" (*https://oreil.ly/fJ9JV*). Among the survey participants, although only 8% currently practice carbon-aware techniques in their development, another 46% were eager to start.

We should also give massive kudos to the public cloud providers for leading by example in communicating and publishing their major advancements in the space. For example, Microsoft announced that Windows Update became carbon-aware (*https://oreil.ly/SUYgi*) starting with Windows 11 in September 2022. Similarly, Google shared that it has been using carbon-aware approaches across the board (*https://oreil.ly/Ctfqb*) since May 2021.

So in this chapter, we will present another way of achieving greenness within our software system: by applying carbon-aware techniques. We will start by addressing how to tell if electricity is clean or dirty and what we can do to our applications with this new piece of information. Then we will move on to our favorite topic of discussion: drawbacks you must consider—so you're fully equipped to respond to any question on the topic with our favorite line: "It depends." Finally, we wrap up the chapter by examining some real-world examples so you will feel inspired to start your own quest right away!

Carbon Intensity of Electricity

Whenever and wherever we need electricity to power anything, we usually plug our electronics directly into a wall socket, and that's pretty much the end of the story. This thoughtless assumption that all electricity is clean, hence low carbon, mostly comes from the fact that we don't smell or see dirt when a wall socket is used. (Maybe school trips to fossil fuel power plants should be a thing?)

How can you, the very end user of electricity, tell whether that energy is clean or dirty? Before we share how you can find out, let's quickly review the distinction between the two states and how to tell them apart.

It's not just the software industry but basically all industries that are now the primary users of a metric called carbon intensity. It measures how much carbon dioxide equivalent (CO_2e) is emitted per kilowatt-hour (kWh) of electricity consumed.

If you remember what we talked about in Chapter 2, *carbon* is a convenient term for us to refer to all greenhouse gases (GHGs). The standard unit of measurement for carbon intensity is grams of carbon equivalent per kilowatt-hour (gCO_2e/kWh). And with this standardization, we can now differentiate the environmental impacts of electricity usage.

Let's say you can plug your laptop directly into a wind farm; the carbon intensity of the electricity you are getting would technically be zero—without considering the impact of the materials making up the wind farm, of course!) However, it's not really possible for anyone to use electricity directly from a wind farm.

Most of us don't have a choice in what we get from the electricity grid; we simply get a mixture of anything accessible at that moment. (Coal-powered electricity with a side of wind-generated sprinkles, maybe?) The carbon intensity of electricity for our day-to-day usage is a mash-up of all the currently available power resources in a country's national grid, which includes lower- and higher-carbon sources.

Electricity grids are a tricky topic, especially how they operate across different countries and how differences in operations can affect a region's electricity market and, hence, the global market. If you want more information on those fascinating topics, we recommend you check out the resources from the International Energy Agency (IEA) (*https://oreil.ly/j7UK3*).

Ultimately, the metric of carbon intensity is what most of us mere mortals need to understand so we can tell dirty and clean electricity apart. Take Google Cloud, for instance; it labels a region as "low carbon" (*https://oreil.ly/qb6w_*) when the grid's carbon intensity stays under 200 gCO₂e/kWh.

Understanding this metric isn't just about software efficiency; it establishes a mental model that encourages us toward a broader goal: the efficient and intelligent utilization of low-carbon electricity!

Variability of Carbon Intensity

By now you are probably familiar with the fact that electricity's carbon intensity has a variability side to it. It's a metric that is affected by geographical location and time of day.

As you'll see in Figure 5-1, some regions, such as Taiwan or the United Kingdom, have the geographical advantage of enjoying very breezy weather all year round; therefore, wind-generated electricity is easy to come by. In fact, it was reported (*https://oreil.ly/uOqdX*) that wind farms overtook gas-fired power plants in electricity generation for the first time in the UK during the first three months of 2023.

In contrast, most Nordic countries have hydropower as their primary renewable energy source since they have the joy of having abundant water resources (mostly from rivers) all year round.

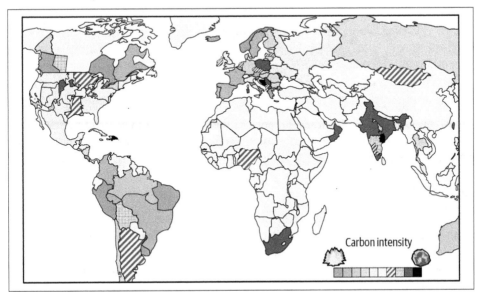

Figure 5-1. A map showing the geographical variability of the carbon intensity of electricity with the trees indicating cleaner energy and the coals indicating dirtier energy

However, even if you are in a region with all the latest in renewable technology, complete with gleaming solar panels covering your entire roof, you may still need to find alternative electricity sources when the sun decides to take an extended break and withhold its rays or the wind stops blowing.

As shown in Figure 5-2, owing to the unpredictable nature of weather conditions everywhere, the carbon intensity of electricity is subject to fluctuations over time.

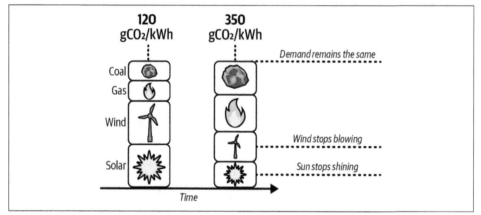

Figure 5-2. A graph demonstrating the variable nature of renewable energy sources. When wind and solar supplies decrease, coal and gas increase, so a constant supply is maintained.

Today, the expectation of a constant supply of electricity is deeply ingrained in modern society, where any minor interruptions, such as power cuts, are seen as exceptions rather than the norm. In other words, almost every single one of us expects to have access to energy at all times and in most places.

So how do the electricity grids around the world deal with the unpredictable nature of renewable energy supplies while supporting the demands of their tiny tyrant customers? We will spend the following section briefly covering the workings of electricity grids and some of the key contributing factors that make up energy markets.

Electricity Demand

Demand for electricity changes throughout the day, and supply always needs to meet that demand. The difficult job of maintaining a reliable service typically falls to each country's national grid. It is responsible for ensuring the delicate balance is maintained between the amount of electricity it delivers and the amount of electricity its customers request.

National grids require the ability to stop and start power generation at a moment's notice to serve this purpose, which is generally much easier to achieve with fossil fuels due to their usual ready supply (although we all saw what happened during the energy crisis in Europe in 2022 (*https://oreil.ly/IJp0v*)).

For example, if the need for electricity suddenly rises or falls, we can rely on coal-burning stations to increase the amount by simply burning more coal or quickly halt the supply by stopping the burning of coal. The *dispatchability* of a power generation source is the term that refers to how swiftly that source can adjust its energy production.

Brownouts versus blackouts

What happens when supply falls short of the current demand? In such cases, a *brownout* occurs, which is a dip in electrical voltage across power lines due to a surge in demand.

A *blackout* is a complete failure of electrical power (i.e., no electricity). This can happen when there is more electricity than required, causing the grid to trip breakers to stop infrastructure from burning out.

In contrast to fossil fuels, renewable sources, such as wind or solar, are less controllable. We cannot control the weather (as much as we might want to), so sometimes we throw away renewable electricity because there is too much of it for a given moment, and we want to avoid a blackout. We call the intentional reduction of electricity supply *curtailment*.

Marginal power

The demand for more electricity at any specific time does not consistently lead to increased production across all power plants—whether they are renewable, low-carbon, or nonrenewable sources. Instead, the required energy is provided by the cheapest power plant with surplus capacity, as power plants are dispatched according to rising costs. The power plant that meets the additional demand is commonly referred to as the *marginal power plant*.

Consider a scenario where our grid comprises 50% solar and 50% coal sources. If we need to acquire extra electricity at any given moment, the immediate consequence is usually increased production from coal-powered plants because, as noted earlier, fossil fuel–based sources have higher dispatchability. In order to meet any abrupt surge in demand, marginal fossil fuel power plants usually step in, leading to extra emissions referred to as *marginal emissions*.

The picture we want to paint here is that balancing electricity demands and the energy market is fiddly. As green software practitioners, we should be aware of these concepts so we can be mindful of our systems' electricity usage and eventual carbon emissions.

Putting It in Practice

Imagine waking up to a superhot day in Hsinchu, Taiwan, before the sun even rises. Groggy and disoriented, you make your way through the darkness toward your air conditioner, hoping to turn up the machine to stop the excessive sweating. You are doing this with little thought because you assume Taiwan's well-developed national grid can handle the surge in electricity demand during such weather.

However, you were not the only one to experience this unbearable heat. Every one of your neighbors has already turned up their machine to the maximum to stay cool.

On a typical and not-so-hot day, electricity demand is relatively steady. Hence, the national grids are fine with maintaining the delicate balance between the electricity they supply and the amount their customers ask for.

However, as you may have guessed, the situation can change rather rapidly, especially during the unprecedented scenarios brought about by climate change. The ever-so-fast increase in demand from everyone can easily lead to blackouts or brownouts. The national grid needs to respond swiftly to avert such situations.

During this morning peak, when most people are still at home getting ready for work, they have to call upon plants with high dispatchability, such as gas-burning ones. These plants increase their power generation quickly by burning more gas. In this scenario, the gas-burning plant becomes the marginal one, as it's the first to dispatch electricity, which unfortunately results in additional marginal emissions.

As the morning goes on, people leave to go to the office one by one, and the demand for electricity returns to a steady level, so the national grid can then uphold its sustainability pledge to utilize more renewable resources.

Since it's a day when the sun decides to play ball, and with electricity demand under control, we are now getting too much solar power. As a result, some of the excess electricity will be thrown away through the process of curtailment.

Tooling

We have spent some time understanding the carbon intensity of electricity, its fluctuating nature, and, most importantly, the contributing factors that affect the scale of its intensity. What sort of tooling is available out there that can help us absorb this information and, even better, consume and act on it in real time?

For practitioners in the UK, there's access to a partnership between the UK's National Grid, various nongovernmental organizations (NGOs), and academic institutions known as the Carbon Intensity API (*https://carbonintensity.org.uk*). This application programming interface (API) is powered by machine learning (ML) to forecast the carbon intensity at least 96 hours ahead for each region in Great Britain.

This enables the API's consumers to schedule their electricity usage to minimize carbon emissions at a regional level. The Carbon Intensity API team's efforts have led to several success stories, wherein their partners have used the product to regulate their devices based on the cleanliness of the current energy, thereby making a significant contribution to carbon reduction.

For engineers outside of the UK, you are also in luck, as there are several frameworks that can help you out on this front, too. First of all, we have the famous Electricity Maps (*https://app.electricitymaps.com/map*). Why famous? Electricity Maps has partnered with several leading software players, such as AWS, Google, and Salesforce, to provide their customers with real-time and global coverage of the carbon intensity of electricity.

Google uses the data to shift its workloads based on the greenness of the current electricity (more on this later) and in its 24/7 carbon-free energy (CFE) reporting. With this collaboration, Google is on track to be the first major cloud provider to operate on 24/7 CFE.

24/7 CFE signifies our capability to consistently align every kWh of electricity consumption with carbon-free generation, round the clock, every day, and in every location. According to the United Nations, achieving this represents the ultimate goal for a "fully decarbonized electricity system" (*https://oreil.ly/7cw53*).

Electricity Map provides "hourly carbon electricity consumption and production data for over 50+ countries globally (and 160+ zones)." The data is available in three distinct time frames: historically, in real time, and as forecasted for the next 24 hours.

SDK, please!

Since we software developers are an infamously lazy bunch, someone has done the hard work and created an open source software development kit (SDK) on top of another carbon intensity API (WattTime (*https://www.watttime.org*)) to enable faster time to market with carbon-aware techniques. (Yay!)

The Carbon Aware SDK (*https://oreil.ly/QsPmh*) by the Green Software Foundation (GSF)) was the star of the show during last year's first GSF hackathon, where participants were able to use the toolkit as a web application programming interface (WebApi) and CLI to integrate carbon intensity information with their solutions.

There were over 50 finished hackathon projects, from Kubernetes extensions to UI design adjustments. Please head to "Real-World Examples" on page 86 to see what caught the authors' eyes.

Carbon intensity is one of the most crucial ingredients when it comes to calculating the total carbon footprint of a piece of software or system. We will present a more detailed analysis of toolings in Chapter 9, with strengths and shortcomings considered.

Demand Shifting

Now that we've established that not all electricity is generated the same way, let's move on to the million dollar question: how do we respond to this newfound information (a.k.a. the metric)?

Once again, carbon-aware computing is about responding to fluctuations in carbon intensity. At its core, the strategy involves relocating your application to a different time or location in response to changes in a critical benchmark.

Load balancing (LB) and content delivery networks (CDN) are well-known techniques that the tech industry uses to redirect traffic to areas best equipped to handle request demands based on the current situation.

If your use case allows flexibility in when and where your software runs, you can consider shifting your workload accordingly.

For example, if your task is not time sensitive (i.e., it doesn't need to be up 99.99% of the time but only once or twice in a given month, as with training an ML model), you should then consider training your enormous large language model (LLM) when electricity is the greenest.

If jurisdictions allow, you can also consider training the model at a location with much lower carbon intensity. But more on this in Chapter 8, where we ponder applying shifting time and place to green AI practices while also examining what considerations are needed at every stage of an ML lifecycle.

Demand shifting can be broken down into time and spatial shifting, with the former usually deemed easier to execute than the latter. This is not only because modification on implementation and deployment may be required but also because local law can be a challenging hurdle to deal with where data is concerned (more on those later).

Time Shifting

Carbon intensity varies throughout the day. As you'll see in Figure 5-3, it follows an inverted bell curve between midnight and 8:00 a.m., so if we can delay the example workload by an hour, we could potentially save nearly 100 grams of CO_2e/kWh. This temporal technique is called *time shifting*, which, in our firm opinion, is one of the low-hanging fruit opportunities that everyone in the business of reducing their software's carbon footprint should grasp with both hands.

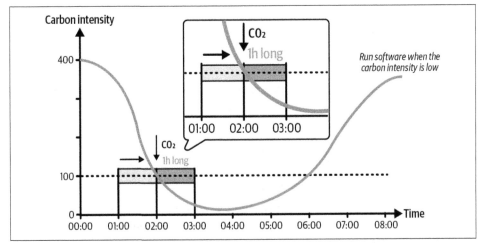

Figure 5-3. An inverted bell curve describing the variability of carbon intensity while demonstrating the time-shifting lower-carbon opportunities it may present

There are many circumstances out there in which we can take advantage of a shift in time to achieve carbon reduction. For example, as previously mentioned, the training stage of an ML model can immensely benefit from running at the time of the day with the greenest energy. Researchers from University College Dublin back this. They reported (*https://oreil.ly/EZkbi*) that practicing time-shifting methodologies for ML models can result in nearly 45% to 99% of software-related carbon reductions.

Another scenario that can hugely profit from time shifting is batch processing. A batch job is a type of workload that groups multiple tasks and executes one after the other without real-time user input. For instance, software updates and system back-ups can happen almost any time in a given period. Microsoft has been scheduling its Windows updates in this manner, resulting in a 99% reduction in carbon emissions.

The last example we want to note is more on you as an end user of video streaming or computer gaming. We are all aware of how much electricity these activities consume. So have you considered exercising flexible viewing such that you pause your 4D streaming when the carbon intensity of the grid is high? Or instead of watching movies on demand, downloading your favorite binge during a clean-energy period? Both of those habits can reduce the overall carbon footprint of internet usage. However, this is an individual action, and we know it is the systemic change we need. It would be much better if this happened automatically, and the good news is it can.

As we discuss in Chapter 7, video streaming services already use caching in locations such as content delivery networks (CDNs) to encourage data to be transferred while the internet is quiet. We would love to see customers' favorite shows automatically downloaded to CDNs or homes during a time when the electricity is greenest. Then we could all leisurely pursue our treasured programs day and night with a clear environmental conscience. And, of course, there is also the potential for a return on dollar savings and an increase in the application's performance.

Location Shifting

The second category of demand shifting, *location shifting*, can be summed up well by citing the words of the famous British rapper Dave, who sang, "If you send me the location, then I'll be right there."

Similar to Dave's commitment in the song, we can respond swiftly and go wherever we're needed upon receiving a location. If we move our applications to another physical location in response to a change in carbon intensity, it's called *spatial shifting*.

Spatial shifting can be a fruitful exercise to reduce overall carbon emissions (see Figure 5-4). For example, if we have a long-running application deployed in the Asian locations of Google Cloud Platform (GCP), and if latency (or any other concern) is not an issue, moving it to a region that naturally has lower-carbon energy sources can massively decrease the carbon footprint of the application.

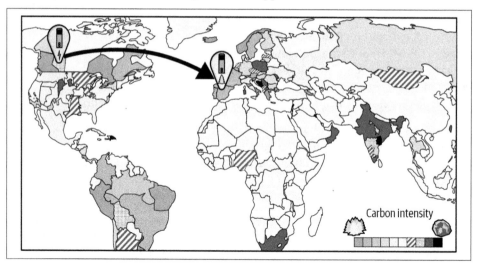

Figure 5-4. A global map showing regional carbon intensities with suggestions for moving applications from a higher-carbon intensity region to a lower one

Relatively short-lived and not real-time computing programs like large-scale data processing and generating 3D animations can also be location-shifting beneficiaries. Those types of scenarios typically just need to get on with it, such as rendering graphics in the 3D animation use case, before producing the end result that most people care about. Location is immaterial.

Demand Shaping

With the previous demand-shifting strategies of adjusting the timing or location for an application, we are still working with the assumption that there is a constant supply of electricity. However, as already explored, renewable energy supply is never really stable or endless. Therefore, we are proud to introduce another strategy within the carbon-aware family to address this scenario: *demand shaping*.

Demand shaping is not new to the computing world. The idea behind it has been exercised many times to fulfill various requirements. For example, video calling applications like Zoom and Google Meet use similar concepts to work with unstable and fluctuating network bandwidth.

During a call, if your network bandwidth is suffering, the application will automatically reduce the video quality. This prioritizes preserving network capability for audio, ensuring that you can still carry on with a conversation, which is the primary objective of a video conferencing call.

Another example we'd like to highlight is how progressive web applications (PWAs) effectively tackle network bandwidth issues through various methods. For instance, the progressive loading technique, also called lazy loading, allows applications to load gradually in stages. This approach significantly enhances the app's performance on slow networks by avoiding the simultaneous loading of all resources.

 We talk more about demand shaping's history in Chapter 7.

In contrast with the previous example where the concerned telemetry is network bandwidth, for carbon-aware solutions, what demand shaping is most worried about is the amount of CO_2e emitted as a by-product of electricity generation.

We can see in Figure 5-5 that if carbon intensity decreases, we should aim to do more in our software systems, and if carbon intensity skyrockets, we should do less. We could make this happen in two ways: firstly, we can make it automatic; secondly, we can let the application clients decide.

The first way should be familiar to most software developers as the technique is well known to engineers who have to deal with patchy networks or other indicators, such as CPU or memory resources, in the on-demand mode of cloud computing.

The latter is closely tied to a key concept of sustainability: consumption reduction. We wholeheartedly believe that we can accomplish plenty by becoming more efficient with resources, but at some point, we may all need to start consuming less (at least until the energy transition is complete). However, this is a book about software, so we will not start a philosophical debate between tribes.

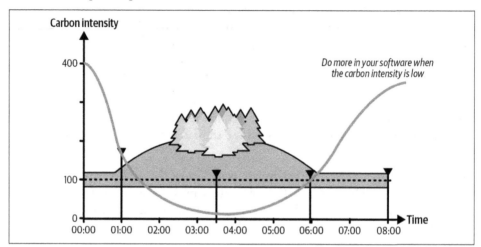

Figure 5-5. A green bell shape over a blue inverted bell curve to indicate doing more in an application when carbon intensity is low and vice versa

Nonetheless, as green software practitioners, we have the opportunity and the ability to steer how our users use our applications, so we can definitely present options to allow them to cancel a process or stop live streaming when carbon intensity is high.

Any Devil's Advocates?

Just like everything else in software, there is a fine line to walk when considering redesigning your application to be more carbon aware. From the previous sections, we gathered that our workload can be carbon aware in two ways: demand shaping or demand shifting, where the shift can be in either time or space. Both are valuable game plans for reducing software carbon emissions; however, careful consideration should be applied depending on use cases and requirements.

Location Shifting Can Be Tricky

Before we discuss the pros and cons of location shifting, we want to debunk the arguments that have been presented against this approach. Folks have expressed their worry that if most of the world moves all its workloads to a region with low carbon intensity, such as France, we will overload it, leading to increases in application latency, making a region more prone to service outages, and potentially degrading a managed service's performance with throttling, etc.

However, we are very far away from this reality. Moving even just one microservice of a software system across regions can be difficult, not only in the technical implementation sense but also in other areas, such as legal requirements for storing data (pesky privacy laws!).

However, this brings us to the point we want to make about moving applications to a different region to achieve carbon reduction when doing carbon-aware computing: thoughtful review needs to be exercised.

For example, one of the most critical aspects of an application is its reliability. Service-level agreements (SLAs) should never be breached, even at the expense of the environment. However, revisiting SLAs is not unheard of for many reasons, such as changes in business requirements or tech stacks.

 A *service-level agreement* (SLA) is a contract between a service provider, such as Azure, and a customer, such as you, an application developer. It documents the service level that the provider promised to deliver for its clients. SLAs typically cover areas such as how long an application should be up for (uptime), when an application should respond to a request (response time), and how long a resolution for an incident should be. There are many brilliant books out there that describe SLAs in great detail; we highly recommend you check out *Site Reliability Engineering* (O'Reilly).

The availability of resources can also throw a spanner in the works; if the region we are shifting our workload to does not have enough resources, then the move cannot be completed. But, of course, we can have enough monitoring in place to make sure we keep track of the carbon intensity as well as the availability of resources to ensure a smooth transition.

Any extra work can increase a team's responsibilities, including setting up additional metrics, all of which can lead to a hike in cloud cost.

Lastly, as mentioned many times, the regulatory side of things could be the biggest hurdle, given that each country has different requirements and laws on how all things software should be governed.

In our opinion, location shifting's counterpart, time shifting, is an approach that may be easier to accomplish. This is because, with time shifting, a lot of the already discussed concerns are not valid.

For instance, we do not need to worry about moving data among countries and trying to be compliant in a new region. We also don't need to be as worried about performance and latency. Lastly, costs should be lower since no additional resources are required and no transfer cost is needed. In fact, latency-insensitive workloads can be much cheaper to operate (for example, by running them in spot instances, as described in Chapter 4).

The final thing we must contemplate is the cost of greener electricity. Currently, we are getting a flat price from our grid provider or even cloud provider in most countries (although not all: Spain and some Northern European countries have already introduced dynamic electricity pricing based on renewables), but there are some complicated behind-the-scenes calculations happening based on the electricity market and the price of clean energy. Dynamic pricing will reach us all eventually. Don't let it surprise you. In the future, carbon awareness will save a lot of money.

Real-World Examples

What a lucky bunch we are! We get to witness the incredible innovations that are happening across all sorts of software businesses in the carbon-aware computing space. We have seen use cases from mobile phones to data centers. Additionally, Carbon Hack 2022, hosted by the GSF, attracted over 50 finished projects of nearly 400 participants to showcase their carbon-aware ideas. Why don't we spend the next section exploring real-life carbon-aware implementations?

Google

Let's start by looking at Google's effort. It began its carbon-aware journey in 2020 with time shifting (*https://oreil.ly/0UwRp*). Every single Google data center, every day, runs a calculation based on hour-by-hour guidelines to help align its computing tasks with times of low-carbon electricity supply. This is done by comparing two types of forecasts for the following day.

The first forecast, provided by its partner, Electricity Maps, predicts how the local electricity grid's average hourly carbon intensity will vary throughout the day.

Google then also creates its own internal power usage forecast for its data centers during the same time frame to complement the data provided by its partner.

Google reported excellent results from its pilot: the pilot effectively increased Google's consumption of lower-carbon energy by aligning load with periods of low carbon intensity.

This result was a milestone because it proved that time shifting is a fruitful tactic. Next, in 2021, Google embarked on a location-shifting quest (*https://oreil.ly/ikeTC*), in which it also reported successfully moving computing tasks that can run from basically anywhere to locations with cleaner energy.

Google initially started this effort with its media-processing domain, where it encoded, analyzed, and processed millions of multimedia files for YouTube, Google Photos, etc. And, of course, none of those efforts affected how the application was supposed to run, meaning no breach of SLAs or SLOs for those applications.

Xbox

In 2023, Xbox consoles also ventured into time shifting (*https://oreil.ly/_U6k6*) after Microsoft's carbon-aware Windows updates enabled it to become the first carbon-aware gaming console.

Xbox now arranges game, app, and OS updates at a specific moment during its nightly maintenance time frame, as opposed to the previous random wake-up between 2:00 a.m. and 6:00 a.m. The console will now be powered up at a particular time when the electricity from the grid is the cleanest (providing the console is plugged in and has access to the internet).

Xbox also announced a new power-saving mode, Shutdown (*https://oreil.ly/sT6Q-*), that can cut electricity consumption by up to 20 times! This new feature saves electricity when the console is off while not affecting the end-user experience in terms of the console's performance or abilities.

iPhone

Apple also has a slice of this carbon-aware cake. With iOS 16.1, iPhone users can now charge their devices with lower-carbon electricity, as shown in Figure 5-6.

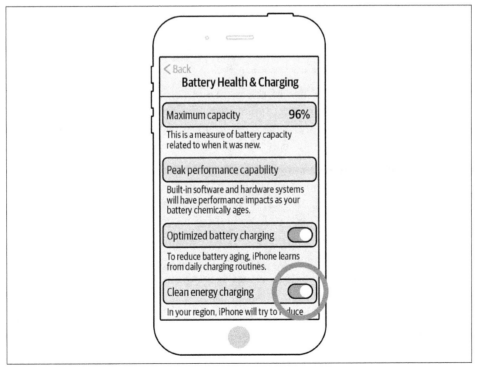

Figure 5-6. A sketch of an iPhone's clean-energy charging feature for iOS 16.1 and above

Carbon Hack 22

The GSF's Carbon Hack 22 (*https://oreil.ly/i2xv4*) attracted many innovative carbon-aware projects, especially around addressing the immense energy requirement for training an ML model. The winner of the hack, Lowcarb (*https://oreil.ly/b_ZA8*), set out specifically to tackle this. The solution was a plug-in for Flower (*https://flower.dev*), a popular federated-learning framework, allowing its users to schedule training jobs on clients in various geographic regions.

The winner benchmarked its solution on an image classification problem, demonstrating an impressive 13% reduction in the training's associated carbon emissions without surrendering "any training speed, final accuracy, or fairness of client selection," which is an essential requirement in a federated learning setup.

 Federated learning is a decentralized ML model-training methodology where the model's training happens across data from multiple locations without the data ever leaving its respective place. Because of federated learning's decentralized nature, preserving fairness in client selection is of utmost importance for the model's accuracy and efficiency.

There was another hack idea (*https://oreil.ly/JqGqF*) we wanted to highlight that focused on the existing gaps in the current carbon-aware markets. Even though many examples have been tried and tested, the global adoption of carbon-aware demand shifting and shaping is still below the ideal level.

One of the main difficulties lies in the increased responsibilities the development team will face. It must now re-instrument its application, determine how to deploy and maintain this new feature, and, most importantly, monitor this new concept without compromising the system's service-level objectives (SLOs).

To help, a carbon-aware solution at the web traffic level was proposed at the hackathon. Instead of instrumenting your already-built web applications with an SDK to react to carbon intensity, the hackathon participants introduced carbon-aware features at the load balancing (LB) or DNS Level.

Suppose your application is multiregion, and you have deployed it across multiple locations. In this case, you could easily employ this idea to preferentially redirect your traffic to the area with the least carbon intensity without much friction (as long as other load-balancing requirements were still met).

Additionally, in many enterprises, a centralized networking team could take on the burden of implementing carbon-aware features for the whole firm. So the application team can enjoy the benefits without any hassle!

You're Carbon and Aware

We hope you are now also a fan of carbon-aware practices and that you feel the urge to grab a large bowl of popcorn to watch how this idea is making waves in all corners of software engineering.

We also hope to have inspired you to embark on your adventure right away. Not only do you understand the different carbon-aware approaches, but you are also armed with resources to debate each strategy's advantages and disadvantages to your heart's content.

Lastly, let's not forget the quick win we all should have on speed dial: the simple time shift for our nontemporally critical applications.

CHAPTER 6

Hardware Efficiency

It's hardware that makes a machine fast. It's software that makes a fast machine slow.
—Craig Bruce[1]

Hardware efficiency? But wait, I thought this was a book about software. After all, we do mention "software" twice in the title. Yes, that is a fair point, but nonetheless, software runs on hardware, and it is well worth diving into a little deeper. No matter if you are a seasoned hardware geek who first learned to code in assembly or someone who just sees hardware as a means to an end, this chapter has something for you.

Hardware in the context of this book means any device that can be used to run software. That covers quite a wide range of different types of devices. Especially given that some enterprising people even implemented the game *Doom* on a pregnancy test (*https://oreil.ly/d5RGS*) (thankfully not controlled using the original input method). In this chapter we will focus on the two groups of more widely used hardware devices: servers and consumer devices like phones, desktops, and laptops. We'll leave the discussion of carbon efficiency in pregnancy tests to someone else.

As we have seen in previous chapters, the main problem we can tackle in data centers (DCs) as green software practitioners is electricity consumption. But for consumer devices, embodied carbon is the greater issue, as it makes up a larger share of the overall carbon footprint of the device over its lifetime. In fact, for smartphones, the manufacturing cost stands for 85%–95% of the annual carbon footprint (*https://oreil.ly/3giTV*) of the phone. We are also using more and more of these devices.

---

1 Dr. Craig S. Bruce's personal website, The Wayback Machine, accessed January 16, 2024, *https://oreil.ly/ZoSBH*.

For example, Deloitte's 2022 Connectivity and Mobile Trends Survey[2] found that the average US household has 22 connected devices.

For these reasons, it is vital for us as software builders to use less hardware and make what we do use last longer. No matter if you are deploying code to the cloud, to a server in your self-hosted data center, or to a consumer device, there are concrete actions you can take. This chapter will tell you to make sure your software is not the reason for customers throwing away perfectly working hardware and encourage you to use your consumer power to make hardware producers green their operations and support hardware for longer. We will also talk about device longevity and how you can achieve it, for example, by extending the lifetime of the hardware within your control and using secondhand hardware.

Another fascinating topic is how to build hardware better or more sustainably. But we are not the experts here. Thus, we will go on only a slight tangent and talk a little bit about what the big players in the industry are doing, as well as recycling and e-waste.

We hope that by the end of this chapter, you, just like us, feel that us software developers can and do impact hardware usage.

Embodied Carbon

Hardware comes with an already paid carbon cost, which we call *embodied carbon*. Manufacturing hardware devices like servers or phones is quite a complicated process. Materials need to be mined somewhere, then shipped around the world (possibly several times) to be assembled—often using an energy-intensive procedure—before the device finally lands in your hands.

This embodied carbon cost of hardware is made up of several components, with integrated circuits being the largest single source of emissions.[3] In Chapter 2, you saw examples of how high this cost could be for end-user devices. In general, getting the exact embodied carbon numbers is not always easy. In Chapter 9, we will show you how cloud providers are reporting on hardware data. The Software Carbon Intensity (SCI) Guidance project (*https://sci-guide.greensoftware.foundation*) from the Green Software Foundation also maintains a list of data sets that provides embodied carbon data from different types of devices.[4]

As software practitioners, we have little control over the embodied carbon cost (except by using our spending power). As a green software practitioner, the only

---

2 "Consumers Benefit from Virtual Experiences, but Need Help Managing Screen Time, Security and Tech Overload," Deloitte, accessed January 16, 2024, *https://oreil.ly/x86sv*.

3 Jens Malmodin and Dag Lundén, "The Energy and Carbon Footprint of the Global ICT and E&M Sectors 2010–2015," *Sustainability* 10, no. 9 (2018): 3027, *https://oreil.ly/k88lj*.

4 "Datasets," SCI Guidance, accessed January 16, 2024, *https://oreil.ly/N8eRG*.

---

remaining thing you can do is to be mindful of the debt that lands in your hand at the same time as your shiny new device and plan for how you will amortize it. There are two main ways to decrease the embodied carbon cost of your software: increase the lifetime of your hardware or increase the utilization of said hardware. This section will cover different ways to achieve these two goals as well as some interesting things for you to consider both as a self-hosted user and as a cloud user.

Device Longevity

How long do end-user devices live? We will give you our favorite answer: it depends. In this case, it depends on the type of device. From a smartphone, you can expect only two to three years of lifetime.[5] Smartphones also have a rapid release cycle. One example is Apple, which releases approximately one new iPhone per year.[6] Meanwhile, the major manufacturers in the gaming industry release new consoles on a roughly seven-year cycle cadence. That means that they design so you can happily play video games to your heart's content until the next model is released, sometimes even longer than that. For example, the Xbox One was designed to last 10 years, and that appears to be holding up.[7] For servers owned by a public cloud provider, the lifetime is four to six years. Microsoft announced the extension of server lifetimes from four to six years in July 2022,[8] Alphabet announced the change in expected useful life of its servers and networking equipment to six years in January 2023,[9] and AWS increased its servers' expected useful life to five years in January 2022.[10] These numbers are the financial practice numbers, and we cannot say for sure how long the cloud providers actually keep their servers. We welcome increased transparency into this data from cloud providers (see Figure 6-1 for lifespans of different devices).

---

5 "Average Lifespan (Replacement Cycle Length) of Smartphones in the United States from 2013 to 2027," Statista, accessed January 16, 2024, *https://oreil.ly/zZhpE*.

6 "List of iPhone Models," Wikipedia, updated January 14, 2024, *https://oreil.ly/WaIgo*.

7 Taylor Bauer, "How Long Will the Xbox One Last into Next-Gen?" Phenixx Gaming, July 22, 2020, *https://oreil.ly/FT5XZ*.

8 Brett Iversen, Satya Nadella, and Amy Hood, "Microsoft Fiscal Year 2022 Fourth Quarter Earnings Conference Call," Microsoft, July 26, 2022, *https://oreil.ly/4Atut*.

9 "Alphabet Announces Fourth Quarter and Fiscal Year 2022 Results," Alphabet Investor Relations, February 2, 2023, *https://oreil.ly/J5T4C*.

10 "Amazon.com Announces Fourth Quarter Results," Amazon, February 3, 2022, *https://oreil.ly/CJETs*.

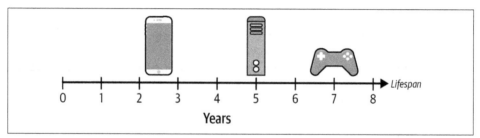

Figure 6-1. The different life spans of a few popular types of devices

What determines that you might only get two years lifetime out of a brand-new smartphone while a gaming console will last you more than three times longer? We can't completely leave out consumerism and the end-user craving for slimmer devices, longer battery life, and better performance. End users have backed smartphone providers into a corner where they need to deliver more performance to be able to adequately compete for market share. This might be changing as consumers grow more environmentally aware, though. One example is the increased growth in sales by the Dutch modular, repairable smartphone Fairphone. Fairphone sold around 120,000 devices in 2022—up from around 88,000 in 2021 and 23,000 in 2018.[11]

But if we go back to the lifetime of electronic devices and what affects it, one thing that causes us to chuck out hardware, perhaps well before its expiration date, is Moore's law.[12]

Moore's law posits that the number of transistors on a microchip doubles every two years, and other forms of progress mean that devices get new features, which developers want to exploit in their new app releases. Mobile phones, for example, have gotten faster, evolved to have dedicated GPU and machine learning chips, and acquired more memory. Apps take advantage of this progress, and that is fine and unavoidable. The same holds true for servers, PCs, gaming consoles, and kitchen ventilators (yes, they come with apps now).

Another thing that impacts longevity is hardware failure, either mechanical or electrical. Of the two, mechanical is more common, simply because mechanical parts face more wear and tear than electrical components. For client end devices, you as a software practitioner have very limited leverage in avoiding hardware failures. What the tech industry needs here is to see hardware manufacturers take more responsibility for designing for longevity. We believe that 10 years of use should be the new standard for device longevity.

11 Natasha Lomas, "Fairphone Nabs $53M in Growth Capital for 'Sustainable' Consumer Electronics," Tech-Crunch, January 31, 2023, *https://oreil.ly/fYXOQ*.

12 Gordon E. Moore, "Cramming More Components onto Integrated Circuits," orig. pub. in *Electronics* 38, no. 8 (April 19, 1965), The Wayback Machine, accessed January 16, 2024, *https://oreil.ly/Wf1xv*.

You might not be able to do much to avoid client-side hardware failures, but you have leverage to avoid the kiss of death by software-defined obsolescence, which we'll dive deeper into in the next section.

Software-Defined Obsolescence

Software-defined obsolescence is what happens when support ceases to be provided to a device. This support could include things like regular updates, upgrades, or fixes. For the purpose of this section, let us consider three different scenarios in which this can happen to client devices:

1. Manufacturer of device ceases support.
2. Favorite/flagship/important/vital software on client device is no longer supported.
3. Minor/additional/nice-to-have software on client device is no longer supported.

In the first scenario, you, as a developer, are still bound by the device support provided by the manufacturer. For good reasons, users should not hang on to their devices once they are out of security support. As software practitioners, the best we can do here is to push for longer support by the manufacturer.

When it comes to smartphones, the company that has the longest OS support is Apple, where the new iOS 15 supports phones that are up to six years old.[13] For Android phones, the market is a bit more diverse; Google, Samsung, and chipset maker Qualcomm have all committed to providing four years of security updates for a large selection of their devices; and Google is promising five years for some of the Pro phones. While this is an improvement on the past, all providers need to improve more, even Apple. Device life expectancies must be much longer than six years to justify the embodied cost of the manufacturing process. To compare, gaming consoles provide several years more of expected lifetime than smartphones; they are built to last. This demonstrates that devices can last longer if manufacturers choose.

Let us consider the second scenario: a user's favorite piece of software is no longer supported on a device. This requires, or at least heavily entices, the user to throw the device away and replace it with a new one should they wish to continue using the software. The device in question might be working perfectly well for other use cases, shining a bright light of responsibility on the software (and by extension, you as its creator). The same can be said for the third scenario, where a nonfavorite piece of software no longer is available to the user on a specific device, although perhaps not to the same extent.

---

13 Jonny Evans, "WWDC: 12 Small but Important Improvements You May Have Missed," Computerworld, June 15, 2021, *https://oreil.ly/sqauZ*.

When a working device is discarded because it is missing a piece of software and the consumer buys a new device, a carbon debt occurs. As green software practitioners, we of course want to avoid this software-caused additional embodied carbon cost. How to achieve this is simple to explain but perhaps a little more work intensive to achieve. The greenest thing to do is to provide backward compatibility and not let your software be a nail in the coffin for a perfectly working device.

Of course, supporting a wider range of hardware versions, with widely varying technical capabilities, increases both maintenance and testing costs. Luckily, on the smartphone side of things, both Android and iOS have some guidance to provide. Android has a guide for how to make your UI remain backward compatible, and this guide includes key learnings:[14]

- Abstract the new APIs.
- Proxy to the new APIs.
- Create an implementation with older APIs.
- Use the version-aware component.

A guide is good, of course, but this will require action and additional work from application developers. Backward compatibility on Android phones is not a new problem. Long ago in 2010, the *Android Developers Blog* ran a post, "How to Have Your (Cup)cake and Eat It Too," outlining some steps to achieve backward compatibility.[15]

Cloud Applications and Services

When you run your software in the cloud, one of the things you pay for is not having to bother with asset management. Someone else is responsible for the servers placed in the server room, including how to run them, when to decommission them, and, to an extent, how to organize workloads running on top of them. This is often very convenient, as it limits the amount of things you need to bother yourself with, and it can also be an argument for why moving to the cloud is a sustainability win. What people mean when they say this is typically that hyperscale cloud providers are more efficient than traditional data centers.[16] This is not magic. Public cloud providers are more efficient because they expend more effort on making their data centers more efficient. After all, selling the cloud is their primary business. For most other companies, something else entirely, like selling clothes, is their primary business.

---

14 "Create Backward-Compatible UIs," Developers, December 27, 2019, *https://oreil.ly/-AY2F*.

15 Adam Powell, "How to Have Your (Cup)cake and Eat It Too," *Android Developers Blog*, July 12, 2010, *https://oreil.ly/xta81*.

16 "Data Centres and Data Transmission Networks," IEA, accessed January 16, 2024, *https://oreil.ly/yMFhb*.

To reap the benefits of all the efficiency efforts your cloud provider has made, you need to work with the tech and not hamstring it by using the cloud exactly like you would a normal data center. Why is this important? In Chapter 2 you learned about energy proportionality for a server. For a data center, we can extrapolate the same behavior, but due to the scale of public cloud providers, it is like energy proportionality on steroids.

Things like PUE and operational costs add on massively in terms of energy cost to underutilized resources. In addition, if you pay for a large virtual machine (for example) but only end up using a small percentage of it, you send the signal to the cloud provider to build more data centers, which in turn means building more carbon-intensive hardware components like semiconductors.

Capacity planning for the cloud providers is a long-haul game, and hardware components come with a long delivery time, something made even more glaringly obvious during the semiconductor shortage in the early 2020s.[17] According to Debra Bernstein (*https://oreil.ly/IB3UC*), senior principal sustainability technologist at Intel, "The actions we take now will make sure we right-size our industry for the future."[18] Chapter 4, on operational efficiency, covered how to help achieve this goal from the software perspective in greater detail, so if you skipped Chapter 4, head on over there for a refresher after you are done with this chapter.

You also want to use the most efficient architecture your cloud provider can offer for your workload. One example of that can be using the AWS Graviton processor-powered instances.[19] These are designed exclusively for AWS and are a good option if you are already hosted in AWS's cloud. The Graviton-based instances consume 60% less energy than comparable non-Graviton instances in AWS. Not all workloads can run on the AWS Graviton, as they implement the Arm64 instruction set. However, a great number of workloads can, and in those cases, a 60% energy reduction for the price of a config change[20] is a low-hanging fruit.

Self-Hosted Data Centers

If you are not writing software for the public cloud, but for your own data center (you are perfectly allowed to call a roomful of servers a data center in the context of this chapter), then you have more choices to make on the hardware efficiency side.

---

17 Wassen Mohammad, Adel Elomri, and Laoucine Kerbache, "The Global Semiconductor Chip Shortage: Causes, Implications, and Potential Remedies," *IFAC-PapersOnLine* 55, no. 10 (2022): 476–483, *https://oreil.ly/p3wbr*.

18 All quotations from Debra Bernstein come from personal communication.

19 "AWS Graviton Processors," AWS, accessed January 16, 2024, *https://oreil.ly/cMkZC*.

20 "Considerations When Transitioning Workloads to AWS Graviton Based Amazon EC2 Instances," GitHub, accessed January 16, 2024, *https://oreil.ly/EBEiJ*.

When you are self-hosted, you own asset management. Yay for complete freedom! Yay, analysis paralysis...? If you are self-hosted, you own your sustainability and efficiency strategy. Completely.

In theory, this means that you can build the most optimized and sustainable data center the world has ever seen. In practice, it takes significant engineering effort to make hardware-efficient decisions. We are not aiming to provide the blueprint for the perfectly green data center, but this section will give you some useful tips to guide you on your journey there. Almost everything that was said about operational efficiency in Chapter 4 is true here as well, so don't skip out on that chapter!

Most importantly, when you are self-hosted, you control the lifetime of your hardware. Extending the lifetime is one of the best, and easiest, ways to decrease your embodied carbon cost. Remember, the carbon debt of producing a server is already paid to the environment, so we can only amortize it and delay further carbon spending. Let's take a look at an example of what this could mean.

We assume the embodied carbon cost of a new server is 4,000 kg of CO_2e, and you originally plan to keep this device for four years. The yearly embodied carbon cost is then 1,000 kg of CO_2e per year. Now if you extend the lifetime of a server from four years to five years, your yearly embodied carbon cost shrinks to only 800 kg of CO_2e per year, or 20% (see Figure 6-2 for examples of this amortization cost).

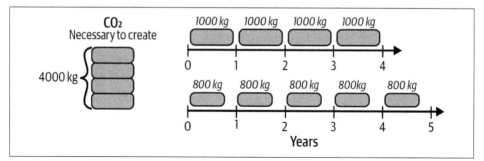

Figure 6-2. Example of how the embodied carbon cost of a server can be amortized over time

When you are on bare metal (e.g., on a dedicated server only used by you typically without an OS or any additional applications), or if you are on prem, you can get down to the nitty-gritty of hardware. Ohm's law dictates that power is voltage multiplied by current, or $P = V \times I$, and that energy is power over time, or $E = P \times t$. Taken together, these two equations show that lower voltage means lower energy spending. On the public cloud, you cannot choose the voltage, but in your own bare-metal setup, you can! This is because any given device has a range of voltage (V) where it will operate as intended. This range of V is fairly tight, and it will need different tuning throughout the life cycle of the hardware. This means that voltage tuning is not really something the everyday software person should or can do, but it is definitely possible and one way to lower the energy consumption on the hardware level. We did promise you nitty-gritty, did we not?

If you own your own data center, you also own the Off button. One of the main benefits of the cloud is that the cloud never sleeps, but your software might actually go to sleep! For example, if your business does not span the globe, you surely have hours of peak demand and hours of little to no demand. During those hours of off-peak demand, you can actually shut your hardware down completely, thus saving considerable energy. "We need to not be afraid to go into low-power states as an industry! Some might not want to take the risk of shutting hardware off, but from a sustainability perspective, it is the right risk to take," says Debra Bernstein. The risk on the hardware side is twofold, both the risk of not having enough capacity in case of sudden increase in demand and the risk of hardware failure on startup. These two concepts were discussed more in depth in Chapter 4, in the section called "LightSwitchOps." The possible sustainability gain of shutting your hardware off is saved energy use from avoiding having those idle servers consuming energy.

 Having to deal with repairs is one of the more tedious parts of asset management. However, if we were to find a silver lining, it would be that hardware failures can in some scenarios give you rare, green insights. For example, is it always your disks that kick the bucket first? This is quite a likely scenario if you have mechanical disks, as mechanical parts are always more prone to failure than electrical components. Knowing this, could you change your software to write to disk less before you actually break the disk? This type of software change that directly impacts your hardware longevity might be rare, but for some it could be a hidden gem.

On the server-creation side, manufacturers invest significant resources to increase the reliability and lifetime of their products. One example is Intel adding aging "odometers" to the chips, which will make it possible to turn off the portion of the chip most likely to fail but still operate the rest of the chip. This is pretty cool, but to reap the benefits, the software needs to adapt. For example, if 2 out of 64 vCPUs are at risk, what layers of software need to be involved to operate using only the 62 good vCPUs? If you are self-hosted, this is an area where you can work together with your hardware provider to overall increase the lifetime of your servers.

Specialized Hardware

If we take a step back from client devices for a while and go back to our world of servers and data centers, one thing to ponder is whether or not specialized hardware is greener than general-purpose hardware. With specialized hardware, we mean things like application-specific integrated circuits (ASICs), field programmable gate arrays (FPGAs), or tensor processing units (TPUs). This type of hardware can typically take the role of processing units, but it can also be used for other purposes.

According to Debra Bernstein, "When it comes to sustainability and general-purpose versus specialized hardware, there is no definitive answer that covers all scenarios. Specialized hardware is good if you deeply understand the problem space and can maximize the utilization of your hardware, because it is more efficient in terms of energy use. It also becomes more sustainable from an embodied-carbon perspective, if you will keep the hardware for longer."

However, if you have a more generic problem space or a newer problem space you might not yet fully understand, then the decision tree grows more branches. You will have to consider whether or not you have the expertise in your organization to write efficient software for your specialized hardware and if this is something you can make a long-term bet on. With general-purpose hardware, you can always repurpose the hardware later on for new problem spaces, thus increasing the lifetime, and ergo get more bang for your embodied carbon bucks. With specialized hardware, this is more difficult, and short-term energy efficiency wins might not outweigh the embodied carbon cost over time, especially if you have to decommission your hardware after a short time period.

One concrete example of ASIC use that is more efficient than CPU use can be found in the field of block ciphers. *Block ciphers* are used to encrypt (or decrypt) large amounts of data, which is something some pieces of software do quite often. For example, transport layer security (TLS), which can be found not only in the IP suite but also in Data Processing Units (DPUs) and the latest Xeon processor,[21] is a cryptographic protocol. In this field, ASICs have been found to be faster and cheaper than other types of hardware.[22]

But what about specialized hardware for specialized software? Yes, this is where we talk about blockchains and crypto and their use of GPUs, as well as AI and ML and their use of specialized hardware like AI accelerators. Even though the GPU was originally designed for processing graphics, it turned out to be ideal for the matrix mathematics involved in machine learning and crypto. And yes, this is where we mention the Jevons paradox again, which you might remember from Chapter 3. The Jevons paradox is the historical observation that when we get more efficient at doing something, it gets cheaper and we all do much more of it. Like we mentioned earlier in this chapter, specialized hardware can be great in terms of energy efficiency for

---

21 "Intel® QuickAssist Technology—Envoy TLS Acceleration with Intel® QAT Solution Brief," Intel, January 27, 2023, *https://oreil.ly/Au4x9*.

22 Bahram Rashidi, "Efficient and High-Throughput Application-Specific Integrated Circuit Implementations of HIGHT and PRESENT Block Ciphers," *IET Circuits, Devices & Systems* 13, no. 6 (September 2019): 731–740, *https://oreil.ly/ldO7a*.

---

specialized use cases. The crux is, when something gets more efficient (e.g., cheaper), you do more of it.

We saw this for some early AI applications like image processing. The chips got more efficient, and thus more image processing was performed, leading to more chips being produced. That in turn means more embodied carbon as the efficiency gains do not map to an equal reduction in embodied carbon. In other words, more chips equal more carbon. To add on to this consideration, you might need to consider more dimensions. For example, does your problem actually need this specialized software solution? This question, for permissions blockchains in particular, has fascinated one of our authors, Sara, since she was in university, and she wrote the first-ever paper comparing the performance of permissioned blockchains with that of distributed databases.[23]

As for the ethics of building specialized hardware for specialized software and its energy use, we'll defer that discussion to another time.

E-waste

Electronic waste is typically shortened to the more sci-fi sounding *e-waste* or the more formal *waste electrical and electronic equipment (WEEE)*. The StEP initiative defines e-waste as "a term used to cover items of all types of electrical and electronic equipment (EEE) and its parts that have been discarded by the owner as waste without the intention of re-use."[24] And we have *loads* of e-waste. In fact, it is the fastest-growing waste stream.[25] According to the UN, the world produced as much as 50 million tons of e-waste in 2019, and it is projected to grow to 120 million tons by 2050.[26] To put that number in perspective, 50 million tons is more weight than all of the commercial airliners ever made. Or if you prefer animal comparisons, 50 million tons is the same mass as approximately 250,000 blue whales (see Figure 6-3.)

The production of e-waste has several consequences for the climate and our planet. In 2019, only 20% of e-waste was formally recycled, despite e-waste containing lots of precious materials such as gold, platinum, and cobalt.[27] Unsafe or informal recycling

---

23 Sara Bergman, Mikael Asplund, and Simin Nadjm-Tehrani, "Permissioned Blockchains and Distributed Databases: A Performance Study," *Currency and Computation Practice and Experience* 32, no. 12 (2020), *https://oreil.ly/jkOYf*.

24 "What Is E-waste?" StEP, accessed January 16, 2024, *https://oreil.ly/zw70N*.

25 Olanrewaju S. Shittu, Ian D. Williams, and Peter J. Shaw, "Global E-Waste Management: Can WEEE Make a Difference? A Review of E-Waste Trends, Legislation, Contemporary Issues and Future Challenges," *Waste Management* 120, no. 1 (February 2021): 549–563, *https://oreil.ly/ubO35*.

26 "UN Report: Time to Seize Opportunity, Tackle Challenge of E-Waste," UN Environment Programme, January 24, 2019, *https://oreil.ly/6XRre*.

27 Ibid.

of e-waste, which happens primarily in developing countries, has high risks of resulting in harm both to the environment and to the people working there. E-waste contains toxic materials such as lead, cadmium, mercury, and arsenic, hazardous both to the planet and people.[28] Of course, e-waste is also a direct indication of how many new devices the world needs to produce. Our society depends more and more on electrical devices, and rare are the cases when a device gets thrown out without immediately being replaced by something new. The result is even more emissions from embodied carbon. Considering the fact that the manufacturing cost accounts for 85%–95% of the annual carbon footprint of smartphones (*https://oreil.ly/UgB_V*), even if the replacement phone is more energy efficient, replacing it is not a green choice.

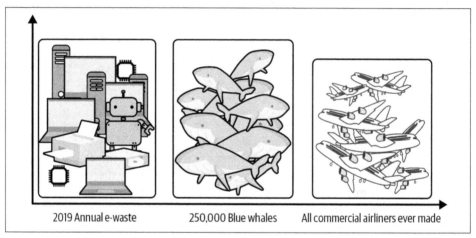

| 2019 Annual e-waste | 250,000 Blue whales | All commercial airliners ever made |

Figure 6-3. A comparison of the volume of e-waste to both 250,000 blue whales and all commercial airliners

---

28 "Cleaning Up Electronic Waste (E-Waste)," EPA, updated November 15, 2023, *https://oreil.ly/yv9gU*.

OK, so the world throws out a lot of electrical equipment. Of course, not all of this is caused by the software industry. Devices that are not traditionally seen as software-running, like refrigerators, TVs, and washing machines, also count as electrical equipment. With the Internet of Things and smart homes, these traditionally "dumb" devices are becoming smarter, thanks to software. This is, again, fine and unavoidable, but it further highlights the responsibility software practitioners have for the hardware life cycle. Not only should we consider servers and laptops within our realm of influence, but if a consumer throws out their perfectly working dishwasher in order to get the ability to control their new dishwasher through an app, then software is directly causing more e-waste.

That was maybe a bit bleak. We do tend to focus on solutions in this book, so let us talk about solutions for a while. What is being done to combat this, and how can you help? You might have guessed it, but the key here is to apply the things we have talked about earlier in this chapter: using your own devices longer and making sure you enable your customers to do the same.

Governments around the world are also doing their bit to help reduce this massive waste stream. In March of 2023, the European Commission adopted a proposal including the right to repair consumer goods.[29] This proposal has been approved by the European Parliament and now only needs to be approved by the European Council to make it a reality. This sends a clear signal to the industry: repairs over replacements. If this proposal passes as is, it will mean legal guarantees to be able to repair goods if it is technically possible. In December of 2022, New York was the first state in the USA to pass a similar bill, requiring manufacturers to repair electronic equipment.[30] In India, new e-waste management rules from the government took effect in April of 2023, providing customers the right to repair electrical equipment.[31] For you as a software engineer, it will likely (hopefully!) mean we will see older client-end devices stay on the market for longer. This in turn makes backward compatibility even more important to your customers.

There are also more avant garde solutions being proposed by our industry. One of those is the concept of a junkyard data center, which utilizes discarded smartphones as a computing resource.[32] This research project showed that for specific workloads,

29 "Right to Repair: Commission Introduces New Consumer Rights for Easy and Attractive Repairs," European Commission, March 22, 2023, *https://oreil.ly/E8qrq*.

30 Senate Bill S4104A, New York State Senate, 2021–2022 Legislative Session, *https://oreil.ly/Z2v0f*.

31 Divya J. Shekhar, "Right to Repair: When Can We Stop Shopping and Start Repairing?" *Forbes India*, May 3, 2023, *https://oreil.ly/KRnKS*.

it is greener (and cheaper!) to use repurposed clusters of smartphones compared to traditional servers, especially from an embodied carbon perspective.

Less avant garde is the robust secondhand market that exists for servers and server room equipment. This can be a great option for both saving cost and embodied carbon.

What Are Hardware Producers Doing to Make Their Operations Greener?

Is the burden all on us as software developers, then? Shouldn't the hardware producers play a part in this? Yes, they should, and luckily for us and the planet, many already have targets set up.

Taiwan Semiconductor Manufacturing Company Limited (TSMC) is the world's largest dedicated independent semiconductor company, and it has set several targets[33] to make its operations greener. These targets include driving low-carbon manufacturing, like reducing greenhouse gas emissions per unit of production by 40% to 2030, using renewable energy, increasing energy efficiency by saving 5,000 GWh cumulatively between 2016 and 2030, and strengthening climate resilience.

Another heavyweight figure in the semiconductor industry is Intel. It has also set several climate targets to green its operations.[34] Intel's 2030 sustainability goals include achieving net positive water, sending zero waste to landfills, and using 100% renewable electricity across its global operations. For its scope 1 and 2 GHG emissions, the 2030 goal is to reduce by 10% to ultimately reach net zero in 2040. Intel's subsidiary, Intel Resale Corporation, also works to help minimize e-waste.[35]

Arm is a British semiconductor and software design company whose primary business is the architecture, design, and licensing of CPU cores that implement the Arm architecture family of instruction sets.[36] Arm is committed to taking a science-aligned approach to cutting absolute emissions, from all scopes, by at least 50% to achieve net-zero carbon by 2030 from an FY19 baseline.[37] Among other things, this includes sourcing 100% renewable energy, cutting energy consumption, and investing in tech-based carbon removal projects.

---

32 Jennifer Switzer, Gabriel Marcano, Ryan Kastner, and Pat Pannuto, "Junkyard Computing: Repurposing Discarded Smartphones to Minimize Carbon," arXiv, October 25, 2022, *https://oreil.ly/eE_7w*.

33 "Climate Change and Energy Management," TSMC, accessed January 16, 2024, *https://oreil.ly/kI_Xs*.

34 "Steadfastly Committed to a Sustainable Future," Intel, accessed January 16, 2024, *https://oreil.ly/zbYSY*.

35 "Intel Resale Corporation," Intel, accessed January 16, 2024, *https://oreil.ly/LYiDI*.

36 "Building the Future of Computing," Arm, accessed January 16, 2024, *https://oreil.ly/aQdPT*.

37 "Our Sustainability Vision," Arm, accessed January 16, 2024, *https://oreil.ly/BQ8f_*.

Apple has several climate targets[38] for its consumer device manufacturing as well. These include producing all Apple devices using 100% renewable energy by 2030 and increasing the use of recycled and renewable material to eventually produce new devices with only recycled and renewable materials.

Microsoft is targeting to be zero waste for all its direct operations, products, and packaging[39] by 2030, and it already has programs for purchasing refurbished devices[40] like Surface and Xbox as well as a recycling[41] scheme.

As the consumer device market is quite large, we won't cover all of the producers and their targets here, but hopefully, this gives you some curiosity to explore your favorite manufacturer a little deeper.

We do want to say that setting an ambitious target is not the same as reaching said target, so we software folks are not off the hook just yet. Collectively, the software industry and the practitioners who make up the software industry (yes, we're talking about you now) have massive consumer power over the hardware industry. You can influence hardware producers to ensure that hardware is produced efficiently and sustainably, as well as push for ease of repairs and recycling.

That Is a Wrap!

No matter what type of software you and your organization write, you run on hardware. In this chapter, we hope that you have been able to pick up some tools to be greener in your utilization of hardware. Not everything will apply to everyone, but if we were to give you a summary of our most important tools from this chapter, they would be the following:

- Make sure your software is not the reason for customers throwing away perfectly working hardware.
- Use your consumer power to make hardware producers green their operations and support hardware for longer.
- Extend the lifetime of the hardware within your control.
- Consider using secondhand hardware.

38 "Environment," Apple, accessed January 16, 2024, *https://oreil.ly/BA2Wi*.

39 Brad Smith, "Microsoft Commits to Achieve 'Zero Waste' Goals by 2030," *Official Microsoft Blog*, August 4, 2020, *https://oreil.ly/_77RY*.

40 "Microsoft Certified Refurbished," Microsoft, accessed January 16, 2024, *https://oreil.ly/PAUxz*.

41 "End-of-Life Management and Recycling," Microsoft, accessed January 16, 2024, *https://oreil.ly/HQHkZ*.

CHAPTER 7

Networking

For never was a story of more woe
Than this of Juliet and her Romeo.
   —Shakespeare

How many deaths have been averted by the invention of TCP/IP?

 Transmission control protocol over internet protocol (TCP/IP, the world's most unhelpful spelling out of an acronym), is the set of simple networking rules, or the protocol, that underpins much of modern communications. One of TCP/IP's fundamental assumptions is that it's not a great idea to assume your intended recipient has always received your message. If Juliet had only applied the principles of reliable communication, then her story would have had a very different ending. In her defense, comms using these rules is slow and often impractical if you aren't passing your messages over wires.

In the developed world, reliable communications underpin our lives. Perhaps it doesn't matter whether they are green or not? Some might argue telecoms is humanity's most important use of energy and must be maintained and extended at any cost.

Are they right?

Are Networks Already Green Enough?

Since our book is one of the first on the subject of building green technology, we ask as many questions as we answer, and that's fine. We're still at the stage of working out how the tech industry needs to respond to the energy transition, and there are few no-brainer moves. Usually, we have to suck our teeth and say, "It depends." Unfortunately, this chapter is yet another example of that kind of mealymouthed equivocation.

Nonetheless, even if we can't easily answer the question, "Are networks already green enough?" there is still a great deal we can learn about being green from networking because it is ahead of the rest of the tech sector when it comes to two techniques that are vital to the energy transition: demand shifting and demand shaping. That is because the developers of the internet have always had to handle the problem of being dependent upon a variably available resource—in their case, bandwidth.

Looking at the Big Picture

In this chapter, we're going to take a broad view of networks and the internet and talk about everything that plays a part in connecting one device with another, whether that device is a phone, a laptop, a VM in a data center, or one DC to another. That means as well as fiber-optic cables and other forms of "wire," we will talk about services like content delivery networks (CDNs), which cache internet content so it's faster for end users to access.

There is a good reason for us to go wide in our definition. For most enterprises, there isn't much you can do about the wires and protocols underpinning your communications because the way the internet functions is a black box to its users, particularly when it comes to routing. That's good. It works. But it means it's not a good plan to start messing around under the hood. However, there are still plenty of choices you can make about how, where, and when you connect to the internet. Some of those are green, and some are definitely not.

 In Chapter 3, we said not to second-guess your compiler. Generally speaking, it's not a great idea to second-guess your routing either: there are risks (*https://oreil.ly/CWLNS*) even if you are an expert.

One thing we can say for sure is that green 6G (*https://oreil.ly/Zn5yg*) isn't going to save us. Even if it turns out to be miraculous, we can't wait that long. Since 5G isn't well deployed yet, 6G might still be a decade or more from mass use. We have to act today to be both greener and more resilient to climate-related infrastructure outages. The good news is we can.

When we need to, we in the global community of internet consumers and suppliers can respond fast to manage our resource use. The proof of that is the way the internet withstood the sudden and unprecedented increase in demand caused by the pandemic lockdowns of 2020. Then, the internet didn't survive because of the laying of new cables. There wasn't enough time for that. Instead, it was kept alive using the same demand-shifting and shaping techniques we described in Chapter 5.

Before we discuss any of that, we need to define what we mean by the internet and which parts are green and which not.

Defining the Internet

The standard answer to the question "What is the internet?" is wires, compute, and storage, and the good news is that being energy efficient is fundamental to most of it.

Because electricity is a big chunk of any network's operational costs, the folk who build telecoms equipment use energy intensity or watts per bit (*https://oreil.ly/ eURWU*) as a key metric and focus on its continual improvement.

Despite this, there are still plenty of carbon efficiency and awareness upgrades that can be made to the internet.

They just probably aren't where you think they are.

What Are These Wires?

The so-called wires of the internet are traditionally broken down into three areas: the backbone, the metro, and the last mile. At each of these stages, the level of aggregation decreases (i.e., each connection is carrying traffic for a smaller number of folk). Sometimes when we talk about wires in the context of the internet, we mean literal copper ones, but usually we're actually describing fiber-optic cables or radio waves.

The *backbone* is how the internet transports the packets of millions of users for long distances and includes the bulk of the world's undersea cables. It is mostly fiber optic, and it is highly efficient because it is in the best interests of the folk who build it to ensure that. You may debate whether sending streamed TV or online gaming packets across the Atlantic is a good use of energy, but because it is being done on fiber-optic cable, it is at least efficient.

The *metro* is what crosses towns and city centers to carry the traffic of thousands of urban users. It is also usually fiber optic and also efficient.

The *last mile* describes the part that gets an individual user their personal packets in their home, while sitting in a coffee shop, or while standing on a train watching YouTube on their phone. In reality, the "last mile" might cover 50 miles or 50 feet, depending where you live. It could be copper wires, fiber-optic cables, or radio waves in the form of 3G, 4G, or 5G. It might even come all the way from low Earth orbit (LEO) via satellite systems like Starlink (*https://www.starlink.com*), OneWeb (*https:// oneweb.net*), or Amazon's Project Kuipe (*https://oreil.ly/EHpbS*).

How Do Compute and Storage Fit In?

For years, compute and storage have played a significant role in reducing the load on the wires and improving efficiency. They do this by providing data compression, clever transcoding, and caching, among other techniques. No one knows how many CPUs are doing this work as part of the internet, but many experts reckon a plausible estimate is one hundred billion.

One hundred billion is also the usual estimate for the number of neurons there are in a human brain, how many stars there are in the galaxy, and Elon Musk's personal wealth in $$$$. That might be a universal coincidence, some kind of existential conspiracy, or a hint that one hundred billion is the number humans pick when they mean, "Err...a lot?"

The person in the street also adds their own compute and storage to the internet via the capabilities of their smartphones, laptops, and other devices. However, most of it resides either in data centers or in "edge" mini DCs located close to where data is generated or near to users (edge DCs are designed to improve response times and require less data to be transmitted on networks at peak times, resulting in faster and cheaper services).

We now understand the components that make up the internet: wires, compute, and storage. But how do they fit together?

 A question you might be asking yourself: are you always better off swapping additional compute—for instance, to do compression—for less data transmission on wires? As usual the answer is "It depends."

As a result of networks and network devices continually becoming more efficient, less than 10% of the electricity bill (*https://oreil.ly/y7oKZ*) of a well-designed modern data center is spent on operating the wires, routers, and switches (although in an older DC, that proportion can be much higher). Basically, fiber networks have become more efficient than computation. The result is that, in a modern DC, you might sometimes be better off sending data uncompressed. However, if your data is highly and easily compressible, if you are sending it at a busy time, or if it benefits from compression hardware like video codec chips (*https://oreil.ly/EFsOW*), then you should compress it.

As always, use the most fitted compression option for the job. There are lots out there, so it is worth putting in some research. Unfortunately, many compression algorithms, which are essentially green tech, have hefty patent costs (*https://oreil.ly/InCPi*). Low-cost, green compression options could be the subject of an entire book, and it would be nice to see one.

More Than the Sum of Its Parts?

The internet is not a homogenous thing. It is a network of networks.

What we refer to as the internet is actually thousands of different networks all connected together. They often operate over multiple data centers and are internally controlled with their own routers and switches using a variety of networking protocols. These smaller discrete networks, which are often owned and run by private companies (*https://asrank.caida.org*), are called autonomous systems (*https://oreil.ly/Yp4J3*). You may never have heard of autonomous systems, but they are the basis of the public internet.

Although some autonomous systems exist only to route data, many also act as ordinary data centers that provide business-as-usual computing services to the companies that operate them.

If you have your own Wi-Fi router for your home network (we'll try not to remind you of the harrowing few hours you spent getting that set up), then in almost all cases, that network is part of an autonomous system belonging to your ISP. You are probably unaware of the huge autonomous system of which your house is a tiny piece.

Whatever size they are, all these networks use electricity, and they have embodied carbon in their wires, physical routers, and switches as well as in their servers and storage equipment (see Figure 7-1). There are networks that potentially could have less embodied carbon, for example, satellite systems like SpaceX's Starlink. But are such systems part of the solution or part of the problem?

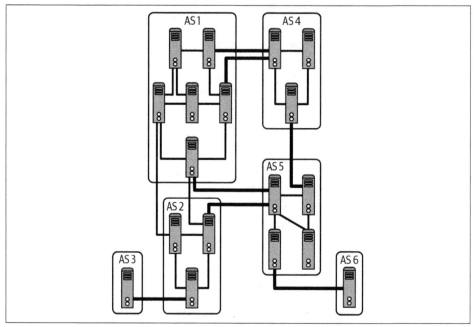

Figure 7-1. The internet is a network of connected autonomous systems

Are Internet Satellites Good or Bad?

Starlink (*https://www.starlink.com*), the communications system from Elon Musk's SpaceX, provides internet connectivity from low Earth orbit (LEO) via a fleet of orbiting satellites. Love it or hate it, Starlink is an ethical and green can of worms. Fortunately, we love opening those.

Putting aside whether or not we like Musk (everything's not always about you, Elon), let's consider the pros and cons of using satellites to extend the internet to parts of the globe that terrestrial connections cannot (or do not) reach. It's an idea that presents an extreme case of the trade-offs of networking, technology, energy use, and the ultimate priorities of humanity. So you might want to grab a snack.

When Sara worked in the operations department of one telco, the company had some stations in the far, far north of Sweden. She remembers, "Wow it was a *pain* when one of those broke. It could easily be a daylong drive plus a good trek for the poor service engineer to swap a faulty part. And if it included climbing, there had to be two people. It was expensive as heck for something that could be a very cheap broken part." Telcos refer to these as "truck rolls," and they are something every ISP wants to avoid if at all possible, which is one of the reasons not everywhere has great internet connectivity.

LEO: Cons

There are some significant downsides to having a huge number of satellites (*https:// oreil.ly/9iNtW*) in low Earth orbit (LEO), and we really could be talking about a *huge* number of satellites.

The trouble is, each satellite can only serve a limited set of users due to wave interference (*https://oreil.ly/9iNtW*). Those annoying laws of physics.

For a full internet replacement, we wouldn't need 100 billion satellites, but we would require a heck of a lot more than the 12,000 initially proposed by SpaceX for Starlink, or even the 42,000 (*https:// oreil.ly/yLhOH*) that count has since risen to. Realistically, because of the colossal numbers required, something like Starlink is not going to be a replacement for the internet and all of its embodied carbon in the near future. However, even without such lofty ambitions, 42K satellites is a lot and it's probably only the start.

The negatives of high numbers of orbiting satellites include:

- The embodied carbon in those sophisticated pieces of equipment, which have a limited shelf/orbit life.
- Risk of collisions, potentially even resulting in a situation where LEO becomes an unusable debris field of smashed satellites—a so-called Kessler syndrome (*https:// oreil.ly/DnkJV*). This is not precisely a green issue, but it is a major concern).
- Photobombing astronomical observations (*https://oreil.ly/P8TYi*) from Earth.
- Energy spent on launches (*https://oreil.ly/Qwybu*). Even if the rocket fuel is hydrogen, that can be carbon intensive to produce).

In 1978, the NASA scientist Donald Kessler raised the concern that if satellites ever began smashing into one another, it could lead to a feedback loop where each crash led to more debris, making another crash with that detritus more likely until all the satellites in an orbit were smashed and there was so much trash up there, you couldn't use the orbit or perhaps even pass through it. This was dubbed a Kessler syndrome.

A Kessler syndrome in LEO would (hopefully) not be apocalyptic because there is still enough atmospheric drag (*https://oreil.ly/ 2be8t*) up there that most of the pieces would eventually fall to Earth and burn up. In other words, it's self-hoovering in a few decades. That is roughly the same kind of time it takes for methane to decay in the atmosphere—another of those cosmic coincidences.

You could argue LEO is therefore a *relatively* safe place to get the hang of the engineering required to handle collision avoidance. It's safer, anyway, than risking a Kessler event in a higher orbit outside of the atmosphere from which Earth would never naturally recover—the resulting space junk would hang around forever.

Nevertheless, the loss of LEO for 20 years would still be less than ideal (a British understatement there). On top of this, due to high-speed collisions, some of the debris would inevitably get kicked up into higher and more dangerously permanent orbits.

LEO: Pros

On the other side of the scales, LEO satellite systems could potentially provide internet connectivity to places that would be hard to hook up otherwise. This includes many parts of Africa (*https://oreil.ly/RKATO*). Satellites also require less terrestrial last-mile infrastructure (thus less embodied carbon) and can be powered directly by solar panels. If we could make them work and get the costs down, they might therefore be a green tool in some situations.

Universal internet access is an important part of the UN's Sustainable Development Goals (*https://oreil.ly/uRiPt*) for humanity, and there are moral, philosophical, and practical reasons why the benefits of connecting everyone on Earth might outweigh the risks and green issues. As well as being an ethical imperative, universal internet access is an important element in global education which, according to Project Drawdown (*https://oreil.ly/uScpL*), is vital for the energy transition. Moving off fossil fuels will be very, very difficult, and the more educated brains from every part of the globe we can get working on the problem and staffing green jobs, the more likely we are to succeed.

Bill Gates extends this fairness and human capital argument in his book *How to Avoid a Climate Disaster* (*https://www.amazon.co.uk/ How-Avoid-Climate-Disaster-Breakthroughs/dp/0241448301*) to suggest that Sub-Saharan African countries should get a free pass on carbon emissions until they can get themselves into a reasonable state with respect to food and energy security as well as education. We can see the point he is making.

Unfortunately, however, even with satellites (and they are not the only option), universal connectivity isn't a given. For example, Starlink is currently too expensive for it to become ubiquitous throughout Africa. In addition, as the Tony Blair institute (*https://oreil.ly/i2XxI*) has pointed out, LEO could be chock-full of cheap satellites and it would still not guarantee a truly global internet because technology is not the trickiest bit of that problem. The cost of smartphones, lack of literacy and digital skills, and lack of accessibility are all greater barriers to universal internet access (never mind Sub-Saharan Africa; there are barriers even in the UK).

So are satellites green or not?

It's hard to guess whether internet satellites will turn out to be a green technology or not, but we do know that a high-scale, efficient green system would inevitably require a heck of a lot of satellites in orbit. That suggests success will rather depend on whether they all crash into one another and wipe out LEO for a generation. However, we do know that "We'll connect Africa!" is not an unchallengeable response to all objections to satellites because, alone, satellites are not enough to achieve it.

The Role of Software

Stepping back, this book is not about hardware, spaceware, or global politics! This is supposed to be a book about software and how *that* can make the internet greener. The good news is, we do have multiple options there, even if they are less sci-fi and more terrestrial.

Software has major roles to play in greening networks:

- It can be used to reduce the amount of traffic transmitted on wires, meaning less infrastructure is required, lowering embodied carbon and electricity use.

- It can spread the traffic load, ensuring devices and cables have a higher lifetime utilization, which again reduces infrastructure requirements and delivers better ROI on embodied carbon.

- It could make the wires, compute, and storage of the internet way more carbon aware (i.e., do more work when and where the electricity is low carbon and less when the carbon intensity is high—a.k.a. demand shifting).

Hurray! That sounds great!

It is. However, we need to be careful about how we tackle internet-scale carbon awareness within networks. There are dangers, rabbit holes, and distractions, and there is a big difference between how risky or effective demand shifting is likely to be depending on where in the network stack it happens.

For example, are we talking about predictable, well established, and well understood techniques at the application level or low-level interventions like routing traffic differently?

Why Can't We Just Make Routing Greener?

The data packets of the public internet get from A to B via physical routers that choose which pipe to send each packet down next. Unfortunately, that is a genuinely difficult choice.

Border Gateway Protocol

Even if you are doom scrolling on the International Space Station or somewhere similarly limited in its connections, there are still a staggering number of different paths a packet from Facebook or X (or whatever it's called today) could take to get to you. The routers of the public internet attempt to pick the best one using something called the Border Gateway Protocol (*https://oreil.ly/OhDVF*) (BGP).

BGP routers don't calculate end-to-end routes for packets. That would be impossible to operate at internet scale because the number of potential routes is too huge. Instead, BGP takes a simpler approach. It calculates which router your packet will travel through next on what *should* be the optimal route to its destination—or at least a good enough one.

A BGP router's decisions are based on a combination of things, including:

- Trying to minimize the number of autonomous systems transited by the packet
- Taking into account policy rules and commercial arrangements between the operator of that router and the autonomous systems it is connected to

Crucially, BGP is only interested in the next "hop" in the route. It doesn't know much about (and can make no guarantees of) the packet's end-to-end journey.

So, given that BGP route calculations are already based on several factors, couldn't greenness just become one of them? For example, if I were routing a packet between places on opposite sides of the world (e.g., from London, UK, to Sydney, Australia), couldn't BGP send it on the route that was more in sunshine—and thus solar powered—even if the darker route would be faster?

That is the question we will attempt to answer next.

The risks and rewards of changing BGP

Technically, BGP could take sustainability factors into account when routing. BGP is just code, and in theory, everything's technically possible. However, would it be the best way to deliver reduced carbon emissions?

Although low-level networking is highly optimized already, there is a heck of a lot of traffic out there (even if networking accounts for just 10% of the internet's gross energy usage, that could still be 30 TW per year (*https://oreil.ly/W2u0j*)). The potential reward for routing it via networks powered by renewably generated electricity is therefore significant.

However, it is not clear that changing or replacing BGP routing is the right way to achieve this payoff. There are several problems with the approach:

- BGP is amazing, but its importance means it is also the weakest link in the stability of the internet. Every time a massive internet outage occurs, we all think, "I bet it's a BGP misconfiguration!" and we're usually right (unless it's DNS). BGP is complex, is critical, and relies on trust and on ISP administrators never making a major mistake. As far as we can tell, there is little appetite among network experts to add further complexity to it, and they have excellent reasons for that attitude. Their main priority is a stable internet, and up until now, BGP in its current form has provided it. Partial outages happen, but the internet as a whole stays up.

- The commercial incentives for autonomous system owners are complex, and it's not straightforward to align them with our green agenda using BGP. Some autonomous systems make their money by being a hop in the internet and may actively want traffic. Others provide their autonomous system as a necessary contribution to the internet but would be very happy if less traffic were routed through it because that traffic is just a cost to them. If being a greener route would garner more traffic, that would be an incentive for some autonomous systems to be green but a disincentive for others. It therefore isn't clear that routing based on greenness would be the optimal way to encourage all networks to go green. The results might be unpredictable.

Mucking around with BGP (*https://oreil.ly/7Nz91*) to enable data to follow the sun or route around carbon-intense regions is therefore something we authors wouldn't want to touch with a 10-foot pole. Our strong suspicion is that the risks and issues with greener BGP routing would outweigh the benefits.

The reality is, although there are problems with BGP, the underlying quality of the routing isn't one of them. If I send a data packet from New York to Paris, once it leaves the data center at my end, BGP will efficiently route it more or less straight to its destination. Unless something goes horribly wrong, we can feel confident it won't end up circumnavigating Earth 20 times and, just as importantly, it will get where it is headed. We shouldn't take that confidence for granted. It was hard won.

We cannot be so sanguine about what our software systems might do to the data *inside* the data center before it leaves. It could be split apart and pass through hundreds of microservices using an energy-intensive variety of service mesh. It could be unnecessarily saved in carbon-intensive storage media. It could be duplicated in multiple regions for a level of high redundancy that isn't truly required.

There are few ways network users (i.e., us software developers) can badly screw up sending a packet. We could send more data than is required, or less, or the wrong data, but those are application-level problems, not routing ones. Software architecture is a lot more likely to make the internet inefficient than BGP.

One day, BGP will have to be replaced because it isn't scalable enough. However, upgrading it will be a major, decades-long undertaking and possibly the hardest challenge the internet has yet faced. As Jon Berger points out, "More of the networking behavior of the internet is emergent than we like to think. Changing as fundamental a component as BGP will not be easy or safe."

Radically improving the sustainability of the internet is something we have to do now. Revolutionizing BGP is also necessary but a long-term project.

We authors would prefer to decouple these two very hard problems, and fortunately, we can. Changing BGP isn't the low-hanging fruit when it comes to greening the internet and isn't a blocking issue. Application-level improvements are well understood, more impactful, safer, and faster to implement. They also have multiple knock-on benefits. As we are about to hear, several of these were demonstrated during the COVID pandemic…

Greening the Internet from the Top Down

It is tricky to tell whether society as a whole learned much from the lockdowns of 2020, but the tech industry did, and we learned it right at the start—within the first few months or even weeks.

The good news is those learnings are extremely relevant to the energy transition, even if most of us didn't realize it at the time.

Lessons from Lockdown

At the start of the COVID lockdowns, the internet had to handle a massive surge in demand as billions of people worldwide switched their face-to-face interactions to virtual conferencing. This was all done without adding any extra network infrastructure.

According to John Graham-Cumming (*https://oreil.ly/nYPrL*), chief technology officer of the CDN firm Cloudflare, "It's hard to imagine another utility (say electricity, water, or gas) coping with a sudden and continuous increase in demand of 50%."

As a result of this unprecedented need for bandwidth, software engineers had to learn about resource management in a hurry. Specifically, they had to rapidly get their head around the concepts of:

- Demand shifting and shaping using clever (often cloud) architectures like CDNs
- Graceful service downgrades
- Efficiency upgrades (which we covered in Chapter 2)

Demand Shifting

As we discussed in Chapter 5, a fundamental feature of renewable energy is that it is not always available. The sun isn't always shining, and the wind isn't always blowing. One of the ways we can deal with such variability is by only doing work when there is clean power available for it, even if that isn't time synchronized with the demand for the work. Achieving this is called demand shifting or time shifting, and an example is provided by CDNs. CDNs handle limited bandwidth rather than limited power availability, but the concepts and techniques are similar.

For decades, internet response times have been speeded up by CDNs. The earliest were marketed as ways for website customers to see images or videos faster, and they achieved that by storing copies of assets all over the world, close to requesting users. CDNs were effectively a magic trick: the asset seemed to have traveled to the user more quickly, but in reality it was already waiting nearby.

CDNs use pretransmission, preprocessing, and precaching of data assets, all of which are demand-shifting techniques.

 Note that "demand shifting" is a misnomer in some cases, including that of CDNs. The *demand* hasn't been shifted, but rather the *work* has been shifted to a different point in time. Fundamentally, the decoupling of work from demand is what we are trying to achieve with demand shifting.

The purpose of CDNs is to improve access speed, and that is great for end-user experience. However, when the pandemic hit, it was their resource management capabilities that proved invaluable.

The premise of a CDN is that it makes smart use of storage. One instance of a large digital asset moves the long distance from the asset's supplier to the CDN, where it is cached. Copies of the asset (let's say it's an HD video) are then sent the shorter distances to their final destinations in the homes of customers who are demanding immediate access to the *Barbie* movie or maybe even *Oppenheimer*. The result is that the overall load on the internet is reduced compared to if all of those giant assets had been sent end to end.

In addition, the size of the asset copy sent from the CDN can be tailored to the end consumer. Someone on a phone might get a lower-resolution, smaller version than someone on a 4K TV. Again, this reduces internet traffic.

That is not the only win. Because the original assets are being moved into position on the CDN in advance, they can be sent when the network is quiet. That flattens peak loads and gets better utilization out of all that embodied carbon in the network. If you know which of your assets folk are going to want to access and when (and you often do, that's what marketing is for), you can make the internet more efficient using a CDN. As we discussed earlier, reducing traffic or smoothing it out to get rid of peaks and improve utilization is green. Less electricity is required to send the data, and less infrastructure needs to be built to transmit it.

Sometimes the huge asset doesn't even get transported over a network at all. Netflix (*https://oreil.ly/zomJx*) sends copies of their films to CDNs in trucks.

Yes, physical trucks. As a wise man (*https://oreil.ly/L8xeY*) named Andrew Tanenbaum once said, "Never underestimate the bandwidth of a station wagon full of tapes hurtling down the highway."

CDNs are a real-world example of the concept of demand shifting, and they were one of the ways the internet survived 2020. However, they were not the only one.

Brownouts, Graceful Downgrades, and Demand Shaping

One way to preserve a service is to plan for how you're *not* going to preserve it.

A brownout is what happens when you drop the quality of energy-related services in an area when there is a shortage of power. They are named after a historical symptom of low-grid power, which is that filament bulbs get dimmer and everything looks a little murky.

A brownout is a physical example of a so-called graceful downgrade: the maintenance of limited functionality in the face of system issues rather than total failure (in this case, a full blackout). Facing COVID-related bandwidth shortages, Netflix did its own version of a brownout. As a graceful downgrade, Netflix cut its network traffic by reducing the quality of its EU service offering by switching its video encodings from high definition to low (*https://oreil.ly/Xz9_v*). Our lockdown movies may have been a bit grainier as a result, but we could still watch them. This was also an example of *demand shaping.*

Videoconferencing (VC) companies like Zoom used service downgrades to achieve a similar effect. VC is a textbook example of where you can perform bandwidth equivalents of brownouts. According to network industry expert Christopher Liljen-stolpe (*https://oreil.ly/wEpPd*), "Current mass-market VC systems are very bandwidth forgiving. That's prevented the [pandemic] meltdown."

VC services make heavy use of QoS (quality of service) techniques (*https://oreil.ly/TxIVp*) of monitoring and prioritization to handle bandwidth variability. For example, high-quality audio is vital to a call but relatively cheap in terms of network usage. Video is way more resource intensive, but its quality can be reduced if necessary without the call suffering too much. Audio data is therefore labeled and prioritized over video data by networks.

VC services also use cunning wheezes like kitten filters and backgrounds, which reduce the amount of video data that has to be sent.

 In the case of high-definition (HD) to standard-definition (SD) encoding changes, "demand shaping" is again a slight misnomer. The demand wasn't changed, but rather it was the service level that was dropped in order to maintain a minimum quality. Kitten filters are definitely demand shaping, though. Customers specifically choose to use a filter that, unbeknownst to them, reduces their bandwidth requirements. For the sake of convenience, we're lumping these together because the effect is similar: bandwidth requirements are reduced.

It's not just VC services that can handle bandwidth variability. Most well-architected applications have some mechanism for coping with dodgy networks because (even without BGP outages) sometimes the internet is flaky.

That is why internet thinking is ahead of the rest of the tech sector on demand shifting and shaping. As software architects, we need to come up with our own cunning wheezes for handling times when energy will be nonexistent or very expensive. We provided some ideas in Chapter 5.

Winter is coming

Dynamic tariffs are a kind of electricity tariff where the costs change from half hour to half hour, depending on what's available on the local grid. Because renewable power is now cheaper than fossil fuels, dynamic tariffs often reflect how green the currently available power is.

Such tariffs have already been introduced in Spain (*https://oreil.ly/wsl7p*) and several other countries and regions in the EU and North America. They are inevitable for the rest of us and will require a shift in our mindsets. We have had decades to get used to designing for flaky internet connections, but most of us still have an old-fashioned view of electricity as 100% available. It's time for us to start thinking about graceful service downgrade options for power in the same way we do for limited bandwidth availability.

So, What Did We Learn from 2020?

The internet is an example of something incredibly resilient. To handle the pandemic, service offerings were gracefully downgraded in thousands of ways by engineers and product managers and by the users who accepted and worked around those degradations. In the face of a crisis, they all pulled in the same direction toward one goal: to keep things running.

The irony is that didn't work so effectively because the internet is ordinarily a solid, reliable platform. Arguably, it worked because it isn't, it wasn't, and it never has been.

The internet is full of flaws. It is a kind of built-in chaos-engineering platform, and every application that runs on it successfully has to be capable of handling issues and outages.

The reality is, it is easier to switch from running on a 90%-reliable platform to a 50%-reliable one than it is to move from 100% reliability to 95%. Few brand-new "Keep going, internet!" levers were pulled during the COVID crisis. They were already tried and tested.

It's amazing what humanity can achieve when we have to. However, things would have been very different if we'd had to pivot from an assumption of 100% internet reliability. When it comes to power resilience, we software engineers are going to have to learn a hard lesson very fast because we too often assume 100% power reliability.

In Conclusion

As a rule of thumb, the lower layers of the internet are efficient but the upper layers aren't, and that is where we should be focusing our attention first. There is plenty of opportunity for improvement at the application level.

Counterintuitively, the low-hanging fruit is at the top of the stack.

In this chapter, we looked at some real-world examples of internet demand shifting and shaping. We also looked at how knowing that a platform is flaky causes engineers to focus more on reliability and efficiency and often therefore results in a more reliable system overall. These chaos-engineering techniques are what kept the internet up during the COVID pandemic, and we need to use similar ones for handling the coming transition to less predictable renewable power.

So what must we do?

- Start architecting everything for dynamic tariffs.
- Make sure that any platform we rely on has a plan for dynamic tariffs, power outages, demand shifting, and demand shaping.
- Stop making the assumption that power is 100% available. Start thinking of it more like bandwidth or connectivity and consider demand management and graceful downgrade strategies.

The commodity tools we have available that already do demand shifting and shaping (for example, CDNs and spot instances) will be vital to the energy transition.

The good news is that during the lockdowns, our industry was able to switch to a new way of doing things fast when we had to. However, the internet had always been flaky, and that meant downgrades, demand shifting, and demand shaping had been vital and familiar parts of application design since the beginning. We are not used to applying the same expectations to electricity from the grid.

We need to get used to it.

CHAPTER 8

Greener Machine Learning, AI, and LLMs

A computer would deserve to be called intelligent if it could deceive a human into believing that it was human.

—Alan Turing

In late March of 2023, Bill Gates wrote in his blog *GatesNotes* (*https://oreil.ly/xmLXk*), "The Age of AI Has Begun," and said that artificial intelligence will be as revolutionary as mobile phones or the internet. That is quite the statement, especially for the two authors who are barely old enough to remember a time without mobile phones or the internet. There is no denying that we live in the age of AI and machine learning (ML). Never before has it had as profound an impact on our lives as it has right now. AI makes splashy headlines in all areas of life, from art to medicine to warfare to school papers to climate.

AI is not new. Alan Turing first suggested the idea of a "thinking machine" in his paper "Computing Machinery and Intelligence" in 1950.[1] In this article he defines the now world-famous idea of "The Imitation Game," which we now call the Turing test. The test is designed to judge whether or not a computer has human, or humanlike, cognitive abilities. This idea was, and still is over 70 years later, captivating and thought-provoking—not only to industry folks like you and us, but also to Hollywood, as evidenced by several adaptations of the idea, such as *Westworld* (*https://oreil.ly/dxKpE*), *Ex Machina* (*https://oreil.ly/UVUgM*), and *The Imitation Game* (*https://oreil.ly/xfKkd*).

Since the first AI models, in the 1950s and 1960s, AI continued to develop at the same pace as Moore's law up until 2012.[2] After that, model size exploded. In the early

---

1 A. M. Turing, "Computing Machinery and Intelligence," *Mind* 49 (1950): 433–60, *https://oreil.ly/kcDuI*.

2 "AI and Compute," OpenAI, accessed May 16, 2018, *https://oreil.ly/B063Q*

months of 2023, the world saw a new paradigm shift with large language models (LLMs) becoming available to the general public through models and services like ChatGPT (*https://oreil.ly/dcK4H*), Microsoft365 Copilot (*https://oreil.ly/UBp8a*), and Google's PaLM 2 (*https://oreil.ly/tPqHP*). LLMs are a type of AI algorithm that uses deep learning techniques and massively large data sets to understand, summarize, generate, and predict new content. These models dramatically increased the amount of data used for training and inference compared to previous language models.

In this chapter, we will focus on how to build greener ML and AI systems, not on whether or not AI will change our lives or take over the world. However, we feel like this is the place to say that we consider climate change to be a larger threat to humanity than the rise of AI.

To understand why AI deserves its own chapter, we'll walk you through the rapid growth of AI usage and AI models—spoiler: it is way, way faster than Moore's law.[3] The bulk of this chapter is dedicated to mitigation approaches across the ML life cycle. The life cycle can be defined in many ways, but for this chapter we will stick with a simplified model (see Figure 8-1). Green AI could be a whole book in and of itself. This chapter is more of a snackable bite size.

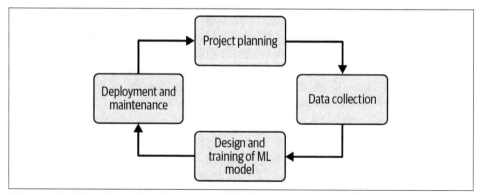

Figure 8-1. A flowchart describing a simplified version of the ML life cycle

Growth in Size and Usage

We have already mentioned that AI models originally grew approximately at the speed of Moore's law. Hardware has always been an enabler for AI. Moore's law was initially enough, but in later years the increased use of parallelization, GPUs, and other specialized hardware like AI accelerators has (no pun intended) accelerated the field further.

---

3 Gordon E. Moore, "Cramming More Components onto Integrated Circuits," *Electronics* 38, no. 8 (April 19, 1965), *https://oreil.ly/r73IX*.

How does model size impact sustainability of ML? Let's look at an example. In 2019 Emma Strubell, Ananya Ganesh, and Andrew McCallum wrote a paper called "Energy and Policy Considerations for Deep Learning in NLP (*https://oreil.ly/NdFIB*)," which by now is heavily cited. In this paper, they characterized the dollar cost and carbon emissions of deep learning in natural language processing. Specifically they analyzed four popular—what they called "off-the-shelf"—models: Transformer, ELMo, BERT, and GPT-2. One of the most cited results from that paper is that training Transformer (with 213 million parameters) with neural architecture search one single time emitted as much carbon as an American car would emit in five lifetimes. This is quite significant. The smaller models in the paper have a smaller carbon cost associated with them, yet many chose to only cite the data from training the Transformer model. This raised the criticism that a model with the size of Transformer would be very rare due to how expensive it was to train, in dollar cost. How wrong they were. Since then, model size has exploded and large models are no longer a rarity. The large models we have seen in 2022, 2023, and 2024 have several hundred billion parameters,[4] which is about a thousand times larger than Transformer.

So we know that model size is growing, causing increased carbon cost for training. However, training is only one piece of the puzzle. It is the area where we as of now have the most research available, which is likely more a reflection of the state of research than the state of software companies' operations. The use of AI features is growing rapidly too. The McKinsey survey "State of AI in 2022" (*https://oreil.ly/Ffv-q*) shows that AI adoption more than doubled between 2017 and 2022, even though McKinsey did see a plateau in the first part of the 2020s. With the true breakthrough of large language models (LLMs) at the start of 2023, it will be interesting to see what the adoption rate looks like in McKinsey's future reports. The same report from McKinsey in 2022 also found that the number of AI capabilities used by organizations also doubled between 2018 and 2022, with NLP taking the lead. The *State of AI in the Enterprise* report from Deloitte (*https://oreil.ly/wW2Ut*) in 2022 found that 94% of respondents say AI is critical to success and 79% of respondents say they've fully deployed three or more types of AI, compared to just 62% in 2021.

To summarize, we can see that the size of AI models is growing as well as the usage of said models. This makes AI and sustainability interesting to talk about, beyond asking ChatGPT if it believes in climate change or not.

---

4 Irene Solaiman, "The Gradient of Generative AI Release: Methods and Considerations," *FAccT '23: Proceedings of the 2023 ACM Conference on Fairness, Accountability, and Transparency* (June 2023): 111–12, *https://oreil.ly/mn57W*.

Project Planning

Project planning is the first phase of most software products. This is where you really have the chance to design for green. Now is a great time to ask difficult questions! Questions like "What will be the climate impact of this new system?" or "How do we plan to measure the impact?" Changing the design when your product is still a paper product is much cheaper compared with when it is already written, deployed, and in use.

If you want to include some carbon-aware features, like demand shaping, this is a great time to start these conversations. Demand shaping means changing the behavior of your product depending on the carbon intensity of your grid, like we talked about in Chapter 5. If you need a refresher, you can think of how the video quality of a videoconferencing call changes depending on your internet bandwidth. The same thinking can be applied to the carbon intensity of the grid. Maybe you serve less computationally intense recommendations when the user's grid is dirty? Project planning is a good time to have these conversations.

Two other things to consider in the early phases are your service-level agreements (SLAs) and service-level objectives (SLOs). According to Adrian Cockcroft, ex-VP of Sustainable Architecture at AWS, "The biggest win is often changing requirements or SLAs. Reduce retention time for log files. Relax overspecified goals."[5] Critically considering what service-level targets your service or customer actually needs and not delivering more than needed can be a big sustainability win.

Data Collection

Data collection is the second phase of the ML life cycle. Data collection means gathering raw data from potentially various sources. These sources could be things like your own internal sales system, the internet, a small part of the internet like a specific forum website, or survey data.

This phase is often seen as a less glamorous part of the ML life cycle. We use all sorts of euphemisms to further emphasize how not fun this part is: "crap in, crap out," "data cleaning," "panning for gold," etc. All these comparisons bring your imagination to dirty manual labor. It is a little ironic that data collection has such a bad rep, when we do know that data quality issues have a cascading effect further ahead in the life cycle, such as reducing accuracy.

As we build larger ML models, they need larger data sets to prevent overfitting and for the data in our model to actually be representative of the full, real-world data. Large data sets can also potentially be reused for other projects later, so they become

---

5 Adrian Cockcroft, personal communication.

even more attractive. Since data sets are growing, it means that green data collection is becoming increasingly important in order to keep carbon cost down. Even so, there is surprisingly little research on how much of the carbon footprint the data collection stands for. But fear not, there are some tools you can use to minimize the footprint of your data collection pipeline.

Firstly, critically think about how much data you actually need and whether there are already open source data sets that could suit your scenario. Using already gathered data means that you do not have to spend additional carbon emissions building your own data pipeline. Luckily for you, there are already lots of data sets available to use, some open source and free, others available at a cost. Just to mention two examples, Hugging Face (*https://huggingface.co*) has over 110,000 data sets available and Kaggle (*https://www.kaggle.com*) has over 300,000 data sets available. Both of these resources are open source and publicly available, and they cover a wide range of scenarios, from images of cats to avocado prices to neonatal mortality in SAARC countries, just to name a few.

Large data sets often carry ethical implications as well. There can be a lack of informed consent in how these data sets are built and used, or it might not even be possible to later on withdraw your consent to being a part of the data set. This has sparked some debate in the art community with the rise of high-quality AI-generated images, but as software practitioners, your code could be used in AI models, so this is a concern not only for artists but for all.

Another example of ethical implications can be seen with the rise of reinforcement learning with human feedback (RLHF). Reinforcement learning first only used *raw data* for training, meaning data that has not been labeled but rather has been only scraped from the internet in massive quantities. This often worked quite well on a technical level, although not always, but that is a story for another time. RLHF did have some issues with content, which soon became too large to ignore. As you can imagine, the internet is full of examples of content that might not be suitable for a professional context or might be downright appalling. To combat this, RLHF was created. It uses a combination of raw data and human-labeled data. This technique is used by newer LLMs. This labeling is the cause for ethical concern. *TIME* reported in January 2023 (*https://oreil.ly/dw0Xj*) how Kenyan workers were paid less than $2 per hour and had to label violent, sexist, and racist data in order to purge the model of undesired content. AI and ethics is another topic that is a book in and of itself, so we'll leave the rest for extracurricular activities for the extra-interested ones.

In times when data collection does not need to happen on demand, consider demand shifting as one way to make use of when and where there is green energy available to us. In Chapter 5, you learned more about how this can be achieved.

Design and Training of ML Models

Up next in the ML life cycle: the design and training of ML models. This is perhaps the most distinctive part of the ML life cycle, where this type of software differs the most from other types of software. It is also an area where we have quite a lot of data and mitigation approaches available to make the phase greener.

Size Matters

Training large models requires significant storage and compute cycles. By shrinking the model size, it is possible to speed up training time as well as increase the resource efficiency of training. This can in turn save not only time but money and carbon. Shrinking the model sizes is an ongoing research area, with several initiatives exploring topics like pruning, compression, distillation, and quantization, among other techniques. As you learned in Chapter 4, being more resource efficient isn't a silver bullet on its own, but rather it unlocks the potential to be greener as you can achieve more with the same hardware and energy. The rise of *edge computing*, in which data is processed by devices or servers at the "edge" of the network (i.e., closer to the end user), and the Internet of Things (IoT) means we are seeing more and more devices with limited capabilities; smaller models will be the way to go for these kinds of devices. Another perk of edge computing is reducing the energy consumption by doing the processing and storage closer to the data source, a sustainability win-win.

One of the shrinking techniques is *quantization*, a technique that maps continuous infinite values to a smaller set of discrete finite values. In the world of ML, this means representing the ML model with low-precision data types, like 8-bit integers, instead of the usual 32-bit floating point. This is a green technique for several reasons. It saves storage space and is thus more resource efficient, just like the other shrinking techniques mentioned previously. Additionally, it allows for some operations to perform much faster with integer arithmetic, which saves energy and resources. When quantization is performed during the training phase, it is called *quantization-aware training*. Meta experimented with training quantization for its LLaMA model in the paper "LLM-QAT: Data-Free Quantization Aware Training for Large Language Models" (*https://oreil.ly/tkohZ*). The company experimented with LLaMA models of sizes 7B, 13B, and 30B, and it showed accurate 4-bit quantization is possible using this technique. This was one of the first instances of quantization-aware training being successfully used for LLMs, which opens the door to more resource-efficient training for LLMs.

Another example of model-shrinking techniques is pruning. This is shown in the paper "PruneTrain: Fast Neural Network Training by Dynamic Sparse Model Reconfiguration" (*https://oreil.ly/VzddI*), in which the authors attempt to use pruning in the training phase to decrease the model size. For an image classification scenario, they could show significant reductions in training time and resource use in terms of FLOPs, memory use, and interaccelerator communication.

 Using smaller models can also be a way to democratize ML research. If training models "worthy" of research publications require massive computational power, the potential contributors are limited to institutions with deep pockets. This can easily cause fairness issues with only a small crowd being able to contribute to cutting-edge research. With smaller models, anyone with a laptop can contribute to the field.

Size Isn't All

While limiting the size of ML models is one great option, there are more available to you when it comes to making your training greener. For example, ML training has the great benefit of very rarely being urgent. Yup, you guessed it: this means it is a great candidate for demand shifting (read more about this in Chapter 5).

Another option, perhaps most widely used for image recognition or natural language processing, is to leverage pretrained models. This can be done in two ways, either by using the model as is or by using transfer learning. Using an existing model as is will make your training phase very green, as you can practically skip the training altogether. And the greenest software is the software that does not exist (it is also the most boring). Just like in the data collection phase, the community has come together, and lots of models already exist and are available to you, either publicly or for purchase. To reuse our examples from before, Hugging Face (*https://hugging face.co*) has over 400,000 models available and Kaggle (*https://www.kaggle.com*) has over 2,000 models publicly available.

If you cannot find a perfect model to reuse but find one that is almost right, you can use transfer learning. The general idea of transfer learning is that you have a model trained on a large data set, with generic enough data to be considered a pretty good model of the world, which you reuse for a new purpose. Let's say you have a model that can detect cats in pictures. You can then use transfer learning to adapt the model to instead recognize monkeys. With transfer learning, you take advantage of the model already created and avoid retraining it from scratch. Instead, you can use techniques like fine-tuning or feature extraction[6] to adapt the model to your scenario.

---

6 "Transfer Learning and Fine-Tuning," TensorFlow, December 7, 2023, *https://oreil.ly/6vs5_*.

This saves carbon compared to a full retraining (and possibly data collection!) of a brand-new model. This technique is also a great one to talk to your CFO about, as it is much more economically feasible to adapt an existing model to a new problem compared to creating a new one from scratch.

Typically, ML models are trained centrally in a data center, which is very convenient when you have centralized data, but different approaches are available. Some of these approaches can be greener if applied with a little thought. One example is training on the edge, which was mentioned earlier in this chapter. Another example is federated learning (FL), which has been in production use by Google since 2017.[7] FL is a technique in which training is distributed across end-user devices, keeping all data local to the device but collaborating on the final model. The paper "Can Federated Learning Save the Planet?" (*https://oreil.ly/mwX43*) looks deeper into the environmental cost of federated learning compared to centralized training in terms of carbon cost. The findings show FL, despite being slower to converge, can be a greener technology than training centralized in data centers. Especially for smaller data sets or less complex models, FL can be a much greener technology.

The advancement of AI is closely linked to the advancement of hardware. OK, that is arguably true for all of the software industry, but this is even more so for AI. Chapter 6 has a deeper dive into the world of hardware and sustainability, so head over there for more content. In this chapter we'll settle for one example: specialized AI chips. AI chips can be used for both training and inference, and they typically include graphics processing units (GPUs), field-programmable gate arrays (FPGAs), and application-specific integrated circuits (ASICs), which are specialized for AI tasks. Because these chips are specialized for the tasks, unlike general-purpose hardware chips such as central processing units (CPUs), they are massively more efficient. Using a specialized AI chip for training can be ten to a thousand times more efficient than using generalized hardware.[8] This in turn yields a massive cost win, which, for example, image recognition scenarios have taken advantage of historically. Of course, we have to consider the embodied cost of any hardware produced as well, but more on that trade-off scenario in Chapter 6.

Deployment and Maintenance

For production companies, deployment and maintenance may very well be where the most carbon is spent. We can't say for sure, as the area is not well researched, at least not with publicly available results. However, logic dictates that with a full

---

7 Brendan McMahan and Daniel Ramage, "Federated Learning: Collaborative Machine Learning Without Centralized Training Data," Google Research, April 6, 2017, *https://oreil.ly/OjVMi*.

8 Saif M. Khan, "AI Chips: What They Are and Why They Matter," Center for Security and Emerging Technology, April 2020, *https://oreil.ly/vDINS*.

training only happening once and inference happening many, many, many times, this phase is where many of us should be spending our time and devoting attention. This might not be true for all ML scenarios, for example, in the research sphere, where models are primarily built for the purpose of writing a paper. But in the enterprise software sphere, where the authors of this book hang out, inference is well worth your attention.

One way to make deployment of your ML models greener is to decrease the size of the model in use. In the training section of this chapter, we saw that quantization, compression, and pruning can be used in the training phase to shrink the model size. These techniques can also be used post-training to decrease the size of the model used when inferencing. Decreasing the size of the final model means two things. Firstly, smaller devices can run these models, which might be great for IoT or client-side scenarios. Secondly, it makes deployment of these models cheaper and greener as smaller models in production means that you can be more resource efficient.

When talking about maintenance of ML models, we must mention MLOps (machine learning operations). *MLOps* is a field that lives in the intersection of machine learning, DevOps, and data engineering (see Figure 8-2). It aims to operationalize the process of taking machine learning models to production and then maintaining and monitoring them. When it comes to making the maintenance phase of the ML life cycle greener, we can conclude that MLOps and DevOps have a lot of things in common, even if they are not identical. As such, we can reuse much of what we learned in Chapter 4 when it comes to reducing the carbon footprint of our operations. The general lessons learned in Chapter 3 will also hold true for writing code to serve ML production workloads, so head back there for a reminder if you need it.

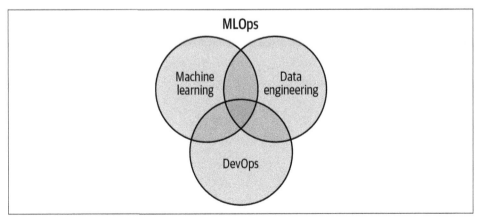

Figure 8-2. A diagram explaining the components of MLOps

Where Should You Start?

We hope that you now have some insights into why AI and ML are interesting to talk about from a sustainability perspective, and that we have provided you with some tools for each part of the life cycle. These tools involve using smaller data sets to make data collection greener and using transfer learning, model reuse, or smaller models to save carbon in the training phase. Likely your next question is, "Where in the life cycle do I spend the most carbon?"

The short answer is that it depends on your project! If you are working with very large models with brand-new data, it makes sense to start looking at your data collection. However, if you are trying to achieve superhigh accuracy or have a research scenario where you will not really use your model after its creation, then look into training cost. If you are running ML operations in your production workloads, chances are high that deployment and maintenance is where you are spending the most.

CHAPTER 9

Measurement

An experiment is a question which science poses to Nature and a measurement is the recording of Nature's answer.

—Max Planck

Metrics, measurements, or monitoring—whatever you choose to call it, software practitioners like numbers and charts that indicate our progress. Perhaps this is due to the intangible nature of our field? Or maybe all types of professionals who dedicate their time to building things are just as obsessed with measurements. Whatever the reason, here are some very commonly asked questions when talking about green software: How can I measure it? How do I know my impact? Which part of my software has the biggest impact? In this chapter, we will dive deeper into these questions and offer you some options for how to answer them.

In a perfect world, every item would have a neat carbon price attached to it, clearly showing the climate impact of each action we took or each product we purchased. That way we could always make informed choices with regard to climate. But as you have noticed in shops, that is not the case today. However, in this chapter, we will go through what "as close to perfect as you can get" would mean for software. Because we are opinionated people, we will also tell you what we would like to see the industry move toward: the real-time monitoring of carbon emissions. And for good measure, we will also tell you what the "good enough" measures are and when and how you can use them.

As with most things, we are of course not the first people to ponder these issues (thankfully). Therefore, we will also go over the current methodologies that other smart people have already put forth for our consideration. The goal is not to rate them but to inform you of their strengths and weaknesses so you can know when to use which and for what.

Does calculating your own carbon footprint sound a bit much? Well, you are in luck, because not only do we already have standards, but there is also tooling available! All the major public clouds have their own tooling, and the wider community has also supplied varying degrees of open source tooling for you to benefit from.

The goal of this chapter is to make you go from "What is my footprint?" to "I know my footprint, so now which action do I start with?"

The Perfect

By now, you know the basic building blocks for what makes software greener, and this gives you an understanding of what you need to measure. You learned in Chapter 2 that energy utilization, embodied carbon in hardware, and the carbon intensity of the grid have a role to play in how green your software is. What would be the perfect way to measure each of these?

Before that, we need to talk a little bit about scope. Today's software is rarely nicely scoped to one single machine over which we have complete control. No, software today spans many machines, abstraction layers, networking, and other types of hardware devices, which on top of it all is frequently shared with other software and/or data. In order to measure the emissions of our software, we need to decide the system limitations of our software. For a web application, that might be the virtual machine in a cloud, the networking equipment to send data from said cloud to the end-user device (e.g., a phone), and said end-user device. It is also useful to consider the temporal boundaries of our software (e.g., how does it behave over time). For our web application, it might consist of active user usage, such as a user clicking on a button, as well as passive usage, such as update installs. We will find that some of these are easier to measure and some are harder or practically impossible due to, for example, limited data access.

The next few sections will introduce how to perfectly measure energy, carbon intensity, and embodied emissions. These values can then be used in one (or several) of the standards that are introduced in "Examination of the Current Methodologies" on page 145.

Perfect Energy Data

Let's start with energy, because likely it is the first thing that springs to mind when you think about how software produces emissions. The perfect source of energy data for your software would be in real time and able to scope to the granularity you currently desire (e.g., on a service or process level, or on a per-line-of-code level). Could you measure this on your own? Yes, but it might be a bit cumbersome.

If your software runs on a device that you have physical access to, then the most reliable way is also the simplest way. Buy a cheap watt-hour meter, plug it into the socket between your wall and your hardware, and you are golden. If you have not used a watt-hour meter before, it is a small measuring device that can measure the electrical power passing through a circuit at a certain time. That electrical circuit can be anything from your entire home to a small hardware device, like your phone. This will always be the best way to measure energy consumption because it will measure exactly what your hardware consumes. There are some caveats to be aware of here:

- Any hardware will consume power when idle. This is called *static power draw*. Consider this a baseline energy consumption. If you are interested in absolute numbers for your application, then you will need to measure the baseline consumption and then subtract it from the overall consumption measured when running the application. (This is something we can also make use of when it comes to energy proportionality, but more on that in Chapter 2.)

- Always start measuring from steady state (SS). You might remember from high school electronic classes (if you took those) that whenever an electrical component starts up, you can observe a transient event, often an oscillation, which is a sudden burst of energy. You don't want to include this in your tests, so start measuring when you can observe SS.

- If your device has a battery, it needs to be fully charged and plugged in when measuring. Otherwise, you will end up measuring the power consumption of charging your battery, which can be interesting, but it's not what we are going for here.

If you do not have physical access to your device, there are multiple ways to instrument your software or hardware to extract this data from the device as well. How you do this depends on how your system looks and operates. It might be possible to get the data from your operating systems or from the orchestrating software you use, for example.

In general, though, this works great in a lab-like environment or for less complex pieces of software. However, doing real-time energy measurements in large-scale systems that span many abstraction layers is another matter, as you will quickly realize. It is entirely possible, but for many of us, it might be more worthwhile to leave the development cost of energy instrumentation up to someone else—like your ISP or your cloud provider. But even when we leave it up to someone else, the criteria mentioned at the start still hold. Ideally, this data should be in real time and provided with sufficient granularity.

One swallow does not a summer make. In the same way, perfect energy does not a perfect carbon metric make. Energy is the first part of the equation, so let's explore the others.

Perfect Carbon Intensity Data

In theory, all energy is created equal. An electron from a solar cell will make your lightbulb light up in exactly the same way as an electron from a coal power plant. In practice, the impact on climate and our perfect carbon metric, however, differs widely. We have already covered this in Chapter 2, so we won't go into further details here. But how can we perfectly measure this?

A simple wattmeter or some code instrumentation won't do the trick here. Generating a perfect carbon intensity signal takes deeper understanding of the energy grid, as well as data access. As with energy data, however, we would like for this data to be in real time and sufficiently granular, this time in regard to location and time of day. We want to combine our energy usage data with the way the energy was created. This way, we will get the carbon metric for the energy portion of our software.

Most often this carbon intensity data will come from third-party providers, either directly from the grid operators themselves or from an organization that aggregates data from multiple grid operators, like WattTime API[1] or Electricity Maps.[2] If you get the data from the grid operators, it will likely be from a public data set of historic carbon intensity, like the data set provided by Our World in Data,[3] not real-time data. Organizations like WattTime API and Electricity Maps provide API-based access to real-time, historical, and forecast carbon intensity data with high granularity. See Figure 9-1 for how the carbon intensity of the grid differs around the world.

Even if we get this data from a third-party provider, there are several types of signals we can get access to here, and they provide us with slightly different types of data. Some examples are:

LRMER
Long-run marginal emission rates

SRMER
Short-run marginal emission rates

AER
Average emission rates

---

1 WattTime, accessed January 18, 2024, *https://www.watttime.org*.

2 Electricity Maps, accessed January 18, 2024, *https://www.electricitymaps.com*.

3 "Carbon Intensity of Electricity Generation," Our World in Data, accessed January 18, 2024, *https://oreil.ly/ GUSm6*.

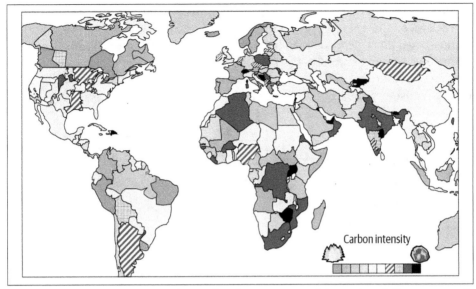

Figure 9-1. A map showing the fictional carbon intensity of the grid in different parts of the world

There is a lot we could say here, but for now let us just consider that perfect data here is likely something you cannot instrument on your own. Fear not: software-based access to perfect data is still possible for many parts of the world. "But wait," you think, "what about carbon offsets? Or power purchase agreements?" In the next section, we will dive deeper into the economic measures of carbon intensity and electricity.

Where Do Market-Based Reductions Fit In?

Let's talk economics for a bit! We promise, only a little bit. *Market-based reductions*, or strategies, are in essence an economic tool to change the carbon footprint of something. We can neutralize emissions and thus claim a lower carbon footprint for our operations. Similarly, we can purchase renewable energy production through an agreement while actually using nonrenewable sources to power our operations and claim carbon neutrality. These are inherently economic measures different from eliminating carbon, but they are interesting and well used, so we want to spend some time talking about them. What does "economic measures" mean in this context? The electrons that we use are always going to be the electrons that we use. Due to the nature of the electricity grids, we cannot pick and choose. What we can pick and choose is what we pay for.

Power purchase agreements (PPAs) are one example of this type of market-based measure. A PPA is a long-term contract between a producer and a consumer of energy, typically guaranteeing that the consumer purchases a fixed amount or percentage of the energy production. This can either be at a fixed rate or at a market-based price, depending on the contract. Figure 9-2 shows an example of what a simple PPA setup between two parties can look like. A PPA agreement can be set in varying degrees of locality, either from a plant right next to your data center (or other planned consumer of energy) or from a plant in a different country.

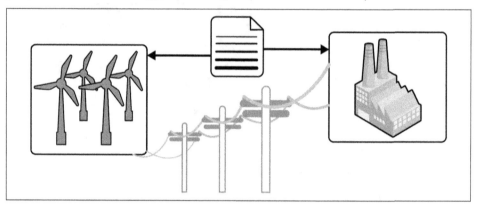

Figure 9-2. A diagram explaining the simplest form of a PPA, where there is one contract between one energy producer and one company, which are located close to each other

This method is often used as a way to finance new renewable energy plants,[4] as it gives the producer certainty of being able to sell the energy it eventually produces. This concept is called *additionality*, and it is something that over time encourages the creation of a fossil-free grid. PPAs are popular. In 2021 more than 137 companies in 32 different countries purchased them. The tech sector is one of the top consumers of renewable energy through PPAs, with Amazon, Microsoft, and Meta being the top three consumers in 2021 and Google coming in sixth place.[5]

Offsetting is another market-based measure that happens after the energy market itself. This is again a relationship between a producer of the carbon offset, or a carbon credit, and a consumer of the same. A *carbon offset* represents a fixed amount of carbon reduction or removal, and this carbon offset can be purchased. These transactions are regulated by governments or independent certification bodies on the voluntary carbon market. Both individuals and organizations can purchase carbon offsets on this market to reach their intended carbon-offsetting goals. The actual offsetting (e.g., not the selling and buying part) can be done in several ways. Perhaps

---

4 Dominik Ruderer, "Infrastructure Solutions: The Power of Purchase Agreements," European Investment Bank, July 12, 2022, *https://oreil.ly/60qbQ*.

5 "Corporate Clean Energy Buying Tops 30GW Mark in Record Year," BloombergNEF, January 31, 2022, *https://oreil.ly/LDNJO*.

most familiar to you are reforestation projects or carbon capture initiatives. As you can imagine, due to the nature of this market, some of these offsets can be hard to track and confirm the validity of, which has been and continues to be a reason for criticism of carbon offsets. One measure to combat this is the existence of several global standards that carbon offsets must meet, such as Verified Carbon Standard[6] and Gold Standard.[7]

There are more tools we could talk about here, like abatements, neutralization, or compensations, but we'll leave this for additional reading by the interested ones. For now, how do these fit into our perfect measurements?

There are different schools of thought here. Some say market-based reductions are fair game and can always be included in carbon reporting. Others say they have questionable effectiveness and should be reported separately. For the sake of measuring software, we think that market-based reductions muddy the picture for people like us, who want to know the carbon footprint of our software in order to make it smaller. Any potential offsets in the future do not impact the current intensity of the software, which is what we care about.

In a net-zero strategy, elimination of emissions is critical to reach our targets for 2045. The Science Based Targets initiative (SBTi) Net-Zero standard,[8] which is currently used by 4,000 corporations, states that most companies will need to set long-term targets to cut 90% of their emissions before 2050. Because market-based reductions make it harder to measure emissions removed from your own software, we consider market-based reductions to have no place in a so-called perfect carbon metric. We should say that this does not mean all market-based reductions are bad or that they should not be used, only that they complicate the actionability of a carbon metric of software.

Perfect Embodied-Carbon Tracing

The final part in our perfect carbon metric is the embodied carbon part. Sadly, this is another piece of data that is difficult to instrument on your own, simply because you rarely produce hardware on your own and thus have limited insight into the process. What you need from your manufacturers is some kind of start value (e.g., a total cost for the manufacturing of the device). The amortization of this spent cost is then something you can have full control over. You can also reason over the cost of recycling or destroying the device at its end of life in the same manner.

---

6 "Verified Carbon Standard," Verra, accessed January 18, 2024, *https://oreil.ly/bpVDN*.

7 Gold Standard, accessed January 18, 2024, *https://www.goldstandard.org*.

8 "The Corporate Net-Zero Standard," accessed January 18, 2024, *https://oreil.ly/M2yPF*.

As you learned in Chapter 2, hardware comes with an already built-in carbon debt. This carbon is already released into the atmosphere, and you cannot change this but only be mindful of this fact. If a hardware provider—for example, of servers—provides a carbon cost per unit, you can then use this unit of carbon emissions and value how you use it. You can model how the impact on your climate changes if you extend the lifetime of this server by one year, or if you are able to effectivize your code or operations to run twice the workload on the same device.

But what if you don't own your own hardware? For example, what if you develop frontend applications or run on a public cloud platform? Does your ISP provide this data?

This data is not very complicated to access if you run your own on-prem data center and deal directly with asset management. But if you do not, then you are again left at the mercy of someone else to provide this data for us. What becomes important then is your—by now very familiar—friend, granularity. You would like to have your service providers give us enough details around embodied carbon that you can understand which actions would reduce the impact.

One example of how to get this data for the public cloud is Cloud Carbon Footprint (CCF).[9] CCF is an open source project, sponsored by Thoughtworks Inc. This tool can measure, monitor, and reduce your cloud carbon emissions of AWS, Azure, and Google Cloud. The CCF has done a life-cycle analysis of many of the machines these cloud providers offer, and this data is open and free to use.

For client-side devices, the situation is tricky. You'd have to be pretty lucky to get your entire user base to provide you with their device age and utilization rates. You also rarely have a service provider you can pose these difficult questions to. In "The Good Enough?" section of this chapter, we will go over some proxies, which can be more useful in this case.

The Future of Perfect Monitoring

Where do we want carbon monitoring of software to go in the future? If you ask us—and since you picked up this book, we're gonna assume you did—it is real-time carbon monitoring.

What do we mean by that? If carbon data became like any other metrics, such as latency and availability, there would be a lot of benefits for our industry. For starters, there already are many principles, practices, and tooling available already for other types of metrics, which could then be reused. There are also a lot of people inside the industry who are already familiar with managing those metrics and who use them in the most effective way.

---

9 Cloud Carbon Footprint, accessed January 18, 2024, *https://www.cloudcarbonfootprint.org*.

How do we then make carbon data just like another familiar metric? There are two things that we think are key: time-series data and standardization of metrics.

Time-series data
> With time-series data, metrics could be easily slotted in with the current industry standard monitoring and alerting tools, such as Prometheus, Grafana, or your favorite monitoring tool. This will allow us to treat the carbon footprint of our software as another golden signal to care about. It also unlocks scenarios such as alerting you when your carbon SLO is breaching, etc.

Standardization of metrics
> Standardization of metrics is another key element. If we make a parallel to what happened with OpenTelemetry, there is now one industry standard for telemetry data, and we can see that it has had clear benefits for the sector. It has reduced data collection complexity, increased data quality, enabled easier comparison across systems/vendors, and started to allow people to work on tooling to analyze those data. Of course, we want the same benefits for carbon data.

Having tools with sufficient granularity in time, location, and software components, which could provide real-time (or close to real-time) data would mean that we as software folks could worry a little less about measuring and a little more about reducing. That seems like a fair deal to us. Having a smaller number of people perfect transparent metrics so they can be consumed by the masses can be a great way to enable more people to reduce their emissions.

Of course, this won't be possible for all types of software. But for software running on larger platforms like hyperscale clouds or well-known operating systems, this is a good solution, which we hope to see the industry move toward.

The Good Enough?

By now, we all understand that "the perfect" might be a little far away sometimes. We don't always have access to perfect data, nor the ability to gather data continuously, and sometimes we don't even have access to *any* data. Does that mean we should give up on measuring? No, but we can approach it from a different angle and keep our scientific approach.

Use of Proxies

Measuring carbon emissions directly is the best way to get to know your carbon emissions (duh). But there are also some proxies that are tied to the carbon emissions you can use as an indication of whether or not you are trending in the right direction.

One of the best proxies is energy, because it is closely related to your carbon footprint. It also has the benefit of being possible to instrument, both on servers and on client-side devices in lab-like environments. One of the best proxies for energy is CPU utilization; it is also easy to instrument, which is a plus. If you are self-hosted, you might also get this data from your energy provider in real time, or at the very least at the end of the month with your bill. As you probably understand by now, energy and carbon do not have a 1:1 mapping, but as far as proxies go, this one is very good.

Cost is another possible proxy, and many green saving actions will also decrease cost. The benefit is that this proxy also speaks the language of your CFO, and you should never underestimate the power of having the CFO on your side. This is not a perfect proxy for a few reasons. One example is that cloud providers do not factor carbon awareness of your workload into your bill. Another example is that electricity cost does not have to be related to the greenness of the production. But in general, lowering your operations costs will lower your carbon emissions, and therefore it is a good enough proxy.

Hardware is a great proxy for part of your carbon emissions! Producing new hardware comes with a significant carbon cost. Due to energy proportionality, running more servers at lower utilization also consumes more energy than fewer servers running at higher utilization. The tricky part here is to consider the system-wide impact. If you are decreasing your hardware footprint in your server hall by sending more computation to the client side, you may actually increase your emissions. Why? Because you are utilizing both the network and the client-side device more, causing higher energy use there. But used with a little bit of system-wide thinking, hardware usage is a great proxy.

For some scenarios, latency or other performance metrics can also be used. This one has more caveats, though, as it requires you to consider how your latency or performance should be interpreted. But in general, it can work a little like this. If you decrease the latency by code efficiency or smarter operations (e.g., not by optimistically throwing an extra hardware cache on the problem), you will use fewer resources on your computer. So far, so good. But, as we pointed out in Chapter 4, alone, this kind of does…nothing (or very little). However, if you pair this with packing things denser on your hardware—for example, by now being able to serve twice as many API requests from the same server—your efficiency goes up. This is where the carbon saving comes in. Performance metrics work in the same way. Using less CPU? Great, that means more resources can now have access to the CPU and efficiency goes up.

Consistent Use of Imperfect Data to Reach Reductions

How scientific is this? Well, it is not as good as our perfect data. But in the real world, things are rarely perfect, and we should not let that get in the way of our taking climate actions. If you are able to keep a scientific approach in how you use your proxy, or possibly even combine several to paint a broader picture, this is an excellent starting point.

If the use of proxies should result in an as-accurate-as-possible result, it does require you to be quite intimately familiar with your software. This might be fine, or you might be willing to risk slightly incorrect numbers in order to not let perfect be the enemy of good. Having a little understanding of how your proxy works will go a long way. But ideally, carbon data should be easy to get, which is why we advocate for real-time carbon monitoring as the goal for the future of our industry.

Examination of the Current Methodologies

As mentioned before, we are not the first ones on the mission to figure out our carbon footprint. There are already some methodologies available to help us to do exactly this. Let's dedicate some time to walking through them together.

We'd like to steal (and possibly misquote) a quote from Dr. Radia Perlman: "Sometimes standards bodies are like sports fans, each only cheering for their own team."

In this book we'll try to be a bit more objective than sports fans, and we also encourage you to arm yourself with knowledge first before judging. Unlike a sports fan, you are also perfectly allowed to have several favorites too.

Greenhouse Gas Protocol (GHG Protocol)

We'll start with the greenhouse gas protocol (GHG protocol), which is perhaps one of the most widely used standards for calculating the carbon footprint of organizations. At least according to themselves, 90% of Fortune 500 companies use this standard.[10]

The GHG protocol is a joint initiative of the World Resources Institute and the World Business Council for Sustainable Development . The work to create the standard was started in the late 1990s and resulted in the first Corporate Standard being published in 2001.[11] Now the GHG protocol also hosts several other standards, but we'll stick to reviewing the GHG's Corporate Standard in this book. The standard comes with a lot of guidance and help available for those who wish to implement the standard, and it is free to use.

---

10 Greenhouse Gas Protocol, accessed January 18, 2024, *https://ghgprotocol.org*.

11 "About Us," Greenhouse Gas Protocol, accessed January 18, 2024, *https://oreil.ly/uzF2c*.

The Corporate Standard covers the accounting and reporting of seven greenhouse gases, as the Kyoto Protocol[12] indicates. The reporting is divided into three parts.

Scope 1:

- All direct emissions from your own corporation; for example, the vehicles operated or the fuel burned by plants owned.

Scope 2:

- All indirect emissions from purchased energy, such as electricity, steam, heat, and cooling.
- In 2015 the Corporate Standard was extended with a comprehensive Scope 2 Guidance (*https://oreil.ly/sJh6M*), which codifies two distinct methods for scope 2 accounting:
  — The location-based method. This method means that the average emissions intensity of grids on which energy consumption occurs is used.
  — The market-based method. This method reflects emissions from electricity that companies have purposefully chosen. This can include energy attribute certificates (RECs, GOs, etc.), direct contracts (for both low-carbon, renewable, or fossil fuel generation), supplier-specific emission rates, and other default emission factors.
- Sounds complicated? Don't worry; the details do not matter a great deal to us in this context. But very simply put: the key difference between the two methods is that the location-based method counts the actual electrons you use, whereas the market-based method counts the electrons you have paid for.

Scope 3:

- All other indirect emissions that the corporation does not own or control. As you can imagine, this becomes a rather large bucket, which fits everything from purchased material to waste management to business trips to product use.

You can see some examples of activities and which scope they belong to in Figure 9-3.

---

12 "What Is the Kyoto Protocol?" United Nations Climate Change, accessed January 18, 2024, *https://oreil.ly/Ck35L*.

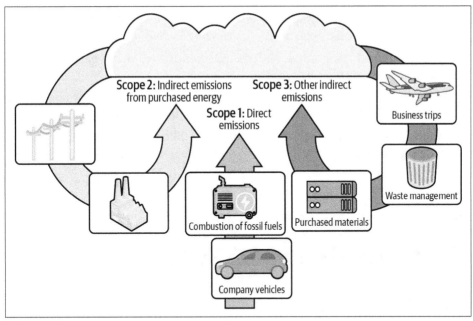

Figure 9-3. An example of different activities and which GHG protocol scope they fall under

Alright, we get it now, but how does it work for software? As it is written right now, GHG protocol is not optimized for software—at least not in the sense that it can give software developers the tools to understand what actions to take to reduce their impact. Let's look at some examples of what we mean by that.

Let's say that you write software, for which you do not provide the primary hosting. An example might be a library or an SDK people can download and use. You might then only host the actual downloading capability, but the runtime is always on someone else's hardware. The lion's share of the emissions stemming from your software will very likely be in someone else's (or, if you are successful, *many* someone elses') scope 2 and/or 3 reporting. What? Yes. Scope 2 because your SDK is consuming energy in your customer's data center, and scope 3 because your software will impact how much or how little hardware they use. Even if you could decrease the energy use of your software, the decrease would primarily be visible in someone else's scope 2 reporting, not yours. Even if you are building an open source service, which you do self-host, part of your emissions will still stem from usage of your service in other pieces of software. And the emissions (scope 1, 2, and 3) from your self-hosting will also count as your customer's scope 3.

Things also get a little harder to follow when we consider different methods of operations. Your choice of infrastructure determines which scope you should report energy and embodied carbon emissions under (see Table 9-1):

- For private cloud applications, the energy usage of your software falls into scope 2, and the embodied carbon of all your servers falls into scope 3.

- For public cloud applications, both the energy usage of your application and the embodied carbon fall into scope 3.

- In scenarios where you are running a hybrid private/public cloud application, part of its emissions will fall into scope 2, and part will fall into scope 3.

- Similarly, for your customer-facing frontend application, energy usage falls into your organization's scope 3 since your customer will purchase the energy to power their device.

Table 9-1. A table showing which scope the energy use and embodied emissions fall under based on your infrastructure

GHG scope	2	3
Private cloud	Energy	Embodied
Public cloud	-	Energy + embodied
Hybrid cloud	Some energy	Some energy + embodied
Frontend	-	Energy + embodied

This makes actionability trickier for folks like us, who want to understand which of our actions had what effect.

Even so, many organizations in the tech sector are currently using the GHG protocol. This means your colleagues and the leaders in your organization already speak this lingo, which can be very helpful when we want to use measurements as a tool for change.

Green Software Foundation's Software Carbon Intensity Specification (SCI)

Next up, the Green Software Foundation's (GSF) Software Carbon Intensity Specification (SCI).[13] The SCI is specifically built for software, and it comes with different limitations and abilities compared with the GHG protocol. Much like the GHG protocol, it also comes with guiding documentation to help you implement it.

The first version, the beta version, was released for COP26 in the fall of 2021. It was quickly followed by the version 1 of the SCI for COP27 in 2022. GSF is working to get

---

13 "Software Carbon Intensity (SCI) Specification," GitHub, accessed January 18, 2024, *https://oreil.ly/ud_hd*.

the standard made into an ISO standard, but as of the printing of this book, it is not there yet. You can follow its progression on the ISO/IEC DIS 21031 page.[14]

The SCI is different from the GHG protocol in that it is not a total for your organization but rather a rate of carbon emissions per functional unit for your software. Reaching a lower number is better, but reaching zero is impossible.

The SCI consists of four key parts:

Energy (E)
> The energy consumed by your software.

Carbon intensity (I)
> The location-based carbon intensity of the energy grid powering your software.
>
> Market-based measures are not allowed in the SCI; only the location-based metrics can be used.

Embodied carbon (M)
> The carbon emitted through the creation and disposal of the hardware that your software is running on.

The functional unit (R)
> The magic thing that makes this standard a rate. This should be how your software scales—for example, per user per device or per API call.

The parts gets combined into the following mathematical formula SCI = ((E × I) + M) per R (see Figure 9-4).

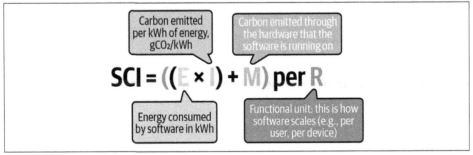

Figure 9-4. The SCI formula[15]

Another key aspect of the SCI is your software boundary. This is something defined by you to delimit your software system in a meaningful way. More is less here. The

---

14 "ISO/IEC PRF 21031: Information Technology—Software Carbon Intensity (SCI) Specification," ISO, accessed January 18, 2024, *https://oreil.ly/IMkyO*.

15 Source: "Green-Software-Foundation," GitHub, accessed January 18, 2024, *https://oreil.ly/iEdSD*.

SCI states that all systems and infrastructure that significantly contributes to your operations should be included inside your software boundary.

Initially we stated that it can never fall to zero. Now that you know the SCI better, you can understand that it is because of three reasons:

1. Unless we make significant scientific progress in the field of hardware, you cannot run software in thin air and thus (M) will never be 0.

2. Since the SCI does not allow for market-based reductions, (I) will always be a number greater than 0.

3. The energy consumed will never be 0 unless the machine is unplugged, at which point it cannot be considered to be a working software system.

The SCI is meant for everyone and all types of software, so this makes it different from other reporting standards.

How can this work in practice? Wonderful Tiny Farm (*https://oreil.ly/hevOX*) has submitted a case study (*https://oreil.ly/poKaL*) to the GSF that we will use as an example. The Farm's software is a .NET application gathering farm insight data, like sunlight and temperature, on a Raspberry Pi.

- Energy (E): 0.003 kWh per day
- Carbon intensity (I): 0.713 kg per kWh
- Embodied carbon (M): 55 kg
- Assume this device is exclusively used for this purpose and has a life span of three years.
- Functional unit (R): per Raspberry Pi device

SCI = ((E × I) + M) / R = ((0.003 × 0.731) + (55 / (365 *3)) per Raspberry Pi = 0.002139 + 0.05228 per day and per Raspberry Pi = 0.052 kg CO_2e per day and Raspberry Pi

This number is fun, but it doesn't do much on its own, so Wonderful Tiny Farm should not stop here and call it a day. No, instead it should inspire the company to take some action. Perhaps this SCI score helped Wonderful Tiny Farm realize that its embodied carbon cost is higher than its energy cost, so elongating the lifetime of its Raspberry PI is a better first step than switching energy providers (which can be step 2).

ISO 14064 Standard

The ISO 14064 standard consists of three parts, called ISO 14064-1,[16] ISO 14064-2,[17] and ISO 14064-3.[18] This is perhaps not very catchy but a rather convenient naming scheme. The standard was first published in 2006, the latest revision was in 2018, and as of the writing of this book, it is currently going through its planned five-year review. The ISO 14064-1 focuses on the reporting of GHG emissions and removals on an organizational level, and we wanted to include it to highlight some similarities to and differences from to other standards we have talked about.

While the ISO 14064-1 is also built on the GHG protocol, the division of emission is a little different. GHG uses scope 1, 2, and 3, whereas ISO 14064-1 divides emissions into direct, corresponding to scope 1, and indirect, corresponding to scopes 2 and 3. ISO 14064-1 also supports market-based reduction techniques, but unlike the GHG protocol, ISO 14064-1 is not free, but access to the documentation comes at a small cost. One benefit of using an ISO standard is that ISO's Committee on Conformity Assessment (CASCO) has produced a number of standards related to the certification process. Your organization can then be ISO certified by a third-party certification body, which can be great for auditability.

Available Tooling

If you don't want to measure yourself or get into the nitty-gritty details of implementing a standard, fear not: you are definitely not alone in this feeling, and there are options for you too! All major hypercloud providers have their own tools for delivering carbon impact data to you based on your usages. There are also other tools available for those who run client-side applications available outside of the cloud. But to avoid comparing apples to oranges, we need to inspect these tools at a closer range first.

Hyperscale Cloud Provider Tools

While there is no official definition for which vendor counts as a hyperscaler, Amazon AWS, Microsoft Azure, and Google Cloud held a combined 66% market share in 2022,[19] so those are the ones we will focus on in this section. Three of the other

---

16 "ISO 14064-1:2018—Greenhouse Gases—Part 1: Specification with Guidance at the Organization Level for Quantification and Reporting of Greenhouse Gas Emissions and Removals," ISO, accessed January 18, 2024, *https://oreil.ly/Nslw0*.

17 "ISO 14064-2:2019—Greenhouse Gases—Part 2: Specification with Guidance at the Project Level for Quantification, Monitoring and Reporting of Greenhouse Gas Emission Reductions or Removal Enhancements," ISO, accessed January 18, 2024, *https://oreil.ly/qt3v2*.

18 "ISO 14064-3:2019—Greenhouse Gases—Part 3: Specification with Guidance for the Verification and Validation of Greenhouse Gas Statements," ISO, accessed January 18, 2024, *https://oreil.ly/SCXzP*.

large cloud providers, IBM Cloud, Oracle Cloud, and Alibaba Cloud, all claim to have a strong focus on sustainability and have objectives for reaching various renewable-energy and sustainability goals. This is great to see, and we look forward to progress across the sector. But in the context of this chapter, as of now none of these three have any carbon-accounting tools available for us to review.

The three big ones, AWS (*https://oreil.ly/1-J6z*), Azure (*https://oreil.ly/cznEG*), and Google Cloud (*https://oreil.ly/Q7veh*), also have strong sustainability commitments. They also provide tools so we can assess our carbon footprint on their platform. This immediately generates some questions for the curious among us. What do they include? Can we compare them to each other? What are they useful for?

Let's compare them to each other (see Table 9-2), shall we?

Table 9-2. Overview and comparison of the three major hyperscalers' carbon footprint tools

	Amazon AWS	Microsoft Azure	Google Cloud
Granularity	Continent level. 0,001 metric ton of CO_2e	Country and region level. 0,001 metric ton of CO_2e	Country, region, and zone level. 0,1 kilogram of CO_2e
Scope 1	Yes	Yes	Yes
Scope 2	Yes Follows the market-based GHG Protocol. (Regional)	Yes Follows the market-based GHG Protocol. (Regional)	Yes Follows the location-based GHG Protocol with hourly emissions factors. Google also promises to also provide a market-based dashboard for its customers.
Scope 3	No (Announced to be added in early 2024.)	Yes Embedded carbon for the manufacture, packaging, transportation, use, and end-of-life phases of data center equipment. Embedded carbon of data center buildings may be included as data becomes available.	Yes Embedded carbon for the creation of data center equipment and buildings. Travel and commute associated with Google data center employees are included.
Allocation type	Not shared	Microsoft allocates emissions based on each customer's relative Azure usage in a given data center region.	Google uses a bottom-up method. Energy used when running a workload is allocated based on each service's CPU usage. Energy used when the machine is idle is allocated based on each service's resource allocation. Overhead energy use is allocated to each machine on an hourly basis, thus trickling down to the first two categories.

---

19 Mark Harnas, "Top 5 Cloud Market-Share Leaders: AWS, Microsoft, Google in Q3 2022," CRN, October 28, 2022, *https://oreil.ly/vD1jC*.

	Amazon AWS	Microsoft Azure	Google Cloud
Time sensitivity	Monthly aggregate Three months data delay	Monthly aggregate 14 days data delay	Monthly aggregate Up to 21 days data delay
PUE	Yes	Yes	Yes
Additional resources	*https://oreil.ly/3LpW8* *https://oreil.ly/ph4fD*	*https://oreil.ly/c_l__*	*https://oreil.ly/LsH9z* *https://oreil.ly/QvQlH*

Open Source Options for the Cloud

Cloud Carbon Footprint (CCF)[20] is an open source project, sponsored by Thoughtworks Inc. This tool can measure, monitor, and reduce your cloud carbon emissions on public clouds. CCF currently cover AWS, Azure, and Google Cloud. They convert cloud utilization into estimated energy usage and then carbon emissions, producing metrics and carbon savings estimates. The emissions shown by their tool are calculated as follows:[21]

> *Total CO_2e = operational emissions + embodied emissions*

Where:

> *operational emissions = (cloud provider service usage) × (cloud energy conversion factors [kWh]) × (cloud provider power usage effectiveness (PUE)) × (grid emissions factors [metric tons CO_2e])*

And:

> *embodied emissions = estimated metric tons CO_2e emissions from the manufacturing of datacenter servers, for compute usage*

Another open source option is Kepler (Kubernetes-based Efficient Power Level Exporter), which is a Cloud Native Computing foundation (CNCF) project from 2023.[22] Kepler can estimate power consumption at the process, container, and Kubernetes pod levels of your software. It does this by reading real-time system metrics for bare-metal deployed software (e.g., when you are running directly on the server without the abstraction of a virtual machine). For virtual machines, Kepler uses pre-trained ML models to estimate the energy consumption. This data can be exported as Prometheus metrics, which makes it easy to track and monitor this data—pretty close to our dream metrics!

---

20 Cloud Carbon Footprint, accessed January 18, 2024, *https://www.cloudcarbonfootprint.org*.

21 "Methodology," Cloud Carbon Footprint, accessed January 18, 2024, *https://oreil.ly/HmNDD*.

22 "Kepler," Cloud Native Computing Foundation, accessed January 18, 2024, *https://oreil.ly/73nTL*.

For ease of comparison, we will use the same format as Table 9-2 to view these open source tools in Table 9-3.

Table 9-3. Overview and comparison of two open source carbon footprint tools

	Cloud Carbon Footprint	Kepler
Granularity	0,001 metric ton of CO_2e	NA (Kepler does not convert energy to carbon.)
Scope 1	No	No
Scope 2	Yes. Follows the location-based GHG Protocol.	Yes. (However, you will have to multiply with the carbon intensity of the grid by yourself, as Kepler only gives you the energy-related stats.)
Scope 3	Yes, only for compute usage type for now due to lack of public data available.	No
Allocation type	This depends slightly on the cloud type, but their model includes compute, GPU, storage, networking, and memory based on the billing information.	Kepler uses a bottom-up by reading real-time system metrics.
Time sensitivity	Depends on the delay of billing data from each public cloud provider.	Live
PUE	Yes, based on public static data from each public cloud provider.	No
Additional resources	*https://oreil.ly/epvKv*	*https://oreil.ly/bUsyt*

Client-Side Tooling

Public cloud tools are great, but not all software runs there. One glaringly obvious example of this is client-side code, like apps or websites. For these scenarios, we are not left in the dark either. There are other tools available, some directly from the major players; others are open source. This is not a complete list by any means; it's a set of examples of tooling to get you started.

For phone apps, both Android Studio (*https://oreil.ly/ItHR8*) and iOS Xcode (*https://oreil.ly/MC0_F*) have options to model energy in the development stage. Turns out, when a resource is limited (like a phone battery), our industry is pretty good at building tools to make you effectively use this resource.

Another tool for mobile apps is Greenspector (*https://oreil.ly/yIsgA*), which actually runs your software on real mobile phones and measures the energy usage. This is pretty close to our dream of perfect energy data! Of course, this will only give you a snapshot, but it can be a number to extrapolate from and something to benchmark against over time.

Green the Web (*https://oreil.ly/Ss48j*) has also gathered a plethora of different tools for different aspects of web development, covering everything from analysis (arguably the most interesting for this chapter) to image compression tools.

If you want to estimate your ML training carbon cost, a set of ML researchers has put together this ML CO_2 impact tool (*https://oreil.ly/-t35S*). It works for several hyperscale clouds as well as on-prem scenarios, and it is open for contributions.

As you can see, these tools all have their limitations or boundaries, but the massive advantage is that you have to do very little to get quite detailed insights into your energy or carbon usage. Paired with a scientific method and consistent measurements over time, these are all great options to lower your software's impact.

You Made It!

You made it to the end of the measurements chapter. Perhaps it was a lot of new concepts and terminology for you, or perhaps this was all old news. Either way, we hope that you now have a better understanding of what you can do to measure your emissions and where you can get help to do the same. Whatever solution you end up using, we hope that you approach your software measurements with curiosity. Ask questions like these:

- Why is this number so high?
- How can I compare it to this other number?
- What if I tweak this operation? How will my number change?

Let the measurements be a conversation starter and, once you get the hang of it, your faithful companion on the road to carbon reductions.

CHAPTER 10

Monitoring

An unreliable person is nobody's friend.
—Idries Shah, *Reflections*

There was once a product called Chuck that was so well built it naturally had 99.9999% availability. (Yup, he was practically always ready to handle any requests!)

Chuck lived a peaceful life free of downtime and outages in Production Land. One ordinary day, much like any other, he was minding his own business and strolling down Production Avenue when he suddenly felt a sharp loss of connectivity and had to sit slowly on the sidewalk. Chuck thought to himself, "Is this it? Am I finally falling over?"

Was Chuck experiencing a once-very-distant-memory network outage?!?!!

Chuck in Production Land is no fairy tale; it's the real-life story of a Google product named Chubby (*https://oreil.ly/2EvHe*) that was very well architected and proved to be so reliable that it led to a false sense of security among its users. They conned themselves into believing that it would never go down and so increased their dependence on it well beyond its advertised, observed, and monitored availability.

We all know that unicorns are mythical creatures that don't exist, and so is 100% uptime for a software product. Even though Chubby rarely faced any incidents, they still occasionally happened, leading to unexpected (and, more importantly, unplanned for) disruptions in its downstream services (*https://oreil.ly/bxD17*).

For Google, the solution to this unicornish scenario was to deliberately bring its own system down often enough to match its advertised uptime, thereby ensuring Chubby didn't overdo it on its availability, thus never again lulling its users into a false sense of security.

The moral of this story is that while striving for the highest possible availability of a product may be an exciting and daring engineering problem to conquer, there are negative consequences that shouldn't be overlooked. These include not only overreliance by users but also software-induced carbon emissions.

Before we continue Chuck's story, we should spend some time defining availability and why the world of tech fawns over it. Afterward, we'll return to basics, examining the why and how of monitoring before taking a detour to discuss why SREs don't think traditional monitoring is enough for this world of microservices we have created for ourselves. Finally, the big gun. We will briefly investigate observability and how it fits in with sustainability in tech. This way, as green software practitioners, we can keep up with the increasingly complex world of distributed systems.

We firmly believe that monitoring software systems' carbon emissions deserves its own shebang (i.e., a chapter)! Not because there is an overwhelming amount of material to examine or tooling to compare and contrast yet, but because it is of the utmost importance for tech professionals to start thinking early on about how being green will integrate with the well-established realms of DevOps and SREs.

It's crucial for us not to reinvent the wheel but to follow the industry standards when figuring out carbon emission monitoring.

Availability as a North Star

A system's availability is about whether it delivers on its intended purpose at any given time. This is often quantified as a probability derived from the ratio of successful operations to total operations—expressed as uptime / (uptime + downtime). *Uptime* signifies when a system is up and running (a.k.a. operational), while *downtime*, as suggested by its name, represents when a system is not. Regardless of the metric used, the result of this calculation is a percentage, such as 99.99%, colloquially known as "4 nines," as illustrated in Table 10-1.

Table 10-1. Availability table expressed per year, per month, and per day

Availability level	Allowed downtime per year	Allowed downtime per month	Allowed downtime per day
90% ("1 nine")	36 days, 5 hours, 22 minutes, and 55 seconds	3 days, 26 minutes, and 55 seconds	2 hours and 24 minutes
99.9% ("3 nines")	8 hours, 41 minutes, and 38 seconds	43 minutes and 28 seconds	1 minute and 26 seconds
99.999% ("5 nines")	5 minutes and 13 seconds	26 seconds	0.86 seconds

Mathematically, those "nines," seen in the first column, are not directly translated into difficulties. However, do not underestimate their significance; the more "nines" there are, the more challenging things become across the board for a system. Why? Because availability doesn't just indicate how much time a system needs to be functional; it also dictates the time allowed for it to be nonoperational. Nonoperational time in this context includes both planned and unplanned downtime.

You can probably imagine, or gather from Table 10-1, the sheer amount of work required to design, develop, deploy, and manage a "5 nines" product that allows only 5.26 minutes of unavailability in the entire year! This substantial workload will also explicitly and implicitly impact the product's carbon emissions.

Availability is just one of the many signals that DevOps and SREs care about. Have you heard the magical tale of the four golden signals or, as we like to call them, the four horsemen of metrics-based monitoring? They represent the foundation of modern monitoring.

Four Horsemen of Metrics-Based Monitoring

In software engineering, *monitoring* involves collecting, visualizing, and analyzing metrics on an application or its system. It's a way for the application's owner to ensure that the system is performing as intended. In other words, we use metrics, or quantifiable measurements, to describe various aspects of software, its network, and its infrastructure.

The four golden signals, as detailed in Google's definitive *Site Reliability Engineering* (*https://oreil.ly/ap76v*) (O'Reilly), include the following:

Latency
Refers to how long it takes for a service to process a request (i.e., the time taken for a user to send a request and receive a response)

Traffic
Measures the amount of demand that a software program experiences (i.e., the total number of requests users have sent in a period)

Errors
Focuses on the unsuccessful requests that the system is handling, indicating the rate at which the system returns error responses to its users

Saturation
Refers to the extent to which a computing resource (e.g., CPU or Memory) is being utilized at a given time

How would this scenario look from a carbon metric perspective? Before we get to that, let's discuss why people get so worked up about those arbitrarily defined quantities.

Service Level Is Why We Are Here

If there is one thing that everyone—designers, developers, testers, managers, and even salespeople—can agree on, it is the desire for customers' happiness. But how do we ensure everyone is on the same page and agrees on what it takes to make this happen? Cue service-level metrics!

According to Google, service-level metrics should be the main drivers behind business objectives, which include user satisfaction. Let's spend the next couple of breaths going over the details so we can agree on the definitions and discuss how carbon emissions can join the pack of service levels.

First up, the *service-level indicator (SLI)* is a direct measurement (i.e., quantity) describing a characteristic of a system. You might have already picked up that any of the four golden signals can be used as an indicator in this context. So, if our SLI is request latency, it means that we are calculating how long it takes for the system to return a response to a request.

Next, the *service-level objective (SLO)* is about how compliant we are with a particular SLI over a specific time frame. This is commonly expressed as SLI over a period of time—for example, request latency for the past 28 days. SLOs are regarded as the fountain of happiness we want all our engineering teams to drink from. We see them as the cornerstone of SRE principles.

We can also use SLOs to drive decision making. For instance, during the planning of the next sprint, if we realize we're not going to meet our SLO for the current month, we can take a step back and figure out why availability is suffering before pushing out new features.

Lastly, *service-level agreements (SLAs)* are the formal agreements between a service provider and a service user. We can think of them as a collection of SLOs, such as uptime, latency, error rate, etc.

So we can see that service-level metrics are a useful tool to steer data-driven decisions. They not only give service providers the opportunity to deliver on their promises that can be tracked and measured precisely, but they also provide us with a framework that can be leveraged by many other disciplines in software engineering, specifically sustainable computing.

When a Carbon Metric Is Ready

Imagine we have it all figured out, like what we talked about in Chapter 9: we have a Prometheus-style real-time carbon metric that is ready to be used by anyone and everyone. Hurray! We can now throw this metric over the fence to our SRE friends so they can start tracking this metric with the rest of the signals.

 A Prometheus-style metric is currently one of the most popular choices for metrics-based monitoring. By following the style, we are collecting data that is readable, flexible, and useable. For example, we can easily deduce that http_requests_total is a metric that calculates the total number of HTTP requests received by a particular system. For more juicy details on why the Prometheus monitoring ecosystem rules, check out *Prometheus: Up & Running* (O'Reilly). (Spoiler alert: PromQL, Prometheus's functional query language, is one of the main stars of the show because it lets its user select and aggregate data in real time.)

Remember our favorite character, Chuck? Let's envision yet another typical day in Production Land. Chuck the Cheerful, who has promised his clients a "1 nine" service for both uptime and renewable energy use, is savoring the last rays of sunshine for the year while diligently working to perform more data manipulation using clean energy. Suddenly, thanks to climate change, heavy rain begins to fall, causing Chuck to lose access to his only clean energy source: solar power.

Chuck is a stickler for best practices and follows SRE principles. He therefore has a system in place to measure and monitor the carbon emissions from his data manipulation, ensuring that he doesn't compromise his commitment to his users in terms of carbon emissions for this particular service.

Faced with having to switch to nonrenewable energy sources, such as coal or oil, Chuck recalls that he still has error budgets—precisely up to three days in this case —left for the month to utilize nonrenewable energy. Unfortunately, he has no error budget left for failing to provide any service at all because he experienced a major outage the week before.

 Error budget describes the leftover SLOs in a given a period of time. In other words, if your availability is "3 nines," that means you have up to ~43.5 minutes for any planned or unplanned downtime.

Chuck thus switches to nonrenewables to maintain all his SLOs. Remember, this is a chapter about monitoring. If Chuck hadn't fallen over last week, he could have turned himself off and saved the carbon. C'est la vie. Error budgets work both ways. They are still the right way to handle carbon emissions.

What we have described here is simply slotting in carbon metrics with what the industry is already doing very well: production monitoring. Again, it's paramount for green software practitioners to not duplicate efforts to create an ecosystem where we can efficiently and effectively monitor environment-related metrics.

Observability

Let's rewind to the early 2000s in Production Land when Chuck's dad, Charles, lived peacefully with many neighbors with whom he was friendly but didn't interact much. During that time, Charles and his neighbors were known as monolithic. They were self-contained applications that didn't need each other to fulfill their one true purposes in their Land.

Fast-forward to 2023, and Chuck not only has to interact with every neighbor on his street, but he sometimes has to reach out to residents at the other end of the city to complete a simple task for users. Chuck and his many neighbors are what we call microservices that make up a distributed system.

Despite the numerous benefits offered by this new consortium of Chuck and his friends compared with Charles's world, it also introduces unprecedented complexity in determining precisely which one of them was the problematic one when an issue occurred. This intricacy in debugging problems, identifying the source of the issue, and understanding the "unknown unknowns" in a distributed system is how observability came about.

The Anticipated Showdown: Observability Versus Monitoring

Observability and monitoring are often muttered in the same sentence, yet they are two distinct concepts. Let's spend a moment to discuss why this showdown was highly anticipated and how, in reality, one doesn't replace the other but complements it.

Even though Chuck and his friends' brand-new world of modern software systems (a.k.a. highly distributed architectures) boasts numerous perks such as flexibility, scalability, etc., which we probably don't need to write about again, an important negative characteristic that is often overlooked is the complexity they bring about, as you'll see in Figure 10-1.

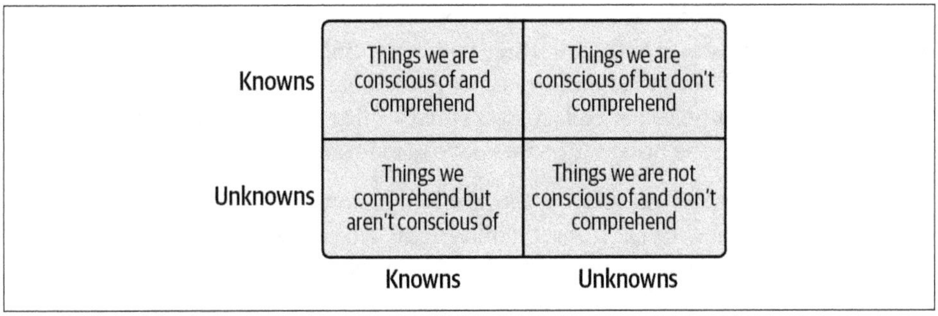

	Knowns	Unknowns
Knowns	Things we are conscious of and comprehend	Things we are conscious of but don't comprehend
Unknowns	Things we comprehend but aren't conscious of	Things we are not conscious of and don't comprehend

Figure 10-1. Four quadrants of the Rumsfeld matrix

Here, we have the Rumsfeld matrix, a handy tool for determining the uncertainty of an issue. For example, in the SRE space, we summarize the difference between monitoring and observability as helping identify "known" and "unknown" bugs, respectively.

We see monitoring as just enough for back-in-the-day monolithic applications because pinpointing where and why things have gone wrong in a self-contained fashion was relatively straightforward. For instance, we could easily collect the CPU usage of an application, plot a graph, and set up an alert to monitor its performance, preventing the software from becoming overwhelmed.

This issue of an overworked CPU is a well-established "known unknown" problem that many monolithic products face. Generally, it's a relatively painless bug to solve because CPU usage is a metric we know how to monitor, and the problem itself is well understood.

However, bugs can become tricky very quickly as we move through the quadrants (a.k.a. facing more intertwined microservices) to things we are neither conscious of nor comprehend (a.k.a. "unknown unknowns"). Consider this: what metrics and dashboards do you need to set up to detect an issue that only affects the Pixel 7A in Taiwan if you are a mobile app developer supporting the past five generations of Pixel phones in over 30 countries?

This is where traditional monitoring falls short: to have meaningful metrics, dashboards, and alerts, you will need to predict what could have gone wrong and where it might have gone wrong. Basically, it's a murder mystery without any clues! If you ask anyone who has held a pager before, they will tell you that dealing with the same incidents more than once in a distributed system was a rare occurrence.

Observability originated from control theory. Specifically, it is defined as a measure of how well the software system's internal states can be understood from its external outputs. This emerging topic allows us to identify not only that something is broken but also where and why it's broken. Neat, right?

Observability is not only about the three pillars of telemetry—traces, metrics, and logs. Observability starts with collecting telemetry, but simply collecting it will not help us understand our system and make it observable. A system is truly observable only when we can utilize the collected telemetry to explain what is going on inside our system based on the observations we have made from the outside.

So monitoring is what will allow us to know that someone in Production Land is facing network issues, but it's observability that will allow us to know it's Chuck's next-door neighbor's bathroom that needs a firewall resync.

Are We Ready for Observability?

So what do you think? Is green software ready for observability? How should we ensure carbon metric moves with the hot new topic?

We did ask you in the previous section, "When a Carbon Metric Is Ready" on page 161, to dream about when we had it all figured out! In this section, we want you to continue this fantasy of ours, where we not only have standardized real-time metrics but also traces that can correlate events happening in intricate distributed systems. These correlations will help us pinpoint which event triggered which component to emit the most energy and, therefore, allow us to treat this bottleneck effectively and directly.

A truly observable system will not only help DevOps and SREs debug and troubleshoot an outage but also assist green software advocates in staying compliant with their sustainability SLOs in the most efficient ways. We want to know quickly which events are the culprit behind the high electricity usage!

We Will Get There

We hope we kept our promise and that this chapter is short and sweet.

We consider this chapter as "Monitoring 101 with a Touch of Green," an introductory guide to monitoring for those less familiar with the field, with our favorite character, Chuck, leading the way as we explore this space through the lens of green software.

Monitoring and observability have been the foundation of modern production system management for quite some time. After all, what's Rick without his sidekick, Morty? We are looking at significant downtime without either of them.

Borrowing from the Ponemon Institute's eye-opening statistics (*https://oreil.ly/ TC86X*), the average cost of downtime per minute is a staggering $9,000, leading to well over $500,000 for an hour of downtime. We therefore need this entertaining duo to help Chuck shorten his outage recovery time, saving us, his overlords, a significant amount of money and, naturally, reducing carbon emissions.

CHAPTER 11

Co-Benefits

The greatest victory is that which requires no battle.
—Sun Tzu, *The Art of War*

We would be lying if we said pursuing green software was an easy quest. We would need to hang our head in shame if we claimed convincing others about the inevitability of sustainability in the tech industry is a simple task. We would have to have a serious conversation with ourselves if we didn't acknowledge that sustainability has now taken a backseat in many organizations during the current economic downturns.

Our original intention for this chapter was to delve deeper into the multidisciplinary aspects of eco-friendly computing and explore the co-benefits of sustainability. By now, you likely understand the interdisciplinary nature of green software, where all areas of concern in software engineering are interconnected, and achieving a delicate balance among them is no easy task.

However, we cannot ignore the unprecedented challenges that most climate advocates have faced over the past several months. For the first time in history, we are witnessing climate records being broken left, right, and center. Yet, investments in addressing climate change are still struggling to become a top priority for many organizations, including those in the tech sector. (Legislation worldwide is slowly catching up to get everyone in the right gear, but the progress is just not happening fast enough.)

Therefore, we are shifting the attention of this chapter slightly. While we will still cover the positive side effects of implementing carbon efficiency in software, we will also provide you with a practical tool—a mental model—to help you demonstrate to your friends, colleagues, managers, and perhaps even your CTO that adopting eco-friendly practices in software operations and development not only benefits the environment (duh!) but also enhances software system performance, reliability, and resilience while reducing costs.

So hold on tight—this chapter is going to be an interesting one!

Is It About the Money?

We are kicking things off with a topic that will literally get you the most bang for your buck: cost-saving as an advantage of going green.

In Chapter 9, we assessed the pros and cons of using cost as a proxy measurement for carbon emissions. In this section, we will examine how and why embracing sustainable practices can enable you to build a budget-optimized product and vice versa.

Why Is Greener Also Cheaper?

A cost-effective workload is one that meets all business requirements with the lowest possible expenditure. So how does a cost-effective workload contribute to sustainability efforts? Let's find out!

There are several well-defined patterns for cost optimization when constructing a budget-friendly product that also delivers business value (e.g., the guidelines provided by public cloud providers like AWS, Microsoft, and GCP). Instead of listing them all here, we will cherry-pick the ones that caught our eyes and also have environmental gains.

Get a good fit

A great way to be cost-effective is to select the resource that best fits your requirements and then use it *as it was intended to be used*. For example, suppose you have chosen cloud provider GCP as your host. In that case, it's worth the effort to explore GCP's cloud-native solutions instead of using the cloud offerings as an infrastructure-as-a-service (IaaS), where you need to build, deploy, and manage your own creation, because that isn't *how GCP is intended to be used*. It wouldn't reduce your ops expenditure by much (if anything) and wouldn't take advantage of the huge investments Google has put into its services.

The term "cloud native" refers to solutions specifically designed to operate within a public cloud environment right from their very start. These solutions typically leverage technologies like containers, microservices, and, most importantly, services.

Let's look at an example of what we mean. Imagine you've been tasked with creating a distributed tracing solution that supports applications in the GCP ecosystem. In this scenario, the best-fitted choice for the data ingestion backend would usually be Google Cloud Trace (*https://oreil.ly/SCA2Y*), which was designed for that purpose. A more labor-intensive option would be to manually configure and deploy Grafana Tempo (*https://oreil.ly/lw3AK*) on top of Google Cloud Storage (*https://oreil.ly/DHUu5*).

By opting for the official service, you're saving on operational and hosting expenses and reducing carbon emissions because that service has been optimized for efficiency in that environment. You are using GCP as it was intended and benefiting from the costly efficiency work Google has already put into it, as well as the work it will do in the future.

 Distributed tracing is the response of DevOps and SREs to the complexity that arises from migration to microservices environments. It enables us to trace a request as it moves through an application. For example, it helps us track a request from the frontend to multiple microservices in the backend and finally to the database.

Another important best practice for getting a great operational fit for your systems is to use dynamic resource allocation to prevent expensive overprovisioning. An example of this is implementing autoscaling wherever possible to accommodate the fluctuating demands of a workload. This approach not only reduces costs but also contributes to carbon efficiency (as we discussed in Chapter 4). Removing idle or underutilized resources is even easier and has the same effect of reducing cost and increasing carbon efficiency.

So how should we tie this all together? FinOps (*https://oreil.ly/INsqX*), from the Linux Foundation (*https://www.linuxfoundation.org*), was created to help organizations regain control of spiraling cloud-computing expenses. It represents a collaborative effort to reduce cloud costs that bridges multiple disciplines, including technology, finance, and business.

FinOps and GreenOps are like sisters from another mother. Both are about optimizing software systems to reduce machine requirements and expensive electricity use. According to Pini Reznik of GreenOps consultancy re:cinq, folks in the cloud can cut bills by up to 50% by using FinOps and GreenOps best-practice tuning and optimization.

Going green really does save you bucks in the bank.

How About Reliability and Resilience?

The second point to ponder is reliability and resilience.

Before we dive into the specifics of why and how operating a reliable and resilient software system contributes to environmental efforts, let's begin by distinguishing between the two terms. They are often used interchangeably, but it's vital to understand their individual relevance to sustainability in this context and distinguish them from the related concept of availability.

Availability is a percentage. A service that has 99% availability is one that responds 99% of the time, even if that response time is slow or otherwise poor.

Reliability is related to a system's ability to consistently and correctly perform *its intended functions over time*. It measures the system's capacity to withstand failures and errors. For example, if your service-level objectives (SLOs) require requests to be processed within 3 ms, and this happens 99% of the time, then it's 99% reliable.

In contrast, *resilience* refers to a system's capability for swift and graceful recovery from failures and disruptions. It demonstrates a system's ability to resume functionality in the face of unforeseen circumstances. Essentially, as detailed in Microsoft's well-architected framework, "a reliable workload is both resilient and available."

Resilience is closely intertwined with operational efficiency and is a huge step forward for both system reliability and sustainability.

Until recently, our primary strategy for providing system reliability was redundancy. We used to maintain duplicate physical copies of a system in a variety of different locations with the aim of guaranteeing there was always ready-and-waiting capacity to failover to in the event of a problem.

The trouble is that maintaining copies is wasteful in terms of hardware and electricity. Those backup systems spend the vast majority of their lives sitting idle because that is their point. Redundancy: the clue is in the name.

Such systems exist solely in the hope they will never have to step in and save the day. Unfortunately, if they are ever called upon to do so, they too often fail. This is sometimes due to a lack of testing but also because when one region has an outage, it is not wildly unusual for the others to hit the same issue. It turns out that, as well as being carbon inefficient, redundancy is not the best solution for reliability.

Building resilience is the more efficient, modern approach to reliability and is more dynamic and effective, as well as requiring less in the way of reserved hardware resources.

Resilience involves the automated and programmatic operational techniques and lightning-fast responses commonly associated with DevOps and site reliability engineering (SRE). These include monitoring for errors, autoscaling, and automatic restarts. The goal is to recover from issues in real time rather than failover to waiting servers, and a resilient system may leverage flexible cloud resources even if it is on prem by default.

Resilience uses automation to reduce time-to-recovery and enhance reliability while getting rid of the need for all those static backups. At the same time, the improved monitoring techniques make the system more aware of its energy and hardware usage, and as efficiency guru Peter Drucker mentioned, what you measure tends to improve.

Example

Let's consider an ecommerce store that sells underwear. We can confidently state that the online shop is reliable because, even during the Black Friday rush, the store can withstand the huge growth in traffic. Customers are still able to browse selections, add items to their carts, and place orders using credit cards without compromising any SLOs, such as transaction latency.

 Latency is about how long it takes to process a request. In real-world terms, this is the time needed for the online store to respond to a button.

Furthermore, we can say that the store is resilient because it successfully and dynamically shifted itself to a different region when the location where it was initially deployed experienced an outage.

What we have just described is a difficult feat in the realm of software engineering—the ability to provide a reliable and resilient service—and behind every such product lies a constant stream of firefighting incidents. We are sure that nearly all SREs, or anyone who has held a pager, can relate to the terrible experience of dealing with an outage of any scale, but we learn from them and improve. In fact, that's why our industry started moving from redundancy to the more sustainable and effective resilience.

If SREs can leverage potential catastrophic outages as a means to persuade their teams and higher-ups of the importance of prioritizing reliability from day one, thereby getting a more robust system, why can't green software engineers do the same to get greener systems?

As stated by green software expert Bill Johnson, "Reliability over time is a great way to define sustainability," and we too see these areas of concern as connected. During the energy transition, a lack of electricity at certain times is going to be a whole new failure mode for systems. On top of that, climate-related weather events are going to increase the failure rate of all physical infrastructure. Resilience makes systems greener and cheaper and, as importantly, more reliable in the face of a changing climate.

Maybe It's Performance?

The human race has always been fascinated by pushing boundaries. We began with physical challenges; for instance, there are many forms of competitive running, such as sprints, marathons, and obstacle course racing. When we exhausted the ideas for physical challenges for the human body, we turned to machinery. There are numerous competitive showdowns between various mechanical devices. There are radio-controlled car racing, boat racing, and, of course, the fast-and-furious Formula 1. Software engineers are no exception. Ask any developer. Isn't a performant system everyone's wildest dream?

A *performant system* in the context of software engineering is one that can handle the demands it encounters *fast*.

How Fast Is Fast Enough?

Before the widespread usage of cloud computing and the emergence of on-demand offerings, many engineering organizations dealing with on-prem setups had to attempt (and sometimes fail) to predict their peak requirements, and they overprovisioned resources intentionally to make sure they could meet their business needs.

Unfortunately, as we have pointed out before, overprovisioning is a wasteful practice.

It increases embodied carbon due to extra wiring and hardware, and it hinders innovation (because setting up a server isn't as quick as Amazon's next-day shipping). It lowers operational efficiency, leading to additional costs and wasteful outcomes across the board, including carbon emissions induced by electricity.

Therefore, striving for an intelligently performant system that doesn't rely on over-provisioning is not just a hardcore badge that every practitioner wants to collect anymore; it's also a vital goal. Why? This is because such a system is also a green one.

Best Fit and Performance

There are many well-established design principles that address performance, but one of the most effective is looking for the best fit between what you want to do and the resources you use to achieve it.

One example is optimizing your compute layer by choosing the appropriate option for your intended use case (in other words, selecting the correct type of machine for your workload—like a memory-optimized one for 4D gaming).

Choosing the best hardware fit not only provides a more performant experience but can also contribute to energy and carbon savings because specialist hardware is much more energy efficient.

 There is always a calculation to be made in terms of the embodied carbon bill from choosing specialist over generalist hardware, but for well-managed, heavily used hardware, electricity use is usually more of a contributor to climate change than the kit's embodied carbon. In good data centers, energy efficiency is usually more important.

Optimizing your storage layer is another well-established approach to performance improvement. Data management has emerged as a field that requires careful consideration. Most enterprises must now meet multiple regulatory requirements for their data storage across many countries and even continents.

For instance, consider a savings account application with data subject to different retention rules. You may need frequent access to a customer's identification details, such as name and account number, while bank statements are required less often and must be retained for different lengths of time in different regions. Deliberately selecting the appropriate storage type for each of those requirements is a must for cost-saving, performance, and sustainability.

As an example, let's consider how you might handle this in the world of AWS. What you could do is consult its object storage performance sheet (a.k.a. performance chart across the S3 storage types (*https://oreil.ly/v6PQl*)). You may choose the glacier-level classes for data that you need to keep for regulatory requirements but that don't require constant access, such as 10-year-old emails. You could opt for the standard class for objects that require frequent manipulation, such as the current month's credit card balance.

As well as better performance, selecting the right storage type will lead to, you guessed it, reductions in embodied carbon and energy usage, as AWS can now be smarter about its resource usage.

It's hopefully becoming obvious where we are heading with this section: most of the best practices in performance have knock-on green benefits through efficiency, a topic we discussed in detail in Chapters 3 and 4. So we can avoid repeating ourselves, please revisit those chapters if you need a quick refresher.

Efficiency is a key driver of both performance and carbon reduction in software, and the result is that greener is usually faster.

It's Got to Be Security!

Many would argue that security is the most crucial regard of any software business. An unsecured product is a betrayal of users. It can lead to significant damage to an organization's reputation, eroding valuable trust not only with customers and vendors but also with regulators.

Information security has always been a complex discipline, and regrettably, it has evolved as drastically as climate change. Attackers worldwide now possess more computer processing power than ever before. They also have access to much larger attack surfaces thanks to the ever-increasing "unknown unknowns" arising from intricate distributed systems (sometimes stretching over multiple hosting providers). Therefore, it would be foolish of us to attempt to provide a comprehensive guide on secure software design. Fortunately, there are many well-written materials available for your reference. In this section, we will pay attention to the characteristics of a secure system that have positive effects on the environment.

 Unknown unknowns, which imply unidentified information (i.e., subjects you are unaware of or do not fully understand), originate from the four quadrants of the Rumsfeld matrix (*https://oreil.ly/ EZsLF*)—a framework not inherently related to software engineering and operations, but nevertheless, a paradigm that has been broadly applied in the field and across various domains to enhance our understanding of certainty and uncertainty when making decisions. For example, in chaos engineering (*https://oreil.ly/O0sHh*), you are encouraged to conduct experiments following the Rumsfeld matrix to figure out which things to break first!

A *secure system* is one that can withstand malicious attacks. Those may range in origin from you absentmindedly clicking on a link that you shouldn't have, resulting in the installation of malware, to a sophisticated distributed denial-of-service (DDoS) attack that disrupts your regular traffic. Either of these scenarios (and many more) can have disastrous outcomes, including revenue loss and reputation damage. One of the less appreciated is wasteful carbon emissions.

Security Is Green

For example, drawing inspiration from CDN company Cloudflare's real-world analogy (*https://oreil.ly/CBBMi*), we can think of a DDoS attack like surprise congestion that obstructs your morning commute to work. Your workplace symbolizes your servers; you represent a regular user trying to access those servers, and the congestion signifies the DDoS attack's malicious increase in network traffic that impedes or even blocks genuine requests.

The increase in network load from a DDoS attack can lead to a surge in energy consumption due to overworking resources such as CPU and memory. Such attacks also waste embodied carbon due to the need for additional hardware to handle malicious traffic while maintaining normal service. In short, DDoS attacks waste energy and cause greenhouse gas emissions with no benefit to anyone (apart from the attacker).

Preventing or closing down attacks like DDoS ones rather than overprovisioning in order to survive them is, therefore, greener and more secure. There is plenty of material (*https://oreil.ly/3_-tq*) out there on the techniques to do this, including reducing your attack surface and rate limiting.

Security expert Ed Harrison pointed out in Chapter 4 that one of the primary ways of reducing your attack surface is also a green technique: closing down zombie systems and servers that are no longer needed.

Secure systems are greener than insecure ones, and a secure system is inherently more credible and dependable. That trustworthiness holds significant value, enhancing marketability and leading to increased sales and adoption. There is, thus, a positive feedback loop between sustainability and security.

But What About Data?

Data is everywhere, quite literally.

The watches we wear, the cars we drive, and even the refrigerators where we store our favorite beer are all examples of Internet of Things (IoT) devices. According to the *State of IoT 2023* report (*https://oreil.ly/ZFbvo*), the world observed an 18% increase in IoT connections in 2022, rising to 14.3 billion active end points. They all gather data, and these statistics are just for 2022 IoT devices—we haven't even touched on the data that will be gathered for LLM models yet.

IoT devices are any machines equipped with sensors that have the ability to collect and analyze data while being connected to other devices through a network (usually the internet).

Such an enormous volume of data can be thought of as an unorganized pile of Lego pieces and, if thoughtlessly managed, has the potential to be just as hazardous (surely, everyone has accidentally stepped on a loose Lego piece and experienced the agony).

This data is going to be transmitted, processed, and stored, all of which has a hefty carbon bill attached. Therefore, at every stage (source, transformation, pipeline, destination, usage, and behaviors), thorough consideration, planning, and management are imperative. Again, plenty of material exists out there on best practices for IoT data management. The bad news is that being green means you are going to have to read it.

Control LLMs

The rise of LLMs and AI (LLMs once again taking the spotlight) has resulted in a wealth of new, well-written material on data management, covering a wide range of topics from data analytics to data engineering and data observability.

The good news is that each of these emerging fields offers practical best-practice guidelines that align well with green software principles, so follow them. For instance, data sanitization typically leads to more accurate and repeatable end results while also reducing the demands on storage and computation. Therefore, clean and correct data promotes sustainability by encouraging efficiency and automation.

Think About Data Models

We strongly recommend investing effort in creating a data model that suits your specific use case and aligns with the needs of both upstream and downstream processes (ideally, your entire organization).

Almost all enterprise engineers have faced the endless need to transform data from one format to another to make it compatible with your systems. These transformations are famous for being resource intensive, even with automation in place. It is, therefore, greener, cheaper, less bug-prone, and more performant to design models that can scale and adapt to new requirements and need less in the way of transformation.

There are many more parallels between sustainability and other data management techniques that we could point out, but it's vital to recognize that the primary challenge in this field is the sheer volume of data, all of which has a potential carbon cost. Following best practices when dealing with data is crucial for reasons of cost, performance, security, and legality, as well as environmental impact.

Actually, It's All of the Above

The wise warrior avoids the battle.

—Sun Tzu, *The Art of War*

We are singing the same hymn again, namely, another quote from Sun Tzu!

What we are trying to say here is that sustainability does not need to compete with the other priorities in software development and operations. If you are a glass-half-full kind of person, the utopia for green software advocates really is a flowery garden where everything coexists in harmony.

We argue that green software practices should be integrated into everything we build, manage, and operate. In fact, they should not merely be integrated but should also serve as the foundation.

Our stance should not come as a surprise to you (unless Chapter 11 is the first chapter you're reading). The very bad news is our beautiful planet is currently facing significant challenges: we are experiencing out-of-the-ordinary droughts, unexpected storms, and record-breaking temperatures every day. The fortunate news for us is that in our industry, a shift to sustainability is aligned with our other priorities. Being green is about being efficient, which means faster and cheaper software, which, as we have seen, can be used to increase security and resilience and thus reduce risk.

In Figure 11-1, we place sustainability at the center of all priorities. You might argue that another, such as performance or security, should be king. However, we will counter with a stern face. Every piece of software needed to become carbon efficient yesterday.

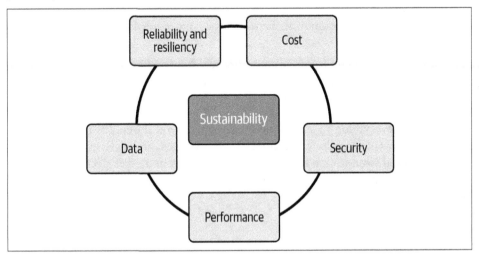

Figure 11-1. A mind map of the computer programming pillars of consideration, with sustainability as the foundation

We have now dedicated substantial time to drawing parallels between sustainability and other tech priorities. This side-by-side comparison is another valuable tool you should add to your toolkit (see Figure 11-2).

For example, if you are engaging in conversations with your data team or chief data officer, you should absolutely seize the opportunity to highlight the strong connection between green software and data engineering.

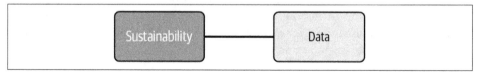

Figure 11-2. Another visual guide demonstrating the close links sustainability in tech has with other focus areas

The strategy of highlighting the alignment between green software and other priorities offers an alternative approach to raising awareness of this crucial topic. While doom-and-gloom tactics may have been productive in the past, they are no longer the most practical option, especially when budgets are tight. We need to show that being green is an opportunity to build better software, not merely a cost.

We firmly believe that presenting green tech in the following ascending order (depending on your level of maturity, as explained in Chapter 12) will give you a massive leg up!

1. Carbon efficiency can be achieved through applying existing best-practice design principles such as the ones associated with performance and cost cutting.

2. Green software is not an ivory tower; it's part of many other well-defined pillars of consideration in computing; hence, it does not require an entirely new stream of workflow.

3. Software will benefit from carbon efficiency being integrated into it from the outset. Therefore, sustainability should be considered a fundamental aspect of all software products and decision-making processes.

Much as with everything in software engineering, careful thought is required. Striking the right balance, making the correct compromises, and determining precisely what is required from both a functional and a nonfunctional perspective will enable you to create a product that is budget-friendly, reliable, performant, secure, *and* environmentally friendly.

Right, We Think You're Ready

You're all set! We hope this roller-coaster ride of a chapter hasn't left you weary.

Our goal was to shed light on the once-not-so-obvious similarities between the design principles of sustainability and other critical aspects of software engineering. We've covered five selected areas with a couple of guidelines, along with real-world analogies. We have no doubt that you are now capable of conducting similar exercises for any other area of concern you see fit (you can do it!)!

While we fully acknowledge that integrating sustainability into any software system isn't smooth sailing, it's worth noting that adding the challenge of convincing others that it's a priority, especially during economic downturns, is like navigating a small boat through a storm at sea.

However, we have complete faith that, after the journey we've taken you on in this chapter, you are now well prepared to engage in conversations with everyone around you about integrating sustainability from the get-go.

Implementing sustainability early not only has numerous positive side effects but also might prove to be less challenging than you initially thought. (Thanks to all the best-practice pioneers who have paved the way for green software.)

CHAPTER 12

The Green Software Maturity Matrix

I can only show you the door. You're the one that has to walk through it.
—Morpheus

The *Green Software Maturity Matrix (GSMM)* is a self-assessment tool from the Linux Foundation's Green Software Foundation.

The GSMM is designed to help organizations understand how well they've already implemented green principles and processes and what to do next. It is part of the GSF's campaign of raising the floor and the ceiling—lifting the behavior of the laggards on green tech and inspiring those doing OK to achieve more by showing what the leaders are up to.

Its intent is to give directions to a well-trodden path so we get the decisive benefit of shared progress on tools and services (see Figure 12-1).

 Anyone can comment on or contribute (*https://oreil.ly/XK7cf*) to the project on GitHub. You don't need to be a GSF member. Anne is the project lead, and she would be very happy to see you.

Note that the GSMM is focused on how, as part of their day-to-day working lives, software practitioners can reduce greenhouse gas emissions. It does not cover water use in DCs, species protection, or any other worthy environmental aim. As we currently understand it, those aims are mostly dictated by data center choice, and developers have little scope to improve on that choice later, particularly iteratively. So decide on your DC wisely.

	Aspiring	Aware	Acting	Awesome	Inspiring
Commitments	None	Carbon neutral	Carbon zero with offsets	10% (offset)	1% (offset)
Footprint	Unknown	Know scope 1&2	Reducing per unit	Reducing absolutely	~Zero
Metrics	None	Report scope 1&2	Daily scope 1&2&3	Real-time	Predicted
Carbon ops	None	Manual	LightSwitchOps	Auto-rightsizing	Carbon SRE
Energy	None	Green hosting	Dynamic management	Demand shaping	24/7 carbon-free electricity
Devices	None	Some targets	10y/90%	10y/95%	Rolling repair
Utilization	None	Some multitenant	All multitenant	Max orchestration	Edge integration
Products	None	Carbon awareness	Demand shaping	Feature tracking	Feature carbon error budgets
Training	Ad hoc	Basic/champions	Advanced	You are the trainer	You are the leader

Figure 12-1. The GSF's Green Software Maturity Matrix

The History of Maturity Matrices

Way back in 1986, when Anne was still wearing fluorescent leg warmers and Sara and Sarah weren't born, the first maturity matrix (sometimes called a maturity model), the Capability Maturity Model Integration (CMMI (*https://cmmiinstitute.com*)), was developed by the Software Engineering Institute at Carnegie Mellon University. It was designed as a framework for assessing and guiding organizations' efforts at process improvement.

Maturity matrices are now used in a wide variety of fields, including project management and cybersecurity, to let companies assess where they stand in terms of best practice. They also point out the practical steps those organizations can take to achieve higher levels of performance.

A maturity matrix usually has five (see the list below and Figure 12-2). The aim is for an organization to adopt better processes and tools to ascend from level 1 to 5:

- Level 1: Aspiring—Processes are unpredictable, poorly controlled, and reactive at best.
- Level 2: Aware—Per-project processes. Often still reactive.

- Level 3: Acting—Processes are standardized, documented, well understood, and reviewed.
- Level 4: Awesome—Processes are measured and controlled.
- Level 5: Inspiring—Continuous improvement occurs based on quantitative feedback.

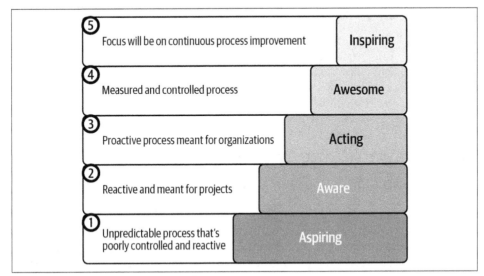

Figure 12-2. Ascending the steps of a maturity matrix

We'll go through the details of how these levels relate to green software next, but we reckon this broadly means:

- Level 1: You are floundering with no organization-level strategy. You have individuals who care or are knowledgeable about being green.
- Level 2: You are starting to get some handle on stuff but without consistency. How advanced you are varies by project and team. You have the bare minimum of emissions data.
- Level 3: You are good. You have basic organization-wide knowledge and decent retrospective data. You have defined processes, which are applied across your organization. You are already acting successfully on green improvements that don't need great data.
- Level 4: You are awesome. You can measure your progress dynamically (i.e., you have got your hands on real-time data).
- Level 5: You have ascended to the next plane of existence. You monitor and improve emissions performance based on real-time data. You give aspirational talks at tech conferences, and what people are aspiring to is what you have been

doing for ages. You are the tech equivalent of a being of pure energy. Think Yoda with a keyboard.

 The audience for the Green Software Foundation's Maturity Matrix is senior folk in tech organizations and internal green advocates. The aim is guiding their high-level journey and giving them something to report progress against.

Consultants also tend to like a maturity matrix because it helps them explain to clients the service they're offering and what good looks like. That makes it easier to persuade those clients to invest time and effort in a project because they know they'll be able to assess progress (and prove it isn't just greenwashing). That's good. We want more folk offering professional services in green software.

Green Software Maturity Matrix

Before we start discussing the details of the GSMM, we need to talk about the good news.

Fortunately, you don't need to wait for great data to start being greener and moving up the maturity levels from 1: Aspiring (where almost all of us are right now) to 2: Aware. That's lucky because, as we discussed in Chapter 9, measuring your greenhouse gas emissions is not yet straightforward. The tools are still evolving.

At levels 1 and 2 of the GSMM, there is effective stuff you can do immediately. The author of our foreword, Adrian Cockcroft, pointed out to us that the ubiquitous quote "You can't improve what you can't measure" (often attributed to the management guru Peter Drucker) isn't true in the case of being green.

There are well-understood actions with guaranteed payoffs in carbon reduction, which everyone can start taking. For example:

- Turning off underutilized machines (a.k.a. zombies) and doing manual rightsizing
- Choosing a hosting location with a greener grid
- Moving some workloads to the cloud and using the services there, or otherwise investigating how you might leverage multitenancy
- Improving your ops skills, for example, by starting to learn about GitOps or SRE principles

Anything you do to cut your hosting bill will cut your emissions, so use that as an initial proxy measurement. You could get started today.

Levels

Let's look in more detail at the levels of the Green Software Maturity Matrix v1.0.

 If you need a refresher on some of these measurement terms, take a quick flick again through Chapter 9.

Level 1

At level 1 of the matrix ("Aspiring"):

- Individuals in your organization care about green targets for technology but have no organization-wide interest, processes, or commitments.
- Some development teams may measure their carbon emissions, but you don't know the overall tech-derived carbon footprint of your company.
- You have no carbon-zero targets or green software strategy (or you have wooly carbon-zero targets like *Net Zero by 2050* (*https://oreil.ly/TEro_*) with no plan behind them).

Realistically, this is where most of us are today. Don't feel bad. It means there are a lot of improvements you can make without that much effort.

Level 2

At level 2 ("Aware"):

- You know your tech organization's scope 1 and 2 emissions, perhaps weekly, monthly, or annually.
- You have a few projects driving carbon reduction within your tech organization, maybe using the data you have but not necessarily.
- Your engineers have had some training in green systems and operations.
- You are doing the no-brainer stuff we mentioned in Chapter 4, like manually turning off zombie services that are no longer in use, rightsizing, or switching what functionality you can to spot instances.

Five years ago, you would have just offset your scope 1 and 2 emissions, labeled your IT systems as carbon neutral, and sent out a self-congratulatory press release. Nowadays, this is only stage 2 of 5 because our expectations have risen: offsets are seen as having limited value, and carbon neutral is fine but nowhere near enough.

Nonetheless, if you are here, you are doing OK. Most folk are not.

"Carbon neutral" was what you used to call yourself if you had bought stuff that was supposed to offset your own carbon emissions. Offsets were things like trees being planted or new renewable power plants being supported. Nowadays, offsetting isn't considered to be that useful because renewables are booming without help and new trees don't store carbon for long enough to make much difference. However, it does show you are measuring your direct emissions, and in the past, being an early customer for renewables was very effective.

Level 3

At level 3 ("Acting"):

- You know your scope 1, 2, and 3 emissions on a daily, weekly, monthly, or annual basis.
- You know your embodied carbon.
- You have been acting on reducing your scope 1 and 2 emissions for a while, and your carbon footprint is going down per some consistent org-specific unit of output (e.g., per order).
- You have defined processes for every team, including regular reporting and reviewing of CO_2 equivalent emissions for all IT-related operations.
- Your product management teams have a remit to avoid waste, for example, by not saving more data than is necessary and not implementing functionality before need (also known as a Lean mindset).
- You can easily switch off zombie or low-use services whenever you like (i.e., you support LightSwitchOps).
- You are aware of the potential trade-offs between carbon emissions from electricity and embodied carbon, and you have plans in place to minimize your embodied carbon footprint, including significantly extending the life expectancy of both the servers and the end-user devices you run on.

Level 3 is good. If you are already here, you are well ahead of the crowd.

Level 4

At level 4 ("Awesome"):

- Your organizational tech strategy has been aligned with being green as a business goal—perhaps for reasons of ESG, cost, resilience, or market access to the EU—and delivery on emission targets is regularly discussed and reported at the senior level.

- Using the basic scope 1, 2, and 3 data you have had for a while, you have already achieved net carbon zero using no more than 10% offsets (*https://oreil.ly/gXdpv*). (Most offsets are problematic, but some are OK and long-term carbon capture and storage (*https://oreil.ly/XDYKb*) is necessary.)

- You have some form of measurement system in place and have good real-time scope 1, 2, and 3 data, and although it's not currently driving the business day to day, the business is aware of it.

- You perform demand shaping, precalculation and caching, or time and location shifting, for example, to adapt your workloads to current conditions. You automatically delete or archive data that isn't in regular use.

- Services no longer in use are automatically turned off, and rightsizing happens automatically (i.e., you apply SRE principles).

- Your applications are Lean, and you constantly review and retire functionality that is insufficiently used.

- Your total IT carbon footprint is going down even as you grow.

- You never cause hardware less than 10 years old to reach end of life either by lack of security patches or lack of backward compatibility in your applications.

- You are actively driving the carbon footprint of your customers to go down (beyond simply their use of your services and devices), for example, by providing scope 3 reporting for your goods and services.

Level 4 is well beyond what most enterprises are doing right now, and there are no commodity services that provide all the functionality required (not even spot instances provide 24/7 carbon-based demand shifting yet). So for enterprises, it is too soon. AWS, Azure, and Google (*https://oreil.ly/wonps*) are only here on some axes.

Level 5

At level 5 ("Inspiring"):

- You have achieved 24/7 carbon-free electricity (*https://oreil.ly/P9jjw*) (24/7 CFE) and require no more than 1% offsets to handle hard-to-shift embodied carbon.

- You have team-level goals for your carbon measurements.

- You and the services you rely on use real-time information, including dynamic grid energy data, to make rapid, quantitative decisions that allow you to optimize for minimal emissions. This could (and probably will) be via a service you use rather than something you built yourself. The data complies with an open standard so meaningful comparisons can be made.

- You are already an SRE-aware organization that thinks in terms of error budgets (*https://oreil.ly/XMvxL*) for outages and downtime, and you now think about carbon emissions having error budgets in the same way as other metrics do.

- Using predictions based on factors such as weather and grid congestion, you change and move almost all of your workloads ahead of time to match your electricity requirements to local green-power availability. Any time-sensitive workloads are highly optimized for minimal electricity use.

- You never cause hardware to reach end of life either by lack of security patches for your software or lack of backward compatibility.

 24/7 CFE is a term used to describe when you are only drawing power from the grid when, at the same time, there is enough carbon-free electricity being fed into that grid to cover your use.

At this stage, you are ready for the energy transition and won't be caught by surprise by new rules or constraints. More rigorous expectations beyond 24/7 CFE will almost certainly be introduced in the future (we don't know what they will look like yet!), but you will be ready for them.

Axes

In practical terms, no business is going to be at the same level across the entire tech organization (except maybe level 1!). Green software maturity will vary team by team. It is therefore useful to break everything down into areas (axes) and define maturity checklists for each:

- Climate commitments
- Carbon footprint
- CO_2 equivalent metrics
- Operational efficiency
- Electricity use

- End-user devices
- Servers
- Product management
- Education

Responsibility for each of these areas will probably sit with different groups or teams, and how green they are may differ wildly (at least to start with). An organization might be level 2 on some of these axes and level 1, 3, or 4 on others.

Axes Checklists

Future tech climate commitments
Level 1: By 2050, you have net carbon zero (*https://oreil.ly/snRA0*).

Level 2: By 2040, you have net carbon zero for scope 1, 2, and 3 (note that you may already be carbon neutral for your scope 1 and 2 emissions).

Level 3: You already have net carbon zero with offsets.

Level 4: You already have net carbon zero with no more than 10% offsets.

Level 5: You already have 24/7 CFE with no more than 1% offsets, monitored by a carbon error budget.

Current tech carbon footprint
Level 1: You don't know what it is.

Level 2: You know what it is (for scope 1 and 2).

Level 3: You know what it is (for scope 1, 2, and 3), and it is reducing per defined unit of output (e.g., orders).

Level 4: It is reducing, full stop, and so is that of your suppliers.

Level 5: It is close to zero.

Resolution of CO_2 equivalent metrics for tech
Level 1: You have no metrics.

Level 2: You have annual, quarterly, or monthly numbers from all suppliers and own systems for scope 1 and 2.

Level 3: You have regular numbers from all suppliers and your own systems for scope 1, 2, and 3.

Level 4: You have real-time metrics through an industry-standard API.

Level 5: You have both real-time metrics and projections through an industry-standard API.

Operational efficiency
Level 1: No rightsizing takes place, and you have zero knowledge about unused "zombie" systems.

Level 2: Occasional spring cleans happen where you manually turn off idle or low-value systems and delete/archive unneeded data.

Level 3: All systems can be safely switched off (a.k.a. LightSwitchOps), and there are regular processes for doing so. You have knowledge of what is running on all your machines, and there are no zombie services. Processes exist for rightsizing.

You save no unnecessary data, and it is maintained in the optimal medium (e.g., tape if the data is not required for real-time queries).

Level 4: You continuously monitor climate metrics. All turning off and rightsizing happens automatically (perhaps through services like burstable instances), and data that is not regularly accessed is automatically deleted or archived.

Level 5: You have a rigorous carbon error budget, including for your scope 3 embodied carbon, and all your resource use is tracked and managed against it.

Electricity use

Level 1: Your systems are always on, and you don't think about electricity.

Level 2: You host in green regions or buy renewable energy.

Level 3: At least part of your systems are dynamically managed based on green electricity availability (either via direct orchestration or through a cloud service).

Level 4: All your systems support demand shifting and shaping based on energy data.

Level 5: You run 24/7 CFE with a rigorous carbon error budget.

Minimizing end-user device embodied carbon waste

Level 1: You have no end-user device longevity targets.

Level 2: Some ad hoc targets are in place for device longevity.

Level 3: You have defined processes in place that ensure 10-year-old hardware is supported by your software for most commonly used devices (90%+).

Level 4: Automated processes ensure 10-year-old hardware is supported by your software for 95% of devices.

Level 5: Automated processes ensure backward compatibility, and security patches are available for all devices (i.e., your software never kills a working device). You support devices that last forever like the Ship of Theseus (this is a potential future requirement for goods imported into the EU).

 The Ship of Theseus is the subject of a famous classical thought experiment about whether an object that has had all of its components replaced remains fundamentally the same object. Philosophy aside, continuous maintenance and repair is a way to minimize waste and thus embodied carbon. We need to treat devices like something precious and worth preserving—e.g., Theseus's ship—not something meaningless and throwaway.

Servers

Level 1: You have no server utilization targets.

Level 2: Some of your systems are using multitenancy to improve utilization.

Level 3: You have defined and tracked utilization targets. All your systems use some form of multitenancy, and any servers you run on have a five-year life expectancy.

Level 4: Optimal utilization is achieved for every server using automated, programmatic orchestration. The servers you use all have a 10-year life expectancy.

Level 5: Hardware use is minimized by using full grid-aware integration with end-user devices, including phones, laptops, smart clothing, fridges, etc.

Product management

Level 1: Your PM teams are not carbon aware.

Level 2: Carbon awareness is part of your product design.

Level 3: All new product design supports demand shifting/shaping, and lean concepts are followed. Your end-user devices prompt for green/off peak charging, and no more data is saved than necessary.

Level 4: Carbon emissions are tracked per feature. Feature use is monitored, and low-use/poor-carbon ROI features are retired.

Level 5: Your features are tracked against your scope 1, 2, and 3 carbon error budget.

Education

Level 1: All your green tech training is ad hoc, driven by the individual.

Level 2: Basic training in green software concepts is available for all software practitioners. Champions are given more advanced training.

Level 3: Advanced training is mandatory for all your engineers and PMs.

Level 4: Only basic training is needed for most because everything is green by default in your platforms.

Level 5: You train others in what you have achieved.

Where Are We Today?

The hard truth is that almost all of us are at level 1 on the Green Software Maturity Matrix right now, and we need to move up.

However, that means the biggest wins are directly in front of us. Low-hanging fruit that gets us from level 1 to 2, like turning off unused servers, could immediately cut greenhouse gas emissions in half, while saving you money and making your systems more secure.

So let's get cracking!

CHAPTER 13

Where Do We Go from Here?

Don't Panic!
—Douglas Adams, *The Hitchhiker's Guide to the Galaxy*

Perhaps we should have had the Douglas Adams quote on the cover of this book because we're not doomers. We believe humanity will adapt to and mitigate climate change and survive and then thrive on our new renewable power sources.

However, not all enterprises, organizations, or software systems will. They will have to adapt or die, as the saying goes.

The good news is that our industry is beginning to wake up. Five years ago, it was controversial to talk about green software at a tech conference because the subject was seen as "political." Now, you would have to be somewhat behind the times (another British understatement) to think adopting green software was anything but a pragmatic move.

The purpose of this book is a practical one. We want to help folk create systems that can handle the transition from the highly dependable, seasoned, but carbon-intensive, fossil-fueled electricity grids of the past to the new renewably powered ones of the future. In addition, those systems need to use hardware more efficiently.

 As an aside, you may have noticed we made no attempt in this book to convince anyone of the reality of climate change. If you don't see any cause for concern in the famous hockey stick graph (*https://oreil.ly/Ole2s*) of global temperature rises over the past millennia, you aren't part of our target audience.

As we said at the beginning, the energy transition isn't going to last forever. Eventually, the solar, wind, nuclear, and battery combo will be humming, and we will have more and cheaper power than we do today. That time will arrive faster than we think. However, in the meantime we are switching humanity over from energy sources with which we have had hundreds of years of experience to brand-new ones.

Let's face it, Homo sapiens got bloody good at fossil-fueling, and we aren't going to be as good at renewables for decades. That means we consumers of electricity need to lend a hand.

Why Us?

The tech industry and its use of electricity isn't the biggest contributor (*https://oreil.ly/1gCCj*) to climate change. Nor are we the most difficult to decarbonize: we aren't agriculture, manufacturing, transportation, or construction. Data centers are the cause of only a few percentage points of fossil fuel energy use (*https://oreil.ly/zmmax*), although if you include embodied carbon waste from all those phones and other devices, our impact is higher (*https://oreil.ly/ck2h-*).

We are not the worst culprit, but that doesn't matter. We are still a culprit. It is necessary for every industry to cut its emissions, and we get no special pass. There is no silver bullet for climate change. We can't just fix one or two sectors to solve the problem. We all have to get our direct and indirect emissions down to close to zero.

Even if we didn't have a social imperative to reduce our emissions, we have plenty of commercial ones. Our industry runs on electricity, and the electricity market is in the process of being revolutionized. Always available, fossil-fueled electricity is being replaced with lower-cost but variable renewables. Batteries and nuclear can provide a degree of availability at times of no wind or solar, but they will add materially to the electricity's cost.

Going green is not just about battling climate change but also about adapting to a new world. Systems that use demand shifting and shaping to run on low-carbon electricity will have far, far cheaper power. It will often be free. That is starting to be true even now, and the companies that can make excellent use of this new power will win.

Power is the carrot, but there is also a stick. At the time of publishing, the European Union will have just introduced a new set of regulations called the Carbon Border Adjustment Mechanism (CBAM) (*https://oreil.ly/r3YfW*). The CBAM imposes tariffs on imports of goods into the EU and on services provided to EU citizens. These tariffs are related to the greenhouse gases emitted directly or indirectly during the production of these goods and services.

In the beginning, those import rules will only apply to heavily polluting industries like steel and coal, but within nine years, the EU expects them to apply to all goods and services. In the future, that means to access the EU market, we'll need to have accurate numbers on our scope 1, 2, and 3 emissions, and we'll pay hefty taxes on them. Tech companies will have to step up and comply with CBAM in the same way we all had to adopt the EU's GDPR—except complying with CBAM will be a lot more difficult.

GDPR applies to any organization that wants to collect data about EU citizens. It came into effect in May 2018, and just before that, there was a scramble by companies worldwide to get their head round it and comply—with hefty fines if you got it wrong.

The lesson here is that the EU knows how to throw its weight around and has plenty of form for doing so. Its attention is now on greenhouse gas emissions, and it has no intention of letting companies from outside the EU, in countries with lower emissions standards, undercut EU businesses.

The problem is that this is tough stuff. Going green is the most difficult challenge our industry has faced. For many companies, it will take 10 years to get from level 1 of the Green Software Maturity Matrix (GSMM), which we covered in Chapter 12, to level 5, and it looks like 10 years is all the EU is going to give us. At best. It might well be less.

Moving Through the Matrix

In Chapter 12, we talked about the GSMM and how we have to move up it. For most of us, that means climbing from level 1 (barely started on efficient and demand-shapeable and shiftable systems) to level 5 (systems that can run 24/7 on carbon-free electricity).

Achieving level 5 is a long-term project. We will have to take it gradually to give new tooling and green platforms time to develop. However, we can all start work immediately on getting to level 2 or 3. For that, we only need operational tools that are already available.

With some focus, we believe most of us could cut carbon emissions from our existing systems in half within six months. That is our challenge for all our maturity matrix level 1 and 2 readers (i.e., pretty much everyone).

The Green Software 50% Challenge

Or How I Cut My Emissions in Half Using Common Household Objects

The excellent news is we can cut emissions by 50% and do it fast without buying expensive tools that don't even exist yet, by exercising the superpower of currently being rubbish. (A much underrated superpower in our opinion.)

The good thing about being at level 1 of the GSMM is that there is plenty of low-hanging fruit immediately in front of you. You have several quick and relatively easy options to cut your emissions:

- Identify and switch off those zombie servers that aren't doing anything (or anything much). Remember, as we discussed in Chapter 4, this alone saved VMWare 66% on its emissions when it moved one data center (DC) in Singapore.

- Do a one-off rightsizing exercise on all your servers, because everything tends to be overprovisioned to start with.

- Turn off your test systems in the evening and on weekends.

- Because of its extreme multitenancy, the cloud already uses only a fraction of the electricity of an on-prem DC. AWS claims to be 3.4 times (*https://oreil.ly/D9mha*) more energy efficient than an average US DC and 5 times more efficient than a European one. Move some stuff to the cloud. (Note: You could also call on your noncloud hosting providers to be more efficient. That isn't likely to pay off inside six months, but you need to play the long game if you want to stay out of the public cloud.)

- If you are already in the cloud, review your instance types. Could you be using spot or burstable instances or autoscaling?

- Many clouds are now offering instances based on more efficient Arm chips (for example, AWS's Graviton that claims up to a 60% reduction in carbon emissions (*https://oreil.ly/88Xoq*) for an identical service).

Let us remind you that cloud veteran Pini Reznik told us that in his experience, "An average cloud system can cut its resource consumption and bills by up to 50% just using ops best practice tuning and optimization." And that's before you move to Arm processors. This is relatively straightforward stuff with a huge impact.

You can measure the scale of cuts you've achieved by the reduction in your like-for-like hosting bills. Hosting cost is only a rough proxy for emissions, but it's good enough at this stage and it's simple to explain and track. No clever tools required!

Hurray! You've saved loads of money, and you are now working on level 2 of the maturity matrix.

Hosting cost isn't a perfect emissions measure, but it will do. It gives you something to track progress against and the ability to do year-on-year deltas. Chapter 9 also describes other possible proxies.

The "like-for-like" comparison could be based on visitor or order numbers. Pick whatever you are already using for your like-for-like reporting. If you aren't doing any, take a look at the retail sector where like-for-like sales is a ubiquitous metric that takes into account a variety of things, including time of year.

The hosting bill reduction is not a straight cost saving because work will be required to deliver it, but it is an emissions reduction.

For this level 1→2 challenge, you should be aiming for a manual audit, rightsize, and cleanup rather than a regular, automated one—that would be better, but don't run before you can walk. Automation needs to happen on a higher rung of the maturity matrix. "The perfect is the enemy of the good," as Voltaire said. We start manually and automate eventually.

What Next?

There are already commodity tools and services out there that happen to be green, mostly because that saves money for the folk operating them. Maybe they are code efficient at scale, like some cloud services, or deliver good machine efficiency, like serverless, or support demand shifting, like spot instances. You need to start using them.

You may have noticed the green platforms that already exist are mostly in the cloud. That's not because Jeff Bezos is secretly a social justice warrior. It's because efficiency is coupled with both being green and cutting operational costs. That means hosted services at scale get a huge win from making themselves efficient. The payoff for the providers—who are the ones that have to put in the effort to achieve efficiency—is far greater than for open source tooling, where you are the one saddled with the hosting bills.

We are consequentialists. We don't care what the motivation was behind a piece of code being carbon efficient; we only care whether or not it is carbon efficient. As we said in the introduction, this book isn't about your soul; it's about your planet. A carbon dioxide molecule has the same effect on the climate whether it was put into the atmosphere by a saint or a sinner.

The behavior of gases is wholly determined by statistics, which makes it the ultimate realm of utilitarianism.

As we said in the introduction, we already know much of what we need to do to cut the next 30% or 40% off our carbon emissions, and again, we don't need to do much measurement to achieve it and nail most of level 3 of the maturity matrix:

- Make sure your hosting provider or operations team has extremely tough carbon-zero hosting targets. Compare them with the cloud and pile on some pressure.

- Ensure machines are hosted on grids and in regions with a high renewable or nuclear mix (AWS currently has 19 sustainability target regions (*https://oreil.ly/ 8O_l3*), for example).

- Choose only green platforms that are committed to a low-carbon future and have a community that will hold them to that commitment. Move to those platforms if necessary.

- Choose an architecture that will support demand shifting and shaping (i.e., usually not always on monoliths).

- Set high bars for operational efficiency and machine utilization, because the best way to both cut emissions and embodied carbon is to use fewer servers. The public clouds are comparatively very efficient. Again, that is because of scale and incentives rather than saintliness. We don't care. In most cases, we can cut our emissions very significantly by moving to a public cloud and using its services well ("lift and shift" buys you something, but you need to move way beyond it).

- Design products and systems to support demand shaping and shifting for carbon awareness.

- Do less and be Lean in your approach. Don't build and save stuff before need.

- Make sure your software is never the final nail in the coffin for working end-user devices because of the lack of backward compatibility or security patches.

- Build basic performance metrics into your systems and do at least basic performance analysis. Resolve any egregious bottlenecks that you find (and you will). They are just bugs that are slowing you down, costing you money, and emitting greenhouse gases. As we said in Chapter 3, performance is often a good proxy for carbon emissions.

- Start to automate the rightsizing you did at level 1 and look at LightSwitchOps so you can turn off systems at will if you think they are no longer used. You'll need some simple metrics for that, too, so you can spot low-activity servers.

- For code that has to run all the time, make it efficient.

Green platforms are a key part of this story. Code efficiency can be difficult and expensive. For most of us, it needs to be something we demand of our tools and platforms rather than build ourselves (apart from fixing those obvious performance bottleneck bugs). We must all put pressure on our suppliers for green platforms and, if they don't comply, switch to ones who will.

This phase of greening your systems is tougher to measure, but it is possible to do so. The public cloud providers now all have basic carbon footprint tools (we talked about this more in Chapter 9). If you are not in the cloud, you need to ask your hosting suppliers to start giving you footprint information. You can still act without data, but you'll be flying somewhat blind, and in the long run, you are going to need it to do business in the EU.

If you manage to get here, you are more or less at level 3 of the Green Software Maturity Matrix.

To Everything There Is a Season

At this stage, we could talk about measurement and tuning systems and getting to levels 4 and 5 of the maturity matrix, but we won't. That's because at this stage, it's of limited use to the majority of folk who will be reading this book. Getting to level 2 or 3 would be a massive achievement in itself.

> We'll cover getting to levels 4 and 5 of the maturity matrix in edition 2, assuming there's sufficient demand to get another edition. Let's call it a cliffhanger. Decent tools and platforms should be available by then. At this point, it would all be custom.

Getting emissions data out of your suppliers and doing the simple cleanup actions we've talked about will take a while. If you've done it already, well done. Now you need to automate it. If you've already done that, you're the ones who should be writing the book.

If you start taking detailed measurements and tuning your code before you've got rightsizing sorted and your ops in good shape and automated, then you're wasting your time. As we have said before, efficient ops is more fundamental than efficient code to green software. You could spend three years optimizing your monolith for efficiency, cutting its CPU and memory usage by 95% or more, but if you run it on the same server, you'll have a more or less identical carbon footprint. Your efforts would be wasted if you didn't get the ops right first.

In terms of priorities, nail operational efficiency and basic performance testing and cost cutting, demand shapeable and shiftable architectures, then worry about code efficiency (and ideally get that through green platforms).

The Cost?

In Bill Gates's book *How to Avoid a Climate Disaster* (*https://oreil.ly/39GBw*), he talks about a "green premium." This is the cost of going green and how we need to reduce it to zero.

In the tech industry, the great news is that hosting costs are not subject to a green premium. When we go green, we reduce machine counts and electricity use and save money. In fact, as we discussed in Chapter 11, FinOps (minimizing the operating costs of a system) is a very effective way to reduce your greenhouse gas emissions. Going green saves money.

Unfortunately, that still doesn't mean going green is a no-brainer for tech. There are real potential dangers, depending on how you do it. Specifically, there are risks to developer productivity if you attempt to make your own code highly efficient, such as reimplementing your systems in Rust or C. You'll soon hit the problem that it can be a lot of work, so there are opportunity costs.

Proposing an approach focused primarily on code efficiency could derail a green initiative, because no one is willing to give up development speed. In an uncertain world, the last thing anyone wants to sacrifice is their ability to react fast. We authors don't want you to either, and we don't believe it is the right definition of green software.

We define green software quite differently.

"All the Things!"

Green is what all software is going to have to be from now on. It's not a niche. So it must fulfill all our needs. It has to be productive for developers, and resilient, and reliable, and secure, and performant, and scalable.

It has to be all the things.

At the start of this book, we defined *green software* as software that is carbon efficient and aware, but that isn't really correct, or at least, it's only partially right. A true definition of *green software* is software that meets all our modern needs *as well as* being carbon aware and efficient.

In this book, we've often talked about this as if to say, "Luckily, with green software you can have it all!" Indeed you can. However, that isn't luck. We are pushing a specific vision of green software that can meet all these needs *because it has to get universally adopted*.

Physically, you could reduce your expectations of many of the requirements previously mentioned to cut emissions. You could at least halve them if you gave up on reliability, for example. You could rewrite your code in C to increase efficiency ten- or even a hundredfold and have your developer productivity go out the window. You could only run when the sun is shining and have the suckiest latency in the world. However, your boss might be less sanguine about the plan.

 In some contexts you could, in fact, downgrade reliability, performance, or developer productivity. In that case, the previously mentioned options would work very well. They are just not the mainline.

Fundamentally, if your green strategy can't work for a business at scale, then it's not green—it's a form of wishful and well-meant greenwashing.

Then How?

The good news is, in the tech industry, we are in the fortunate position of being able to avoid most of the costs of going green. Even better, we can improve our performance on all of our other goals while at the same time reducing emissions. We can have it all!

How?! The same way that we have made most of our astonishing progress in the past decade: via code reuse.

Code Reuse

For highly efficient code that is hard to write or for hardware-efficient multitenancy platforms are hard to maintain, then we need to make sure they get used loads and loads of times by loads and loads of people to make them both work well (because test in production has always been a thing) and worth the investment.

In the tech industry, that means one of two things: open source or services, particularly services provided at ultra scale.

Security experts have a saying: "Never roll your own cryptography" (*https://oreil.ly/tNNmq*). The reason is that it's extremely hard to get security design right. Nevertheless, we still have security. We just use security and encryption products and services, of which there are plenty, rather than attempt to implement security by ourselves. We have high expectations that those tools and platforms are secure. We demand it. If they weren't, we wouldn't use them.

If we use tools that do their job well, in addition to security, we get developer productivity, scalability, performance, and resilience (usually those are also requirements placed on a security tool or service).

Now is the time for us to start having the same expectations of our platforms for carbon efficiency and awareness. We need that *as well as* scalability, ease of use, security, resilience, and performance. All at low cost.

It is achievable.

However, we must demand green platforms that deliver all the things, because if we don't ask, we don't get.

So, What Is Green Software?

Green software isn't carbon-efficient and aware software. Or it isn't *only* that. Low or zero carbon is necessary, but it isn't sufficient.

Productive for developers, cheap, resilient, secure, performant, and scalable. Green software has to be all these things, too, before it can eat the world. That means we need to demand tools and services that enable us to do it all. We need such green platforms. Then we must use them.

It won't be easy. But it will be green.

Epilogue

> There is much good work to be done by every one of us and we must begin to do it.
> —Wendell Berry

You are probably thinking, "Finally, these three have finished!" Hold your horses—we are not done quite yet.

We have talked about carbon throughout this book, but we can't ignore the fact there are other environmental impacts that we also need to pay attention to. Water supply (especially clean), plastic pollution, and ecological damage from mining precious metals for hardware, to name but a few.

Water is starting to get a lot of attention because our latest tech sensations, large language models (LLMs), require a boatload of DCs to train and operate. However, there is still not enough noise about the other aspects, and this is where you can come in.

We techies are famously good at solving problems, so we ask your help to kick off conversations about all the stuff we haven't talked about so far. Reading this book was merely the start.

Until next time, ciao from Sara, Sarah, and Anne! The saga of *Techies for the Planet* shall be continued in edition 2 of the book!

Index

Symbols

---

ability to avoid most costs of going green while improving on traditional goals, 201

carbon footprint, GSMM axis checklist for, 189

need for cutting carbon emissions, 194

potential dangers of going green, 200

temperature

departures (°C) from 1961 to 1990, 16

keeping global mean temperature rise to 2°C, 19

tensor processing units (TPUs), 100

time shifting, 119, 188

(see also demand shifting)

about, 80

easier than location shifting, 85

and spot instances, 63

time-critical, always-on tasks, 10

time-series data (for carbon), 143

tools, 5

for carbon intensity of electricity, 78-80

more targeted carbon footprint reporting tools, 9

traffic, 159

transcoding, 110

transfer learning, 131

transformations of data, 176

Transformer model, 127

transportation, 17

trunk rolls, 113

Turing test, 125

Turing, Alan, 125

turning off machines, 70, 71, 186

turning things off, 196, 198

shutting down hardware, 99

U

UK, Carbon Intensity API, 78

UNFCCC (United Nations Framework Conventions on Climate Change), 19

unknown and known bugs, identifying, 163

unknown unknowns, 174

uptime, 158

user devices

carbon emissions from, 11

carbon-zero, need for long lifetime, 11

users

how end users will use products, 20

steering away from creation of unnecessary emissions, 20

utilization, 4

(see also machine utilization)

improving for the internet using CDNs for demand shifting, 120

increasing for hardware, 27

V

version control system (Git), 59

video calling applications, working with fluctuating network bandwidth, 83

video codec chips, 111

video streaming, time shifting for greener electricity, 81

videoconferencing (VC) companies, use of service downgrades, 121

virtual machines (VMs)

cloud, 39

Kepler estimates of power consumption for, 153

lightweight VMs, use by AWS services to encapsulate jobs in cluster scheduling, 62

voltage, 98

W

waste electrical and electronic equipment (see e-waste)

water supply, 202

watt hour meters, 136

watts, 21

watts per bit metric in telecom equipment, 109

WattTime API, 138

WattTime carbon intensity API, 79

WBSCD (World Business Council for Sustainable Development), 20

weather versus climate, 18

Weaveworks, 60

web application programming interface (WebApi), 79

web applications, system limitations of software, 136

web development, tool for measuring carbon footprint, 155

web traffic level, carbon-aware solution at, 88

WebAssembly (WASM), 39

Wi-Fi, 110

wind, 1

About the Authors

Anne Currie is a tech veteran who has been a part of the industry as a developer, senior manager, and startup founder for nearly thirty years working on everything from high performance C software in the 90s, to e-commerce in the 00s, to modern operations in the 10s. She is a campaigner for future-proof, sustainable systems and regularly writes and speaks on the subject. She is a community chair of the Green Software Foundation, and co-founder of tech consultancy Strategically Green. She is also the author of the scifi Panopticon series.

Sarah (Chun-Wei) Hsu strongly advocates green, sustainable software. She regularly speaks and writes on the subject and serves as the chair of the Green Software Course project for the Green Software Foundation. In collaboration with the Linux Foundation, the group recently launched a free online educational course titled Green Software for Practitioners (LFC131) to assist software practitioners in building and maintaining greener applications. She currently works as a Site Reliability Engineer on a distributed platform on Google Cloud.

Sara Bergman is a Senior Software Engineer working as a backend engineer with people experiences in the Microsoft ecosystem. She is an advocate for green software practices and frequently speaks about green software publicly in conferences, meet-ups and podcasts. She is an individual contributor of the Green Software Foundation, where she has contributed to several projects, including the Software Carbon Intensity specification and the GSF newsletter.

Colophon

The animal on the cover of *Building Green Software* is a blue-headed racket-tail parrot (*Prioniturus platenae*), a colorful parrot native to the western Philippines, particularly around the island of Palawan.

These medium-sized parrots are known for their vibrant plumage. Adults are typically olive and green with a yellow belly. Their most striking feature is, of course, their blue head, although this coloration is less pronounced in females.

Blue-headed racket-tails prefer the quiet seclusion of humid lowland forests. They are social creatures and can be found flitting through the trees in small flocks. Their diet consists mainly of fruits, seeds, and nuts.

The blue-headed racket-tail is classified as Vulnerable by the IUCN. Habitat loss due to deforestation is the biggest threat to their survival, though trapping for the pet trade is another concern. Conservation efforts are underway to protect these beautiful birds and their dwindling habitat. Many of the animals on O'Reilly covers are endangered; all of them are important to the world.

The cover illustration is by Karen Montgomery, based on an antique line engraving from *Histoire Naturelle*. The series design is by Edie Freedman, Ellie Volckhausen, and Karen Montgomery. The cover fonts are Gilroy Semibold and Guardian Sans. The text font is Adobe Minion Pro; the heading font is Adobe Myriad Condensed; and the code font is Dalton Maag's Ubuntu Mono.

O'REILLY®

Learn from experts.
Become one yourself.

Books | Live online courses
Instant answers | Virtual events
Videos | Interactive learning

Get started at oreilly.com.

Printed in the USA
CPSIA information can be obtained
at www.ICGtesting.com
JSHW051412240624
65300JS00012B/486